no lonesome road

don west

no

lonesome

road

selected prose and poems

Edited by

Jeff Biggers and George Brosi

University of Illinois Press

Urbana and Chicago

The prose and poems of Don West are reprinted by permission of
Linda McCarthy, administrator of the Don West Estate.

Library of Congress Cataloging-in-Publication Data
West, Don.
No lonesome road : selected prose and poems / Don West ; edited
by Jeff Biggers and George Brosi.
    p.   cm.
ISBN 0-252-02887-2 (cloth : alk. paper)
ISBN 0-252-07157-3 (pbk. : alk. paper)
1. Appalachian Region, Southern—Poetry. 2. Appalachian Region,
Southern—Civilization. 3. Mountain life—Appalachian Region,
Southern. 4. Mountain life—Poetry. I. Biggers, Jeff, 1963–   .
II. Brosi, George. III. Title.
PS3545.E8279A6   2004
811'.54—dc21   2003010930

contents

selected poems

acknowledgments

Jeff Biggers would like to thank a legion of Don West associates and friends for their editorial insights, research assistance, interviews, access to personal papers, and general support, including: Bob Henry Barber, John and Jean Biggers, Joyce Brown, Mike Clark, Peter Cole, John Crawford, Anthony Dunbar, Philip Fraley, Elaine Gerger, Robert Gipe, Chris Green, Harvey Klehr, Carrie Noble and Michael Kline, P. J. Laska, Helen Lewis, Ted Olson, Edwina Pendarvis, Rachel Rubin, John Salmond, Clancy Sigal, James Smethurst, Jim Webb, and Jack Wright.

Special thanks to Yvonne Farley and James Lorence for playing the roles of research guides and mentors. Special thanks as well to Warren Doyle for providing access to his personal papers on Don West and to Jancy Davis, who donated the invaluable Mike Ross Papers to the Southern Labor Archives at Georgia State University.

Profound gratitude to the librarians and research assistants at the ACLU Archives at Princeton University, Atlanta-Fulton Public Library, Berea College, Disciples of Christ Archives, the Appalachian Collection at East Tennessee State University, FOIA/Federal Bureau of Investigation, Frostberg University, the Southern Labor Archives at Georgia State University, Gilmer County Public Library, Library of Congress, Lincoln Memorial University, New York City Public Library, Northwest Georgia Regional Library, Oglethorpe University, the Reference Center for Marxist Studies, Vanderbilt University, Walter Reuther Library of Labor and Urban Affairs at Wayne State University, West Virginia University, Western Illinois University, University of Arizona, University of Illinois, University of Kentucky, University of North Carolina, University of Wisconsin, and Wisconsin Historical Society. In terms of this anthology, material was also gathered from the Ann and Carl Braden Papers, Highlander Folk School Papers, Howard Kester Papers, George Meyers Papers, George Weissman Papers, Mike Ross Papers, and the Freedom of Information Act files from the Department of Justice and Federal Bureau of Investigation on Don West.

Sally Maggard and the Appalachian Studies Association got the Don West train in gear in 1999. Under her tenure as editor, parts of my introduction first appeared in "The Fugitive of Southern Appalachian Literature: Reconsidering the Poetry of Don West," *Journal of Appalachian Studies* 5:2 (Fall 1999): 159–80. © 1999 by the Appalachian Studies Assocation. Reprinted by permission. Special thanks to Hedy West.

And special thanks to Judy McCulloh for her patience and support in bringing this collection to publication and to my coeditor, George Brosi, for his keen insight and hard labor.

Soprattutto, grazie a Carla Paciotto, la mia inesauribile fonte d'ispirazione.

· · · ·

George Brosi would like to thank his wife, Connie, and their seven children, Brook, Berry, Blossom, Sunshine, Sky, Glade, and Eagle for their understanding and support during the course of this project. Special thanks goes to Berry for his research in New York City and at the Stanford University Library and to Sky for checking the Yale University Library for sources.

Thanks to colleagues at the Berea College Appalachian Center for their invaluable assistance, especially Gordon McKinney, Jack Wright, and Genevieve Reynolds. Special thanks to the student workers Danessa Pollard, Jim Fershee, and Abbie Tanyhill. Additional thanks to colleagues and students at the University of Kentucky, Eastern Kentucky University, and Somerset Community College, especially Bridgette York Smith.

Thanks to Don West's daughter, Ann Williams, and his granddaughter, Linda Williams McCarthy, for their help.

On trips to learn more about Don West, thanks to Helen Lewis of Morganton, Georgia, to C. W. Conner of Ellijay, Georgia, and to Robert Mealer on Turkey Creek. Thanks to Leeanne Garland, the archivist of university archives and special collections at Lincoln Memorial University's Carnegie Vincent Library in Harrogate, Tennessee, and to the good people of the Bell County Courthouse in Pineville, Kentucky. Thanks to Rebecca Ware, Mike Mullins, and all the folks at Hindman Settlement School for their help.

Thanks to Pat Taylor, Steve Gowler, Jennifer Morse, Josh Young, Susan Henthorn, Harry Rice, and Josh Strawser at Berea College's Hutchins Library and Special Collections for their assistance tracking down materials. Thanks to Steve Stone, Kristy Melton, and Susan Wheatley at Eastern Kentucky University's Crabbe Library. And thanks to Kate Black, Claire McCann, Teresa Burgett, Mary Vass, Roxanna Jones, Kandace Rogers, Carla Cantagallo, Paul Page, and Ed Hager at the University of Kentucky Libraries and Special Collections.

Thanks, finally, to all who have kept the legacy of Don West alive.

introduction

Jeff Biggers

In the spring of 1946, the country still emerging from the aftermath of the Second World War, a slender volume of poetry, *Clods of Southern Earth*, emerged as the featured title of the New York publishing house Boni and Gaer. The noted "first-time" author was Don West, an "unknown" Georgia farmer and educator. At the time of their press announcement, the veteran publishers Charles Boni and Joseph Gaer had already received 12,300 prepress orders for the collection; the *Atlanta Constitution* would report that the publication set a record for sales of a first book of verse (Hite 1946). Over a thousand copies were sold in one book signing in Atlanta; subsequent newspaper reports hailed the book as a best-selling phenomenon, with nearly a hundred thousand copies sold (Sibley 1952; Graham 1989).

Clods of Southern Earth broke ground in more than one way. Written in the simple verse and rhyming quatrains of folk ballads and regional speech, it was a fearless paean to southern Appalachian culture and dispossessed sharecroppers, miners, and mill workers with "callused hands." The volume was a prophetic call in the South for integration and civil rights; West's unusual introduction marked the beginnings of an early historical analysis of the "Mountain South" and underscored his defiant efforts to recognize a mountain heritage that had been in the forefront of the American Revolution, the antislavery and Underground Railroad movements, and contemporary struggles for displaced mountaineers, tenant farmers, and union workers.

Despite the Boni and Gaer marketing blurbs, *Clods of Southern Earth* was not Don West's first book of poetry. Nor was he an unknown Georgia farmer. According to John Egerton in *Speak Now against the Day*, an epic chronicle of the generation in the South prior to the civil rights movement, West had "gained near-legendary status as a sort of phantom revolutionary who left a trail of radical poems and sermons in his wake" (1994:159). As a poet and an activist, West's readings and speeches drew large crowds; as a gifted organizer, he had cultivated a faithful following in the southern fields, mines, and mills; publication in leftist newspapers and journals had brought his work to a national audience.

By 1946, West had already left his native Georgia mountains to study literature and religion at Lincoln Memorial and Vanderbilt Universities, published several collections of poetry in the nascent forefront of modern Appalachian literature, traveled across Europe, cofounded the Highlander Folk School in Tennessee, which would later serve as a leading training center for the civil rights movement, and escaped from Atlanta under a sack in a car, wanted dead or alive for defending a radical African American on trial for leading a hunger march. Blazing his own Appalachian trail on an Indian Chief motorcycle, at times imprisoned and even beaten, reviled by newspaper editors across the South, monitored intensely by the FBI, and soon to be burned out by the Ku Klux Klan, West had organized textile workers in North Carolina and coal miners in Kentucky. He had also served churches in Ohio and Georgia as an ordained Congregational minister, had become a popular figure in Greenwich Village literary circles, and had drawn national attention for his innovations in rural education in Georgia. By the late 1960s, as the founder of the Appalachian South Folklife Center in West Virginia and an active pamphleteer in the tradition of his exemplar Thomas Paine, West would serve as one of the inspirations for the folk revival movement.

The legacy of this phantom Appalachian revolutionary had strangely disappeared into the Appalachian Mountain fogs by the mid-1980s; West's several collections of poetry went out of print and became difficult to find. His work was rarely included in anthologies, curriculum lists, or histories of southern or Appalachian literature. Any archives or collections of his personal papers disappeared or were lost to various fires. He died in virtual obscurity in 1992.

In his own words, West's journey had been a long and rocky road, but not a lonesome one. Few figures in Appalachia, the South, or the country had experienced a more daring and extraordinary life.

Mountain Boy

Born in the shadow of Burnt Mountain in Gilmer County, Georgia, in 1906, the eldest son of a farmer, Don West came from Appalachian mountain families that had celebrated their nonconformity with the antebellum South for over a century. They wore more than the bib overalls of dirt farmers who raised corn on steep slopes and dug ginseng for cash; they wore the conflicting southern history and heritage of mountaineers like blue badges of courage. Some members of West's family had been Union soldiers in the Civil War in a part of Georgia that had flown the Union flag; his grandfather, Kim Mulkey, a towering man with a beard to his chest, raised West on stories of their mountain traditions of resiliency, independence, and opposition to slavery.

This sense of his heritage wasn't only a matter of pride for West. It transformed his vision from being in the ranks of displaced poor whites to being part of the continuum of an extraordinary Appalachian history that had settled in some of the most difficult terrain in the country while producing the first declaration of independence, one of the first abolitionist newspapers, the trails for the Underground Railroad, and soldiers on the frontlines for freedom. For West, it also reached deep into the lowland South, back to the declaration of James Oglethorpe, Georgia's founder, against slavery in 1776.

Until the age of fifteen, West lived on a hundred-acre farm off Turkey Creek, which adjoined the farms of his uncle and grandfather. Then his father joined the tides of other mountaineers drifting from the area for jobs in the factories, mills, and large farms, settling in the Georgia lowlands as a sharecropper. West lost a couple of fingers on his left hand in a farm accident as a youth; despite the incident, he continued his studies, earning a chance to attend the Berry School in Rome, Georgia, a missionary boarding school developed for indigent mountain children. When the film *Birth of a Nation* was shown on campus, he organized a student protest against its blatant glorification of the Ku Klux Klan (Wigginton 1992). Later expelled from the well-known school for supporting a controversial faculty member, West eventually aired his view of the institution's patronizing and missionary role among mountain kids in an impassioned letter to the *New Republic* ("Sweatshops in the Schools" 1933). He left the school without a diploma.

After working for a telephone company for a brief period, stringing cables through the Georgia mountains, West hitched his way to Tennessee, where he enrolled in a work-study program at Lincoln Memorial University (LMU). Nestled at the foot of the Cumberland Gap, the university had been founded after the Civil War in gratitude for the mountaineers' contribution to the Union effort. West arrived on campus with $1.65 in his pocket (West 1986). Within two years, he became president of the YMCA, class president, and captain of the track team.

A fellow LMU student, Jesse Stuart, who would eventually emerge as one of Kentucky's most popular and prolific writers in the mid-twentieth century, became a companion, and the two made a formidable pair; both were over six feet tall, outstanding and popular athletes and students; both were from poor mountain families and had worked full-time before entering college, making them easily contemptuous of the college's paternalistic regulations. Another classmate, James Still, from Alabama, went on to achieve an even greater reputation among contemporary literary critics for his classic novel, *River of Earth* (1940), and his acclaimed stories and poetry. The three young men would soon appear in the front ranks of the region's modern literary movements (Drake 2001).

At LMU, West also met an aspiring visual artist from eastern Kentucky, Mabel "Connie" Adams. The couple eloped during a break from classes, with Connie's sister, Addie, and Jesse Stuart serving as the only witnesses at a church near Middlesboro, Kentucky.

Falling under the wing of the novelist and literature professor Harry Harrison Kroll at LMU, West began to weave his oral traditions into a literary reflection of his own times. Kroll, who also served as Jesse Stuart's literary mentor at the university, had been a former sharecropper. His writing provided critical portraits of ethnic unity and class conflict in the South, and he would eventually author over twenty novels and nonfiction books, including the bestseller *Cabin in the Cotton*. More importantly for West, Kroll urged his students to write in the language of their communities, saying, "'These are things in your own backyard that need to be written'" (qtd. in Richardson 1984:76).

In his senior year at the university, West led a student strike in protest against what he perceived as paternalistic college rules. He was expelled in the process. The freshly radicalized student body redoubled its protests, resulting in West's reinstatement.

Beyond activities on the school campus, LMU's central location in Appalachia allowed the young student to observe labor conflicts that were brewing in mining camps in Kentucky and textile mills in North Carolina. West later reported being affected by the extraordinary violence against textile workers in Marion, North Carolina, where six mill strikers were shot down in the streets by gun thugs and sheriff deputies in 1929 (West 1971b). This experience also exposed West to union organizers and radical organizations for the first time, planting the seeds for some of his more militant associations; the unforgettable images of misery and blatant lawlessness would soon emerge in the young student's poems and sermons.

Remarkably, all three of LMU's future literary luminaries—Don West, James Still, and Jesse Stuart—choose to study at Vanderbilt University after graduating in the class of 1929. Unlike Still and Stuart, West did not pursue the heady corridors of the Southern Agrarian literary movement at Vanderbilt's English department. Instead, he entered the School of Religion; he declared that he felt a calling to become a preacher. His family, especially his influential grandfather Kim Mulkey, had long been fervent Baptist stalwarts in northern Georgia.

At Vanderbilt, West studied under the auspices of Willard Uphaus, who eventually became the director of the World Fellowship Center and an imprisoned social activist, and Alva Taylor, who was a leading figure in the Social Gospel movement, which incorporated concepts of social justice and equality with the modern Christian experience. West joined a lively cadre of students that included Howard Kester and Claude Williams, both of whom would become leading figures in several progressive southern organizations and movements.

Once again, West's experience was not limited to the campus. Many faculty members and students at Vanderbilt, led by Taylor, performed relief work during a dramatic strike in the coal-mining town of Wilder, Tennessee, throughout the early 1930s. Saddled with a debt-ridden system of servitude that paid two dollars a day for a sixteen-hour shift, the miners languished in hunger (Dunbar 1981). Despite drawing national attention, the strike reached a tragic breaking point when the labor leader Barney Graham was brutally murdered in April 1933. The strike was crushed. West, along with other divinity students and faculty members, performed the funeral.

Clodhoppers Unite!

By the time West arrived at Vanderbilt University, he was writing and publishing poetry in a number of journals, including the *Letters* literary magazine at the University of Kentucky. In 1931, his first collection of poems, *Crab-Grass*, rolled from the presses of a local printer in Nashville, dedicated to "my mother and father, mountain woman and man." The slim hardback volume was a celebration of Appalachian culture, written in a mountain vernacular about his "lil' ole mountin home," "a-fox huntin'," "push-back holler," and coaxing crops from the red Georgia earth.

Kroll wrote a foreword for the collection, commending West for the "sternly beautiful mixed with the whimsical light and airy" (1931). Stuart added an introduction. *Mountain Life and Work* magazine praised *Crab-Grass* for its "observation, acquaintance, and affection" but added, "of fortunate expressions and memorable lines one would like to find more" (Smith 1932:26).

In a voice shared miles away by his urban counterpart, Langston Hughes of the Harlem Renaissance, West wrote in sing-song verses and quatrains of rhyme and mountain speech. Hughes had the blues and jazz, while West "spun a melody of corn blades" (West 1940:64) in the sharp tunes of the hollows or the rhythm of the cotton mill work songs. In the title poem, West muses:

> It wonders me whut fer
> Ye'r made,
> Crab-grass,
> Allus pesterin' around'.
> In th' corn down th' creek
> An' taters in th' new-groun',
> Crab-grass,
> Allus pesterin' aroun'. . . .

West's poetry also drew on his own family's displacement from the mountains and their hand-to-mouth survival as sharecroppers. He echoed the sentiments from the ballad "Hard Times Cotton Mill Girls," which West had learned from his aunt, who had drifted into the textile mills. According to West (1979), his aunt made four dollars a week for sixty hours of work in the mills. In an early poem, "Dark Winds," West laments:

> Sad winds,
> They've blowed sorrow an' sufferin'
> Frum northern mills,
> An' drug my people
> Down frum th' hills.

In addition to publishing his first book, another critical development in West's young life occurred at Vanderbilt through Alva Taylor's encouragement. He won a scholarship to visit the folk schools in Denmark, which would remain a strong and often unrecognized influence throughout the rest of his life.

Inspired by the theologian N. F. S. Grundtvig, who had collected hundreds of folk songs and poems from Danish peasants in the mid-nineteenth century, the schools believed in the "living word" as the primary source of education, with books a distant second. The folk schools sought to bring displaced and illiterate Danes into the workings of the liberated nation. Beginning each day with traditional songs, the schools stressed the value and common sense of village people who lived off the land; the performing arts were part of one's connection to the soil and nation. Peasants were educated through a curriculum built on their cultural heritage and experiences. By the early twentieth century, the folk school had been credited as the most successful adult education experiment in the world.

West's trip to Europe not only stimulated his thinking about rural education but also exposed him to an intensely political milieu. He witnessed a European Left that was considered a legitimate social force, with socialist and communist movements operating as integral parts in the political milieu.

Imbued with a deeper sense of the possibilities of cooperation among common folk, West returned to complete his thesis at Vanderbilt, writing a sociological portrait of a mountain community, "Knott County, Kentucky: A Study," surveying much of the area on horseback. The thesis would be a window into West's vision and life's work, especially in the field of adult education (Glen 1988). Championing the unique character, strengths, and forbearance of the Appalachian community, incorporating elements of folk school schemes for community development, and analyzing the economic realities of industrialization, West concluded with a literary exhortation to himself and his fellow Appalachians:

Mountain Boy
You are more than a dirty child
In patched overalls.
You mountain boy . . . !
The hills are yours.
The fragrant forests,
The silver rivers
Are your heritage.

Dreamers. Thinkers.

Rise up, young hillmen.
Sing your ballads.
Dream your future.
Up and down your valleys,
Over the ridge-roads.
Climb your jagged mountains.
Gaze into blue space . . .
Turn your thoughts free.
Nourish your imagination.

What will you do for your hills,
You mountain boy?

In 1932, West taught briefly at the Hindman Settlement School in Knott County; he also recommended Hindman as a place for Depression-era employment to his fellow LMU and Vanderbilt student James Still, who remained in the area as a writer and librarian and became a literary fixture until his death in 2001 (Still 2001). Anxious to launch his own school, West toured the region and then partnered with Myles Horton of Savannah, Tennessee, who had also made a pilgrimage to Denmark. They founded the Highlander Folk School at Monteagle, Tennessee, that fall. Modeled after the Danish folk schools, Highlander was intended to be a racially integrated school that would teach Appalachians about their progressive history and culture and train activists and union organizers for a "new social order" (Wigginton 1992) in the South. Highlander would later become a critical center in the civil rights movement, training Rosa Parks, among many others.

By 1932, West had also published two more chapbooks of poetry—*Deep, Deep Down in Living* and *Between the Plow Handles*—which took his increasingly fervent political views one step further to the radical Left. The collections also marked West's divergence from a strictly Appalachian perspective on politics.

Although Don West and Myles Horton would remain complimentary of each other for the rest of their lives, their varying personal approaches and political ideas on how to bring about change in the South diverged. West and his wife finally decided to leave Highlander in the fall of 1933 to launch a library project in Kennesaw, Georgia.

As the nation and the world became more deeply entrenched in the Depression, West recognized the extraordinary demands and circumstances of the times. By 1933, he had personally witnessed the rise of Hitler in Germany and had passed through a reign of terror and depravation conducted against coal miners and mill workers in the Mountain South.

The critical elements of West's own vision and writing were drifting inevitably into the tide of leftist literary movements across the United States in the 1930s. The forces tugging at his work, however, were wildly diverse: West found himself a promising poet, an Appalachian nativist, an ordained Congregational minister and follower of the Social Gospel, an educator and founder of a "mutual aid–guided" Danish folk school, a labor organizer sympathetic first to the Socialist and then the Communist Party, and a militant committed to radical change.

The Depression had ushered in a period of intense scrutiny of the American identity, opening the door for West's writing. After Black Thursday in 1929, the literary world had become a forum for debate over the essence of American form and expression. Writers, photographers, music recorders and oral historians, muralists, dancers, and actors were funded by federal work programs and sent out into the countryside to document the American experience. At the same time, leftist publications prompted by the Communist Party and other radical organizations were launched in an attempt to reach the "toiling masses." According to the literary critic Cary Nelson, "for a brief moment in American literary history, writing poetry became a credible form of revolutionary action" (1996:32).

West's work started to appear regularly in leftist and Communist publications such as the *Liberator, New Masses, Anvil, Partisan Review,* and the *Daily Worker;* his poetry and essays were also published in mainstream religious and regional publications such as the *Christian Century* and *Mountain Life and Work.*

West had also made the first of many journeys by motorcycle to New York City, where he would ease into a vibrant political and cultural scene among other leftist and communist writers during the Depression (Byerly 1992; Wald 2002). Mike Gold, one of the deans of the flourishing proletarian literary movement, announced West's arrival on the national literary stage in a column in the *Daily Worker* in January 1934. In comparing West to Robert Burns, Gold declared: "Such poets delight in health and nature, but their very sensitivity makes them feel acutely the bitter lot of their brothers. Robert Burns became a revolutionary, and Don West has also traveled the road that leads from poetry to action" (Gold 1934). In a subsequent *Daily Worker* interview

Don West on his Indian Chief motorcycle in the 1930s.

with Edwin Rolfe, who became one of the celebrated poets to emerge from the Abraham Lincoln Brigades in the Spanish Civil War, West made the distinction between his earlier "folk poems, not really revolutionary," and forthcoming political work in a new collection, to be called "Southern Folks" (Rolfe 1934).

In 1934, West published a poem entitled "I Am a Communist" in the *Daily Worker,* the official publication of the Communist Party, with his byline and his Georgia address. This poem and its transformation—West would later change the title and theme to "I Am an Agitator"—shaped West's life and work for several decades; it also marked one of the most unique incidents in American literary history, whereby a poet's literary work would be used against him repeatedly for decades by numerous southern newspapers and U.S. congressional investigators. West wrote:

> I am a Communist
> > A Red
> > A Bolshevik!
> Do you, toilers of the South,
> > Know me,
> > > Do you understand?
> Do you believe the lies
> > > Capitalists say
> > And print about me?
> > > You farmers,
> > Share croppers,
> > > Renters,
> Factory Workers,
> Negroes, poor whites,
> Do you understand me,
> > Do you see
> > That I am you.
> That I, the Communist,
> > Am you—?
>
> I am Don West, too.
> > The poet
> The working man.
> > But the poet
> Is a cry for justice.
> The Communist is the tempered soul
> > Of a hundred million toilers
> > Marching to victory

A new world
A working man's world!

I am the son
Of my grandfather.
His blood pounds thru
My veins, and cries out
For justice!
I am the poet
Who sings to the south
And she responds
With sobs of misery!

I'm not foreign
No body
With calloused hands
Is foreign to us—
I'm Don West
Raised on a Georgia farm—
The son of my mother
And a Communist. . . . (West 1934b)

The poem was emblematic of a literary phenomenon in the burgeoning leftist political and labor movements during the upheaval of the Depression; thrust onto the front pages, poets often had access to thousands of daily readers who would have never otherwise seen their work. Often dealing with particular events and immediate issues, poems were being shaped and written for a spoken-word dynamic; verses were appropriated and passed out at daily gatherings. Some read like visionary headlines, such as West's "Angelo Herndon's Dream," which was also published in the *Harlem Liberator* (Smethurst 1999).

West had moved to Atlanta to assist the Angelo Herndon Defense Committee in 1934. A young black activist affiliated with the Communist Party, Herndon had been arrested and sentenced to twenty years on the chain gang for leading a protest of unemployed people in 1932. He had been found guilty of "insurrection," the charges originating from a law dating back to 1866. When the case in the pre–civil rights era of the South became a national headline event, inching toward an eventual Supreme Court decision and exoneration of Herndon, the local prosecutor accelerated his crackdown on radicals with warrants of arrest for "circulating insurrectionary literature" (Martin 1976:110). West, who had already shifted his work underground under the alias of David Lee, became the prime target, "wanted dead or alive," and he narrowly escaped arrest by hiding under a trapdoor in a basement. Covered with sacks, he fled Georgia in the back of a car on a summer night in 1934 (Solomon 1998:248). In a dramatic essay in the *New Masses,* West recounted his escape, the origins of his involvement in the legal struggle, and his role as an organizer for the Communist Party. Written in the heat of the moment, the twenty-eight-year-old declared:

> One day a *Daily Worker* came to my hands. It was news! In the South the Reds were hard to find because of the illegal situation. I talked with Socialist leaders—Clarence Senior, Norman Thomas. It was no use! But I still had hopes in the Socialist Party. I rode a motorcycle from Atlanta to New York to see Clarence Hathaway. He was the only real Communist I knew anything about. Four days I stayed with him. He was considerate, kind, the most human person I thought I'd ever seen. How different from the tales we heard in the South about long-haired Bolsheviks with a knife between their teeth and a bomb in each pocket ready to cut loose on the first person they met!
>
> I returned to the South to be state organizer of Georgia for the Communist Party! (West 1934a:15)

West never turned back on his militancy. He soon headed up a Communist-supported defense committee for cotton mill workers in Burlington, North Carolina, in the fall of 1934, after a cadre of strikers had been arrested in a bomb plot. On behalf of the International Labor Defense, West wrote an introduction to a widely distributed pamphlet, *Burlington Dynamite Plot,* about "the story of a thrilling drama" in the labor movement (Pickard 1934:2). Operating under the alias Jim Weaver, West solicited the involvement of noted Carolinian intellectuals and writers in the trial, including the Pulitzer Prize–winning playwright Paul Green, until West's identity was publicly exposed. While working on this case, West was briefly jailed in Danville, Virginia, as a result of the betrayal of a paid informant, who had claimed to be sympathetic to the cause. Afraid of extradition efforts by nearby Georgia for his earlier warrants, West fled the state and became an underground labor organizer in the volatile mining communities in Kentucky under other aliases (West 1975a:45; Salmond 1998:422).

The brutality of the period did not elude West. Years later, he would recall his experiences in the Kentucky mining camps in an essay on Appalachian history: "I remember a night on a mountain road above Harlan town in the 1930's. Six operator gun thugs with deputy badges and a young native organizer. Beaten unconsciousness, thrown in the brush for dead, he came to hours later, crawling from the nightmare, stumbling down the mountainside to where a friendly old couple tended him in their humble cabin. A few nights later, in a fourth rate Hazard hotel, beyond sitting up, unable to pay for food or lodging, dirty, hungry, listening to every footstep in the hall outside with fearful uncertainty. Organizing the poor in the 1930's was risky and extremely uncertain. I speak from experience here" (West 1969:6).

West, along with two other men, had taken jobs at the coal mines in Kayjay, Kentucky, in order to organize for a union; it was later revealed that one of the three was an agent (Duke 2002). West was eventually arrested and held in jail for six weeks in Pineville, Kentucky. He was accused of conspiring to overthrow the government and shared a cell with three men on death row. During this time, desperate for money to support himself and his family, West wrote Jesse Stuart, asking whether Stuart could repay some of the money West had lent him when they were students at LMU and at Vanderbilt. Stuart wrote back and informed West that any money he sent would go to a cause that he didn't support and refused to help. After this experience the two former best friends never truly reconciled (West 1981). Released on a five-thousand-dollar peace bond and ordered by the judge to leave town, West nearly drove off the mountain road through the Cumberland Gap when his car's wheels almost fell off. The lug nuts had been loosened.

These episodes only galvanized West's resolve. Returning to Kentucky under the alias George Brown, West served as the state organizer for the Kentucky Workers Alliance for the Unemployed, which had originally been aligned with the Socialist and Communist Parties in 1937 and later split over political differences. The organization assisted unemployed workers throughout the state. On one tour to the eastern mountains, West—who would eventually use his own name—and his associates found people living in deplorable conditions, "in some instances, they even found mountain families living in dark, damp caves; hunger and privation were everywhere" (Cooper and McElfresh 1973:91). As part of his efforts, West led several hundred unemployed miners to the National Hunger March on Washington in the 1937, protesting the disparity in wages for southern workers. During this unsettled time in West's life, his wife Connie became pregnant and retreated to Pleasant Hill, Tennessee, where the famed "Doctor Woman of the Cumberlands," May Wharton, delivered their first child, Ann (West 1981).

On a national level, West's work was included in a Communist Party–supported national anthology published in 1935, *Proletarian Literature,* which sought to illustrate the explosion of literary work over the past five years. Editors at the *Partisan Review* were astonished at the readership's preference for West's work over more party-controlled "intellectual writers" (Gilbert 1968:59).

Throughout this period, West performed his poetry and speeches on the radio and at some of the largest rallies in the Depression-era South and Appalachia. Often a headliner at the events, West's "accustomed eloquence," according to Giles Cooper, the head of the Kentucky Workers Alliance, brought "cheering and waving, from start to finish" (Cooper and McElfresh 1973:125). West had discovered that the social gatherings of his readership—protests, church services, funerals, and union meetings—could be stirred by poetry readings.

A fictional character strikingly similar to West would eventually be immortalized as "Tod North, the People's Poet," in Clancy Sigal's 1961 underground classic novel *Going Away;* one of Sigal's protagonists hails the exploits of a Georgia farmer-poet, a drinking partner of fellow mountaineer Tom Wolfe: "Hardly anyone on the Left, in the late 1930s, wasn't aware of Tod North's name and work. . . . Even my father, who never read poetry, sometimes declared aloud Tod's verses" (Sigal 1961:278).

While West was thoroughly left-wing in his commitment, his work was by no means predictable or malleable. His writing took on an increasingly complex outlook, reflecting the multifarious forces behind his work and itinerant life.

Like the midwesterner Meridel LeSueur, another literary figure who came of age in the radical 1930s, West had always maintained a certain distrust of the New York–based publishing circles and leftist organizations. At the first American Writers Congress in 1935, when the chasm between poetry and politics was keenly bridged in the exuberance of the "angry decade," LeSueur voiced concern about the lack of roots and sense of place in the new wave of literature. As he became more involved in organizing militant strikes, West also began to question the long-term commitment of the largely middle-class East Coast leftist activists and writers to his region. West would eventually dismiss outsiders who needed to "sow their radical wild oats" at the expense of Appalachian needs (West 1969:6). Throughout his life, West sought to validate homegrown movements and literary expressions in an attempt to dispel any need for direction or interference from outside forces.

At the same time, he felt compelled to deal with the "cracker–white trash–hillbilly" stereotype in many East Coast publications, including leftist journals, which had gained notoriety as early as the 1880s. By the 1930s, after Georgia farmers had gone through a decade of turmoil due to the boll weevil, the tribulations of the sharecropper had made it to the front page of the public consciousness in a flood of conflicting articles in national magazines. Far from a progressive heritage, the mountaineers and displaced farmers were depicted as followers of the social trinity of despair—illiteracy, lynching, and tenancy—and saps in the shadows of demagogues.

In addition to the general dismissal of southern rural culture, West had to confront increasing mass-media appropriations of his own Appalachian culture, including the selective constructions of idioms and historical events that would wind up in popular literary caricatures and historical misinformation about Appalachia. Dating back to Mary Murfree's popular novels in the late nineteenth century, which meted out stereotypical portraits of backwoodsmen, mountaineers had been treated to a cavalcade of caricatures and bizarre reflections of their lives; Al Capp's *L'il Abner* cartoon, which would reach over fifty million readers with its depictions of ignorant and moonshined residents in Dogpatch, debuted in 1934, the same year West entered the national literary scene (Rubin 2003).

In jest to both sides of the political spectrum, West played with his own regional prejudice in his poem "Clodhopper."

> Who said:
> "Clodhoppers of the world,
> Unite!
> You have nothing to lose
> But your clods—
> Unite!"
> [. . .]
> Oh, I'm the clodhopper
> That makes the tall corn grow,
> The artist that smears dignity
> Through the speckled cotton patch.

Aware of the regional literary geography and his place in it, West was also one of the lonely voices in the South to challenge the Vanderbilt Agrarian poets and their reckoning of an antebellum past that his own mountain heritage had long ago rejected. While the crush of the Agrarians' Apollo and the New Critics took place in an academic realm outside of his readership, West played the rebellious voice of Pan in the defining terms of southern literature. Like the Agrarians, West celebrated a preindustrial southern past, though his was rooted in the Watauga Association, in what later became East Tennessee, the first self-governing community in the United States, or found on the pages of *The Emancipator,* one of the first newspapers in America dedicated to abolition, based in the southern Appalachians. In a parody of the landmark Agrarian collection *I'll Take My Stand,* West retorted with "They Take Their Stand—For some professional Agrarians":

> In Dixie Land they take their stand
>   Turning the wheels of history back
> For murder, lynch and iron hand
>   To drive the Negro from his shack.

They never delve in politics,
    That's all too commonplace, they say.
Their thoughts must go to subtle tricks
    Befitting noble gents like they.

These fundamental conflicts over the value and focus of folk cultures and the variance of historical experiences among working-class and farming communities in the Mountain South defined West's departure from mainstream literary movements in the South, such as the Agrarians, and ultimately planted the seeds of his severance from national literary critics and chroniclers. According to the West Virginia poet P. J. Laska, who worked with West in the 1970s, West's eventual disappearance from the literary canons in the South and even in Appalachia dated back to his orientation in this period: "Because he had a real audience of working people who admired his work, he knew who he was writing for, and didn't give a damn about the opinions of academic critics who have never had the folk experience. That is why if you take Don out of the context of history and struggle and place him in the context of ignorance, elite bias and creeping monoculture, he suffers a loss of stature. Don has to be read and appreciated as a folk-poet in a time when there was more access and linkage than our current set-up allows" (Laska 2002).

Like Langston Hughes, West intended to give poetic meaning to folk traditions outside of mass culture. This included a preindustrial South with its own heritage, prior to a "preproletarian culture" defined in the *New Masses.* West didn't wish to elevate his folk traditions—oral traditions of poetry, storytelling, songs, and even preaching—to a "higher art" or within forms of academic or standard language. Such a rendering would have transmuted the essence of "folk" culture or "living word" and denied its inherent value and contributions: choosing a "high" form would have been an implicit designation of "low" to his own vernacular. West believed that poetry in the language of "his people" was not only an expression of his own culture but an act of resistance in return.

By seeking out publishing organs with national readerships, West ensured that his so-called mongrels would no longer be frustrated by their marginalization; the "cracker" and "hillbilly" could now be part of the pages of books and national journals on their own terms. Unlike the revisionist face of the Agrarians, West didn't demand acceptance of his culture or writing from academia, the North, or urban centers. He viewed the act of writing poetry as a legitimate and natural expression of his heritage and times and an unaffected progression of his oral and literary traditions, not the means of an academic career or salary.

Clods of Southern Earth

Don West possessed the commanding presence of his grandfather. With a dry wit and a riveting voice, he relished being on stage like a preacher. He would hook a book of poems in a hand that was missing a couple of fingers, stubs set like inadequate book markers. He traveled the back roads of the South and Appalachia like a swashbuckler on his infamous Indian Chief motorcycle. Armed with a book of poems and a Bible, he would eventually carry a .38 revolver. In the mid-1930s, he organized a brigade of Appalachian miners for the Republicans in the Spanish Civil War; his wife's only brother, Jack Adams, would never return from combat, cut down with many other Americans in the Abraham Lincoln Brigades at the merciless Battle of Ebro (Cooper and McElfresh 1973).

One of his first short stories, "Thoughts of a Kentucky Miner," had to be published under a pen name, Mack Adams, in *Mountain Life and Work* in 1936, which had blacklisted him from publication. The same magazine would reject work under his own name, including a poem, "A Time for Anger," that was later set to music by the popular folk trio Peter, Paul, and Mary. In 1937, on behalf of the Kentucky Workers Alliance, West published a booklet of labor songs, *Songs for Southern Workers,* written to popular tunes. Modeled on the *Little Red Songbook* published by the International Workers of the World, the booklet was widely used around the South.

On a national level in 1939, West's work created a flicker of controversy in the literary world when he was singled out for writing "propaganda art" in the critic Cleanth Brooks's study, *Modern Poetry and Tradition.* Brooks had chastised a poem from the *Proletarian Literature* anthology, "Southern Lullaby," which included, "Eat, little baby, eat well / A Bolshevik you'll be" (Brooks 1939:51; Hicks 1935:199).

West's fourth book, *Toil and Hunger,* was published in 1940 by Hagglund Press, a radical fugitive printer then based in San Benito, Texas. Allan McElfresh, who had worked with West in the Kentucky Workers Alliance, reviewed the book for *Mountain Life and Work.* He singled out the poem "Ballad Singer" as an example of West's "mastery of poetic simplicity, structure and lyricism" (McElfresh 1940:31).

> He sang in quiet places
> Along his mountain ways
> Where wrinkled human faces
> Showed tracks of weary days.
>
> He never heard the praises
> Of fame and loud acclaim

Don West at Bob Snyder's house in Beckley, West Virginia, after the 1974 Antioch College–Appalachia graduation. He lost fingers on his left hand dynamiting a stump on a farm as a youth.

Which oft the headline raises
Around a polished name.

But he saw furrowed faces
And gripped the calloused hand
Of men in quiet places
Where lonely cabins stand.

By the late 1930s, however, concern over domestic issues became more and more overwhelmed by the war clouds looming in Europe and Asia, and work for organizers dried up. West returned to the ministry briefly, serving as the pastor of a Congregational church in Bethel, Ohio, and then a parish in Meansville, Georgia, in the early 1940s, where he also published a newsletter, the *Country Parson*. During the same period he contributed articles to various publications, including a regular column on religion, "The Awakening Church," for the *Southern News Almanac*, a leftist tabloid out of Alabama (Kelly 1990:196). After one of his deacons led a mob in beating an elderly black man who was accused of brushing against a white woman, West resigned his position and never pastored a church full-time again. He ended up taking a job on a Mississippi River steamboat, based in Memphis, for the rest of the year.

Retreating to his family's Georgia farm for a short period, West attempted to take a break from the political fray. Along with freelance writing for several newspapers, he worked on a novel that was never completed. He declared in letters to his friends and colleagues that he had "severed my former political connections," in a cryptic reference to the Communist Party, though he remained committed to its leftist cause (West 1939). Through the generosity of a sympathetic preacher in Cincinnati, West had been able to purchase a small farm, once owned by his paternal grandfather, near Cartersville, Georgia. It was here that their second daughter, Hedy, was born in 1938 (West 1981).

Ironically, it was during this period, at the onset of the Second World War, that the FBI launched what would become an intense thirty-year monitoring of West's life; in an internal memo from the Department of Justice on December 1, 1941, West was listed by the Special Defense Unit as part of a group of "individuals believed to be the most dangerous and who in all probability should be interned in event of War" (FBI Memorandum 100-20396-5).

In 1942 West took a job as superintendent of a school in Lula, Georgia, attracting national attention again for his ideas about cooperative learning and community development. *Seventeen Magazine* featured the school "that runs the town" ("Plumb to Yonder" 1946), while the New York–based magazine *Reader's Scope* highlighted the school's role in organizing farm cooperatives, establishing a school newspaper and radio program, and developing cottage industries (Davis 1946). West initiated student reforms and led his teachers in basing their curricula on student-centered concepts of teaching. West's wartime stationery trumpeted the school's motto: "Education for Victory over Fascism Both Foreign and Domestic."

The tenure at Lula was an impressive and largely overlooked achievement in West's life. By 1945, his work brought him a prestigious Rosenwald Fellowship for graduate research and study at the University of Chicago and Columbia University. Endowed by the former president of Sears, Roebuck, and Company, this foundation had become a major philanthropic channel for research and education in the South, funding leading educators, writers, and artists, including Zora Neale Hurston, C. Vann Woodward, and James Weldon Johnson, among others. After this period of study, West returned to Atlanta and taught creative writing and education courses at Oglethorpe University (Egerton 1994).

By the time of the release of *Clods of Southern Earth* in 1946, West had published and performed his poetry throughout the country, especially in the South and Appalachia. Most of the poems in the volume had previously appeared in smaller chapbooks or magazine and newspaper publications; all references to communism or Bolsheviks had been removed. He had helped to create an extraordinary poetry circuit among new readers and towns in the South and Appalachia and around the nation. He had also developed a vast network of friends, unions, and organizations that considered him, in the words of Alva Taylor, "'the poet laureate of the New South'" (qtd. in West 1951). He had even been featured as the prototype for a populist leader in Henrietta Buckmaster's historical novel *Deep River* in 1944, which had become a wartime bestseller.

The favorable reception of *Clods of Southern Earth,* therefore, like his own performances in the fields, churches, and union halls, was inevitable. Published in 1946, in a postwar period that had narrowed the public debate to a stultifying orthodoxy, its success was nothing less than remarkable.

The literary reception of *Clods of Southern Earth* was mixed at best and regional in tone. Ironically, the literary South welcomed West's celebration of racial unity and his mountain roots. His often didactic poems for the rights of farmers, miners, and displaced southerners and Appalachians as well as his plea for civil rights were accepted and generally praised within the context of his political and cultural role in the South. Despite the headlines of lynchings and the outbreak of the Cold War, the South and Appalachia recognized West as their native son.

The *Atlanta Constitution,* a newspaper that would eventually hound West as a communist pariah, found him to be a "strong writer . . . who occasionally achieves literary art—as when he gives you the real essence of the mountaineer" (Hite 1946). The reviewer called him a "Walt Whitman in overalls."

Seeking to place West within the context of the literary South, the reviewer concluded that, "Some readers may not care for Mr. West's style, but no one can fail to find in these poems a challenge" (Hite 1946).

Echoing such sentiments across the Midwest, the *St. Louis Post-Dispatch* declared: "He speaks a language the workers understand, and highly articulate, translates their troubles into shining and searing words" ("Georgia Poet" 1946).

While dismissing Jesse Stuart's "repudiation of a mountain town" in his new book, *Foretaste of Glory,* published the same year, *Mountain Life and Work* embraced West's volume in the same issue: "Regardless of whether or not one thinks poetry should preach in just this way, here is poetry and here is a sermon. He is deaf indeed who will not listen, and look and think deep" ("*Clods*" 1946:26).

The literary reviews in New York City were less favorable. Nash K. Burger, writing for the *New York Times Book Review,* excoriated West's "homespun" collection as propaganda for the Soviet Union, mocked his portraits of textile workers "with gaunt eyes," and insinuated that the author was out of touch with the real South. "West's South . . . is a romantic, simplified South which will be readily recognized by every schoolboy from Moscow to Vladivostok, but it has several features that will bewilder most Southerners, white and black—and especially those white 'workers' who have just gotten through sending Bilbo and Rankin back to Congress" (Burger 1946). Burger's reference to the southern demagogues underscored the northern intellectual's distrust of West's "crackers."

The *New York Herald Tribune Weekly Book Review* was untroubled with West's politics but dubious of his literary form. According to the noted poet and reviewer Ruth Lechlitner, "Although the militant regionalism of his general theme is over-simplified and over sentimentalized, Don West's love for the Georgia countryside and its people is genuine and compassionate. It is not his subject matter, but his form that often fails him as a poet of the people." In contrast to Carl Sandburg, who published *Poems of the Midwest* in the same year, she added, "West would be a much more memorable poet if he used a strong stressed, near-Biblical form" (Lechlitner 1946).

Most of West's readership would never read a single review. In 1947, *Publishers Weekly* noted the participation of tenant farmers and unions in the marketing of the book, including the role of Rev. Claude Williams, West's former classmate at Vanderbilt, once aligned with the Southern Tenant Farmers Union ("Boni and Gaer" 1947). The Southern Conference for Human Welfare gave copies to new subscribers to its journal (Dunbar 1981:213). West himself was shocked to find a receipt in his publisher's New York office from a Tennessee union that had ordered a thousand copies for their members as Christmas presents. Huge book signings followed in West's hometown base in Atlanta. Though unconfirmed, the volume was later reported in the *Atlanta Journal and Constitution* (Sibley 1952; Graham 1989) to have sold nearly a hundred thousand copies.

Delighted by the success of *Clods of Southern Earth,* West wrote to Myles Horton in 1946 of this "pleasing experience after so damn many years of scraping bottom" (West 1946). Unfortunately, the poet didn't have much time to enjoy the celebrity status associated with his book. In 1948, when the Progressive party nominated Henry Wallace as a presidential candidate against Truman, Dewey, and the Dixiecrat Strom Thurmond, West became a delegate of the Progressive party in Georgia; West had earlier made a failed bid for a local office in the Lula area on behalf of the Progressives. His maverick role in the Wallace campaign heightened criticism from all sides, including liberal newspaper editors, elements of right-wing racist organizations, and ideologues in the Communist Party.

The hostile air of the Eugene Talmadge administration in Georgia, which had earlier declared that "any person in the university system advocating Communism or racial equality" would be removed (Anderson 1975:175), still permeated the times. Ralph McGill, the legendary editor of the *Atlanta Constitution,* wrote numerous editorials red-baiting West during the campaign, holding him accountable for his earlier political activities and publications, including the poem "I Am a Communist," which he had published in the *Daily Worker* in 1934 (McGill 1948). To further exacerbate his precarious situation, West had publicly defended Rosalie Ingram, a black woman who had been sentenced to the electric chair, along with her two children, after the children shot and killed a white man who had broken into the house and attempted to rape their mother. Before the end of 1948, West lost his job at Oglethorpe, despite being selected by the students as one of the most popular professors ("Prof. West Chosen" 1947). Connie West also was fired from her job as an art teacher in the public schools.

Eventually, elements of the Klan would add their own touch, burning down his family home and barn. West ended up losing his lifelong collection of books, handicrafts, his grandfather's tools, and all of his manuscripts as well as the library of the novelist Olive Tilford Dargan, who had feared this kind of retribution for her own leftist sentiments (West 1981). Years later, West would write one of his poems, "For These Sad Ashes," as an inventory of the literature and arts that had been burned:

> But they burned them
> And their ashes are part
> Of Georgia's red dirt
> Where wind-bent weed roots now feed.

These were trying times. The fervent movements of the 1930s and 1940s had become dormant; many of the points of struggle, such as workman's compensation, labor contracts, social security, and unemployment insurance, had actually been won. The nascent steps of the civil rights movement would not be taken until the Montgomery bus boycott in the mid-1950s. The rising tide of McCarthyism unleashed in 1950 against "internal subversion of Communists" would begin to crush liberals and radicals like West.

Even his longtime friend Langston Hughes, who had been West's academic neighbor in Atlanta in 1947 as a guest professor, would release a new collection of "lyrical poems," marking a temporary departure from politics.

West returned once again to the family farm. He raised and peddled corn and vegetables. He wrote occasional feature stories and editorials on rural communities for Aubrey Williams's *Southern Farmer,* a journal based in Alabama that claimed a circulation of one million. In 1951 West briefly worked for the Home Missions Council of North America, a precursor to the Division of Home Missions of the National Council of Churches, serving communities of mostly Mexican migrant workers in southern Texas.

West's next book of poetry, *The Road Is Rocky,* appeared in 1951, with a small New York publisher, New Christian Books; a similar chapbook also appeared in Texas. Addressing a national readership, steeped in biblical language and imagery, and divided into three parts—"A Time for Anger," "A Time for Rejoicing," and "A Time for Love"—many of the poems challenge the literary community to confront the darkness of McCarthyism and the nation's enduring disparity. Others address the role of women in West's first major forays into love poetry. Several of the poems also chronicle West's travels and work among farm workers in the American Southwest; he dedicated the book to two union organizers based in Texas.

In the book's inside cover, the fellow Georgia poet Byron Herbert Reece hails West as "a People's Poet," in the tradition of Robert Burns and John Greenleaf Whittier, who speaks "his heart against the vicious and tyrannical." Hughes proffered a blurb: "these are the poems of our heartbeats and our longings from the cotton South to the orange grove West, as American as Route 66." Despite a marketing plan among unions and churches, the book lacked the momentum and timing of *Clods of Southern Earth.* It received no reviews in the mainstream national press.

Hughes's *Montage of a Dream Deferred* would be published that year to poor reviews and attacked in the *New York Times* as showing the "'limitations of folk art'" (qtd. in Rampersad 1989:192). William Carlos Williams would also make a strong attack in the same year on the quality of Carl Sandburg's *Collected Poems.* As the critic Donald Davidson had once written in a survey on southern literature, all books dealing with "poor whites" were disregarded, since they were the result of a state of mind that was "not quite healthy" (Cook 1976:187).

Ever more scornful of mainstream literary circles, West had a self-proclaimed working stiff write the introduction to his new book. Roy Smith, a plumber and superintendent who had worked in Georgia on various WPA projects, declared, "Don West is the poet laureate of the common people of the South, if not all America. . . . Big shots in the literary world are shocked when a man like Don West comes up from a Georgia sharecropper's stock . . . with a book of poems that gets mass distribution. They can't understand. These poets who write little pettyfogging nothings for each other, to be circulated in a few hundred copies, can't understand when textile workers, coal miners and sharecroppers buy and read a book of poems" (West 1951).

The virulence of the McCarthy era finally arrived at the Wests' farm in the early 1950s. While plowing the fields down by the Chattahoochee River, West was handed the first of several subpoenas he would receive in the 1950s to appear before congressional committees, including the House Committee on Un-American Activities. West would always invoke the Fifth Amendment or refuse to cooperate. Most of the accusations implicating him came from an informant, Paul Crouch, a disgruntled Communist Party organizer whose fabrications, inaccuracies, and contradictory stories ended up discrediting his testimonies (Alsop and Alsop 1954). Nevertheless, any direct connection with the Communist Party dogged West for the rest of his life. One of the most telling inferences ironically emerged in the 1970s from West's longtime friend Hosea Hudson. He wrote about their comical experiences at a Communist Party "national training school" in New York in 1934 in his memoir, *The Narrative of Hosea Hudson, His Life as a Negro Communist in the South.* Due to an editorial oversight, West's last name, interchanged with the pseudonym of Jim Gray, was disclosed in the book (Painter 1979).

After the fallout of the bitter 1948 Wallace election, the *Atlanta Journal* noted that West had long cut ties with all political organizations; West, according to one unidentified source, claimed "he was too rugged for the Communist Party" ("Rows with Miss Tontak" 1949).

In a rare public admission regarding his political past, a beleaguered West had confided in Celestine Sibley, a reporter for the *Atlanta Constitution,* in 1952, after returning from a day of peddling vegetables in Atlanta:

> "They won't let me alone," he [West] said. "Twenty years ago I wrote a poem which appeared in *The Daily Worker.* I was a Communist then. Any young person who is not a rebel is not worth his salt.
>
> "I am not a Communist now. I am a Georgia farmer.
>
> "When I worked for the people's Progressive Party the Communists fought, opposed and attacked me as much as Ralph McGill has."

Reminded that he never denied editor McGill's charges that he is a Communist, West said:

"I don't think it does any good to deny or claim. I believe in the teachings of Jesus. I believe if there is one thing you can live by it's His saying, 'By their fruits ye shall know them.'

"I'll be content to be known by my fruits." (Sibley 1952)

Nearly a half-century later, Sibley, who became a leading chronicler of southern life and culture, listed West's poetry among her favorites (Sibley 1998).

In 1955 West returned to the fray when he agreed to edit a newspaper, *The Southerner,* for the Union Assembly of God, an unusual church in Dalton, Georgia. The church's mercurial minister, Rev. C. T. Pratt, had served as one of the cochairmen of Henry Wallace's Georgia campaign. The paper chronicled the poor living and working conditions in the area and served as an organ for a subsequent effort to unionize the chenille workers in the local textile factories. West's background as well as the controversy surrounding the strike eventually caught up with him. Recycling the columns and issues from the *Atlanta Constitution* in the 1940s, the Dalton newspaper editors hounded West for months for his radical political affiliations; his "I Am a Communist" poem was reprinted and widely distributed in a special "Don West supplement." The anticommunist hysteria reached a boiling point; a lynching party against West was disbanded at the last moment. *The Nation* magazine noted that even the Dalton newspaper editors had become alarmed by the "impending mob action" (Weissman 1956:149).

After admitting that he had once invoked the Fifth Amendment before a grand jury, West refused to cooperate with a staged cattle call to submit to a "loyalty oath." He resigned from the newspaper and left town, though not without violence. When a car full of gun thugs attempted to drive him off the winding mountain curves on the outskirts of town, West shot out the tires of the charging vehicle with a .38 pistol, allowing for a narrow escape.

Ironically, in this same period, internal memorandums at the FBI, dated 1955, noted that due to West's lack of contact with revolutionary or communist associations he had been dropped from the Security Index investigations (FBI Memorandum 100-20396-139).

Undaunted by the Dalton experience, West attempted to launch his own newspaper, the *New Southerner,* from Aubrey Williams's publishing operations in Montgomery, Alabama, in 1956. "Dedicated to the rights and interests of Negro and white working people of the South," the newspaper floundered after a few issues, unable to locate financial support.

Returning to Georgia, West relied on his farm to make ends meet once again. He sold his surplus vegetables on the streets of Atlanta, often going door-to-door. His wife Connie was forced to take a teaching job in Florida, again splitting up their family. The Klan continued to make regular cross-burning visits to the farm. West was subpoenaed in 1957 to appear in Memphis for congressional hearings on internal security, where he invoked the Fifth Amendment, adding, "I am working only on the matter of running a farm, trying to making a living." In 1958 West was once more called to testify at another House Un-American Activities Committee hearing in Atlanta, while his wife languished in critical condition in a Kentucky hospital, recovering from a serious car accident.

Exhausted by the turmoil and persecution in the South during this period, with his wife in need of further medical care, the Wests packed up and found work as teachers in Baltimore in 1960, where they remained for several years. Connie had secured a job teaching art in the public schools, and Don taught at various institutions, including a rabbinical academy. He also received a Rabinowitz grant for research and study on the history of Appalachia at the Library of Congress.

Within a short time, however, the tug and pull of leftist political movements became irresistible for the longtime firebrand. While living in Maryland, West became one of few "Old Left" activists to reach out to the emerging antiwar, civil rights, and "New Left" student movements in the 1960s. He attended National Council meetings of Students for a Democratic Society—as did his former coworker, Myles Horton. While suspicious of the middle-class counterculture trends, West openly embraced the identity politics and radical causes of the Black Power and American Indian movements and the growing revolutionary upheavals in Latin America and the Third World. Still, his heart remained closest to the ongoing struggles of his native Appalachians.

Down Here in Appalachia

The Wests' exile from the Mountain South was short-lived. Living on one salary in Maryland, the couple had put aside their savings for several years. After a tour of the region, they purchased a six-hundred-acre farm in southeastern West Virginia with the hopes of launching another folk school. In 1965 the Appalachian South Folklife Center was "dedicated to a mountain heritage of freedom, self-respect and independence with human dignity." The center sponsored adult education and farming classes, a summer camp, and a mountain music and poetry festival, coordinated the Heifer Livestock Project in the area, and provided social services and outreach programs to families in the hardest-to-reach hollows. Once again in the national spotlight, West was featured in *National Geographic,* which profiled his effort at the center to teach "mountain children the value of their cultural heritage" (Hodgson 1972:125).

By the early 1970s, the Folklife Center had attracted throngs of Appalachians, college students, activists, and folk-song enthusiasts during a revival of folk music and mountain culture. West found himself to be a mentor for a new generation of young activists and writers inspired by the Appalachian Identity Movement and other regional-consciousness efforts. Serving as a trustee and faculty member at the Antioch College's Appalachian Center in Beckley, West Virginia, West was, according to his longtime colleague Yvonne Farley, "a living connection to history who filled in the blanks on our Appalachian heritage by making the historical connections from Georgia to West Virginia" (Farley 2002). For the poet P. J. Laska, who took part in the noted Soupbean Poets collective in the 1970s, his Appalachian group's literary efforts were a "natural outgrowth of Bob Snyder's educational idea and Don's historical record of struggle against the exploitation and colonization of the Region" (Laska 2002). Laska added that West's "influence can be seen not so much in the style of what we wrote as in the stance, which was both radical and angry—and sometimes splenetic" (Laska 2002). In the foreword to a pamphlet of poetry, *A Time for Anger,* the Appalachian Movement Press editor and activist Tom Woodruff declared, "Don West gave us the spirit and moral support needed to start and to continue our efforts despite the mass of non-support and criticism all around us" (Woodruff 1970).

Back on the poetry-reading circuit, West maintained a busy schedule, performing his work around the county on fundraising trips for his Folklife Center. Once again, it was the performance of his poetry that kept his literary work alive.

More radical than ever, many of his poems laced with a bitter edge, West returned to publishing in the 1970s, opting for personal control and a West Virginia printer at the Appalachia Movement Press in Huntington. The press produced low-cost pamphlets on myriad themes related to Appalachia. One of West's poems, "Appalachian Blues," became a symbolic indictment of the machinations in the region in the 1960s, fingering the disastrous impact of poverty relief programs, missionaries, folk music collectors, and corporate control:

> Down here in Appalachia,
> Government-designated "poverty area"
> blue thoughts stagger
> up the valley
> whisper on mountain fogs—
> [. . .]
>
> You do-gooders
> missionaries of numerous persuasions
> soul-savers who paint outside privies
> poverty warriors who play at being poor

and gather us together
to tell us what our troubles are,
long haired hustlers
expert at proposal writing
lengthy verbiage
for Federal grants. . . .

West became more adamant about the singular nature of his background and heritage—what he termed "Appalachian values." He implored Appalachians to reject the materialistic creeds of the day. In the poem "Mountain Heritage," he pleaded:

Listen
You mountain kid
Old woman or man,
I would call you back
To your own heritage . . . !

Must we, too, be lost
As America is lost
In a thicket of violent greed?
Are we too lost to recognize
Our own broken image?

In his most prolific period in years, invoking the spirit of the revolutionary pamphleteer Thomas Paine, West published a number of pamphlets about Appalachia, including *People's Cultural Heritage in Appalachia, Songs for Southern Workers, Romantic Appalachia; or, Poverty Pays If You Ain't Poor,* and *Southern Mountain Folk Tradition and the Folksong "Stars" Syndrome,* examining the region's abolitionist traditions and heroes, economic and social conditions, and music and customs. He sought to chronicle the continuum of a uniquely progressive Appalachian heritage of defiance and independence. He drew haunting parallels between the prophetic and mostly dismissed mountain voices in the antislavery movement during the Civil War and the overlooked activists in his own times. His articles and interviews began to appear regularly again in regional magazines.

Often misinterpreted as romantic, West's work expressed a profound love for his preindustrial land-based mountain culture and yeomanry, championed Appalachian resistance to outside control, and dealt with the stereotypes and misinterpretations that had been grafted onto mainstream interpretations of the sociocultural evolution of the mountaineers. The region's labor movement battles of the 1920s and 1930s became an increasingly common chorus in his poetry, functioning as a sort of litany of Appalachia's bitter labor triumphs amid industrialization's displacement. West's work, indeed, blatantly overcompensated for what he perceived as the disregard of the mountaineer's progressive spirit, seeking to fill in the gaps of unrecorded history and neglected recognition of the Mountain South's cultural heritage. In this way, West's prose and poetry defiantly emphasized a positive, meaningful, and vital view of the Appalachian commoner. Taking this view one step further, he saw his work as a cultural bulwark of sorts: a sharp riposte to the deluge of mass media images of *Dogpatch, Snuffy Smith, The Beverly Hillbillies,* and Jack Weller's dreary missionary viewpoint in *Yesterday's People,* which continued to disparage the Mountain South as a quagmire in the backwash of history.

In the footsteps of Burns and Hughes, West had once been a darling of the urban literary parlor rooms, only to spurn their advances, beset by a lifelong hatred for the outside economic and cultural control of his region. "Southern Appalachia is a colonial possession of Eastern-based industry," West wrote. "Like all exploited colonial areas, the 'mother country' . . . will do about everything—except get off the backs of the people, and end the exploitative domination" (West 1969:6). His poetry and prose openly detested academics, literary critics, urban VISTA workers, missionaries, hippies, liberals, and Lil' Abner as much as the Ku Klux Klan, U.S. Steel, Consolidated Coal, company thugs, and Rockefeller.

In unabashed terms, West celebrated his beloved preindustrial heritage, the land of his grandfather Kim Mulkey, and a still displaced and exploited readership in the southern Appalachians. Invoking the lyrics of Florence Reece's Appalachian labor ballad, which had been written when West came of age politically during the bitter coal mining strikes in Harlan County, Kentucky, in 1931, West answered his own question to the literary world: "The poet can never be neutral. There is the inevitable question: Which side are you on?" (West 1982).

West's most ambitious project was the publication of *O Mountaineers!* in 1974, a collection of poems written over forty years. Aubrey Williams, the one-time ardent New Dealer and fellow southerner who had earned the loathing of both communists and anticommunists, wrote the collection's introduction. He declared that West "will go down in history as one of the true poets America has produced."

While West had regained a certain prominence among a New Left and Appalachian readership by the 1970s, national critics and academic anthology chroniclers overlooked or dismissed the collection and the nature and role of his work. This end result, of course, was nothing new to West or any of his closest readers; in fact, realizing his work had little chance in academic circles against the prevailing influence of his modernist peers, West went out of his way to taunt the critics. His publicity for *O Mountaineers!* restated his anti–

literary establishment pronouncements of the 1940s and 1950s: "Don West is not much like most of the other poets. His poems aren't the fancy, frilly, big worded say-nothings that serve only as mental exercises for the upper classes."

According to the poet and novelist Michael Henson, West continued to openly violate established assumptions about poetry, "that it must be 'literary' in its sources, complex in structure, and morally ambiguous," and in effect, his work was a "declaration of war on them" (Henson 1983:55). For these violations and the fact that the university-educated West had chosen to write in a "simple and accessible style," Henson added, poets such as West could "virtually guarantee that they will never be studied seriously" (Henson 1983:55).

Despite this increasing disappearance in the official canons of southern, Appalachian, and even social protest literature, West performed his work around the country until his late seventies. In many ways, he represented the academic's nightmare of political poetry: he was a folk poet who had commanded a considerable and responsive readership for over half a century, independent of literary journals, academia, and critics.

As a poet of the dispossessed, West had decidedly become dispossessed, excluded from and contemptuous of the publishing industry. Still managing to sell his poetry in the thousands, West relied on an underground network of readers to keep his work alive. In his last volume, he declared, "Purposely this book is not copyrighted. Poetry and other creative struggles should be levers, weapons to be used in the people's struggle for understanding, human rights, and decency" (West 1982).

Recognizing the range of West's readership, a small but aggressive Minneapolis press published *In a Land of Plenty: A Don West Reader* in 1982. Dispelling any reports of West's demise or the folly of self-publishing ventures, the book sold over six thousand copies in two printings. The West End Press publisher John Crawford considered West to be one of "the best living examples of oral culture, and [he] deserved a national audience" (Crawford 1999).

In the second edition of the volume, West included one of his first rhyming quatrains, "I Cannot Sing," written in 1933, which had served as a signature work of his themes over the past fifty years:

> I cannot sing within myself
> Of trees and flowers a-bloom
> While sad-eyed children still look out
> From many a barren room.

> I cannot sing just for the few
> Who live in wealth and ease,
> While there are those whom hunger gnaws
> And winter weather freeze.

For I must sing my simple songs
Of men who till the soil,
Of those who sweat in mill and mine
Or other honest toil.

I know of loving and of loves
That are unsatisfied,
From empty hearts from circumstance
Where kindled hope has died.

These are the themes my songs embrace—
An earth with love and strife.
I sing of them because they are
The stuff of living life.

Reviewing the collection for the *Appalachian Journal,* the novelist Richard Marius declared in his first line that, "It is hard to say anything bad about a good man like Don West" (Marius 1983:361). Marius chided West's glorification of the poor and his narrow view of poetry; conversely, as Marius pointed out, this political motive provided both "the power and curious tedium" (362) of West's work.

On Cabin Creek

During the 1980s, West and his wife retired from full-time activities at the Folklife Center, spending part of the year in St. Petersburg, Florida. After a heart attack and bypass surgery, along with a struggle with cancer, he retreated from public life and the projects at the Folklife Center, though he insisted on settling into a coal camp house in Cabin Creek, West Virginia, one of the hubs of the infamous coal wars. The move to the coal camp house was a symbolic act of moving back into the heart of his life struggles. Years before, West had written:

And there may be a tomorrow
On Cabin Creek
a clean tomorrow,
child of hope and hurt and solidarity.

The shadow of his political activities would eventually consume his legacy, especially within Appalachian and southern history annals. After filing for his FBI records through the Freedom of Information Act in 1982, West received over twelve hundred pages documenting his life and activities; hundreds more pages were included in the Highlander Folk School files. The records indicate that the FBI had closely monitored West's life for over thirty years.

In the winter of 1983, West made a long-planned trip to the Soviet Union, leading an Appalachian Peace Delegation on a visit to various sites, including selected coal mines. The trip drew little media attention, though. By the end of the Cold War, an octogenarian West saw his image shift from being a radical to becoming the "heart of the hills, a romantic hero," in an *Atlanta Journal and Constitution* profile (Graham 1989). A newspaper in Florida, where West spent the winters, hailed him an "American legend" (James 1989).

In 1987, the Appalachian Writers Association honored West for his lifetime contribution to literature; despite the honor, West's work still failed to be included in many of the regional anthologies and histories. After his wife and partner for sixty-three years died in 1990, West fell into further isolation on Cabin Creek.

When West died in 1992, the *New York Times* obituary outlined his activist history and educational achievements over several paragraphs. The article simply mentioned that he "wrote poetry that had been widely read in the South" (Saxon 1992).

A preacher, labor and political organizer, farmer, teacher and professor, editor, and writer, West had simply referred to himself as a poet in a *Mountain Life and Work* interview in 1971 that looked back at his life's work. He declared, "I think human nature potentially can be very beautiful and very lovable and very peaceful. . . . I think it is. When it is warped and twisted, it becomes otherwise. I guess basically I am a poet, and being a poet—that is what I always wanted to be—I think you could not believe any other way" (West 1971b:13).

Works Cited

Alsop, Joseph, and Stewart Alsop. 1954. "Information on the Informant." *Washington Post*, April 16.

Anderson, William. 1975. *The Wild Man from Sugar Creek: The Political Career of Eugene Talmadge.* Baton Rouge: Louisiana State University Press.

"Boni and Gaer." 1947. *Publishers Weekly,* March 22.

Brooks, Cleanth. 1939. *Modern Poetry and the Tradition.* Chapel Hill: University of North Carolina Press.

Burger, Nash. 1946. "Homespun Poems of the South." *New York Times Book Review,* July 28.

Byerly, Victoria Morris. 1992. "What Shall a Poet Sing? The Living Struggle of the Southern Poet and Revolutionary Don West." Ph.D. dissertation. Boston College.

"*Clods of Southern Earth,* by Don West." 1940. Unsigned review. *Mountain Life and Work,* Fall, 26.

Cook, Sylvia Jenkins. 1976. *From Tobacco Road to Route 66: The Southern Poor White in Fiction.* Chapel Hill: University of North Carolina Press.

Cooper, Giles, and Allan McElfresh. 1973. "They Fought Hunger! The Story of the

Kentucky Workers Alliance during the 1930s." Manuscript. University of Kentucky Library, Special Collections, Appalachia.

Crawford, John. 1999. Telephone interview by Jeff Biggers. August 20.

Davis, Griffin. 1946. "From the Hills of Georgia." *Reader's Scope,* January, 40–43.

Drake, Richard. 2001. *A History of Appalachia.* Lexington: University Press of Kentucky.

Duke, David C. 2002. *Writers and Miners: Activism and Imagery in America.* Lexington: University Press of Kentucky.

Dunbar, Anthony. 1981. *Against the Grain: Southern Radicals and Prophets, 1929–1959.* Charlottesville: University Press of Virginia.

Egerton, John. 1994. *Speak Now against the Day: The Generation before the Civil Rights Movement in the South.* New York: Alfred A. Knopf.

Farley, Yvonne. 2002. Telephone interview by Jeff Biggers. April 10.

Federal Bureau of Investigation. 1941. Freedom of Information/Privacy Acts Section. Subject: Donald Lee West. File 100-20396, sections 1–4. December 1. Memorandum 100-20396-5.

———. 1955. Freedom of Information/Privacy Acts Section. Subject: Donald Lee West. File 100-20396, sections 5–7. June 24. Memorandum 100-20396-139.

———. 1957. Freedom of Information/Privact Acts Section. Subject: Donald Lee West. File 100-20396, sections 8–9. October 26. Subject's Testimony, Internal Security Subcommittee Hearing, Memphis, Tenn.

"Georgia Poet Points to the Plight of Downtrodden." 1946. *St. Louis Post-Dispatch,* April 14.

Gilbert, James B. 1968. *Writers and Partisans: A History of Literary Radicalism in America.* New York: Wiley.

Glen, John M. 1988. *Highlander: No Ordinary School, 1932–1962.* Lexington: University Press of Kentucky.

Gold, Michael. 1934. "Change the World." *Daily Worker,* January 19.

Graham, Keith. 1989. "Heart of the Hills: Poet of the People Goes from Radical to Romantic Hero as Time Marches On." *Atlanta Journal and Constitution,* July 20.

Henson, Michael. 1983. "Naked Words That Have No Subtle Meaning: Poetry and Teaching in the Writings of Don West." In *Appalachian Studies Conference 1983.* Boone, N.C.: Appalachian Consortium Press. 54–60.

Hicks, Granville, ed. 1935. *Proletarian Literature in the United States: An Anthology.* New York; International Publishers.

Hite, Alex. 1946. "Poetry Books Are Written by Georgians." *Atlanta Constitution,* August 4.

Hodgson, Bryan. 1972. "Mountain Voices, Mountain Days." *National Geographic Magazine,* July, 118–46.

James, Sheryl. 1989. "A Radical of Long Standing." *St. Petersburg Times,* March 22.

Kelly, Robin D. G. 1990. *Hammer and Hoe: Alabama Communists during the Great Depression.* Chapel Hill: University of North Carolina Press.

Laska, P. J. 2002. E-mail interview by Jeff Biggers. May 4.

Lechlitner, Ruth. 1946. "Overalls Poet." *New York Herald Tribune Weekly Book Review,* September 8.

Livingstone, Sir Richard. 1945. *On Education.* Cambridge: Cambridge University Press.

Marius, Richard. 1983. "Don West's Sermon on the Mount." *Appalachian Journal* 10.4 (Summer): 361–62.

Martin, Charles. 1976. *The Angelo Herndon Case and Southern Justice.* Baton Rouge: Louisiana State University Press.

McElfresh, Allan. 1940. "Toil and Hunger." *Mountain Life and Work,* Fall, 31.

McGill, Ralph. 1948. "All Right, Here It Is!" *Atlanta Constitution,* October 18.

Nelson, Cary. 1996. "Poetry Chorus: Dialogic Politics in 1930s Poetry." In *Radical Revisions: Rereading 1930s Culture.* Ed. Sherry Linken and Bill Mullen. Urbana: University of Illinois Press. 29–59

Painter, Nell Irvin. 1979. *The Narrative of Hosea Hudson: His Life as a Negro Communist in the South.* Cambridge, Mass.: Harvard University Press.

Pickard, Walt. 1934. *Burlington Dynamite Plot.* New York: International Labor Defense.

"Plumb to Yonder." 1946. *Seventeen Magazine,* June, 103–45.

"Prof. West Chosen Student Advisor." 1947. *The Stormy Petrel* (Oglethorpe University), November 7.

Rampersad, Arnold. 1989. *The Life of Langston Hughes, 1941–1967: I Dream a World.* Oxford: Oxford University Press.

Richardson, H. Edward. 1984. *Jesse: The Biography of an American Writer.* New York: McGraw-Hill.

Rolfe, Edwin. 1934. "Hounded by Georgia Terror, Don West Fights for Herndon and Atlanta 6." *Daily Worker,* June 11.

"Rows with Miss Tontak Hurried Barfoot Decision." 1949. *Atlanta Journal,* June 29.

Rubin, Rachel. 2003. "Voice of the Cracker: Don West Re-invents the Appalachian." In *Left of the Color Line: Race, Radicalism, and Twentieth-Century Literature of the United States.* Ed. Bill Mullen and James Smethurst. Chapel Hill: University of North Carolina Press. 205–21.

Salmond, John. 1998. "The Burlington Dynamite Plot: The 1934 Textile Strike and Its Aftermath in Burlington, North Carolina." *Northern Carolina History Review* 75.4 (October): 398–434.

Saxon, Wolfgang. 1992. "Don West, 86, Dies; Fought for the Poor, Workers and Blacks." *New York Times,* October 2.

Sibley, Celestine. 1952. "Neither a Red nor Scout Organizer, Poet Don West Answers Senators." *Atlanta Constitution,* August 14.

———. 1998. "Old Favorite Poems Can Be as Warming as the Hearth." *Atlanta Journal and Constitution,* November 23.

Sigal, Clancy. 1961. *Going Away.* New York: Dell.

Smethurst, James Edward. 1999. *The New Red Negro: The Literary Left and African American Poetry, 1930–1946.* Oxford: Oxford University Press.

Smith, May B. 1932. Review of *Crab-Grass,* by Don West. *Mountain Life and Work,* July, 26.

Solomon, Mark. 1998. *The Cry Was Unity: Communists and African Americans, 1917–1936.* Jackson: University Press of Mississippi.

Still, James. 2001. *From the Mountain, from the Valley: New and Collected Poems.* Lexington: University Press of Kentucky.

Wald, Alan. 2002. *Exiles from a Future Time: The Forging of the Mid-Twentieth-Century Literary Left.* Chapel Hill: University of North Carolina Press.

Weissman, George. 1956. "Pulpit for Unionism." *The Nation,* February 25, 149.

West, Don. 1931. *Crab-Grass.* Nashville: Art Print Shop, Trevecca College.

———. 1932a. *Between the Plow Handles: Poems.* Monteagle, Tenn.: Highlander Folk School.

———. [1932b]. *Deep, Deep Down in Living.* N.p.

———. 1932c. "Knott County, Kentucky: A Study." Bachelor's thesis. Vanderbilt School of Religion.

———. 1933. "Sweatshops in the Schools." *New Republic,* October 4, 216.

———. 1934a. "Georgia Wanted Me Dead or Alive." *New Masses,* June 26, 15–16.

———. 1934b. "I Am a Communist." *Daily Worker,* March 13, 5.

———. 1939. Letter to Howard Kester. December 14. Box B3. Manuscripts Department. Wilson Library. University of North Carolina at Chapel Hill.

———. 1940. *Toil and Hunger: Poems.* San Benito, Tex.: Hagglund Press.

———. 1946a. *Clods of Southern Earth.* New York: Boni and Gaer.

———. 1946b. Letter to Myles Horton. April 5. Box B29. Highlander Papers. Wisconsin Historical Society, Madison.

———. 1951. *The Road Is Rocky.* New York: New Christian Books.

———. 1969. "Romantic Appalachia; or, Poverty Pays If You Ain't Poor." *West Virginia Hillbilly,* March 29, 1–6.

———. 1970a. "Freedom in the Mountains: Appalachian History." *Mountain Life and Work,* December, 20–22.

———. 1970b. *A Time for Anger: Poems Selected from "The Road Is Rocky" and "Clods of Southern Earth."* Huntington, W.Va.: Appalachian Movement Press.

———. 1971a. "The Heritage of Appalachian People." *Mountain Life and Work,* May, 3–7.

———. 1971b. "Mountaineers Fighting For Freedom: An Interview with Don West." *Mountain Life and Work.* January, 6–13.

———. 1971c. *People's Cultural Heritage in Appalachia.* Huntington, W.Va.: Appalachian Movement Press.

———. [1972a]. *Romantic Appalachia; or, Poverty Pays If You Ain't Poor.* Huntington, W.Va.: Appalachian Movement Press.

———. [1972b]. *Southern Mountain Folk Tradition and the Folksong "Stars" Syndrome.* Huntington, W.Va.: Appalachian Movement Press.

———. 1973a. *Freedom on the Mountains: Excerpts from a Book Manuscript on Southern Mountain History.* Huntington, W. Va.: Appalachian Movement Press.

———. [1973b]. *Robert Tharin: Biography of a Mountain Abolitionist.* Huntington, W.Va.: Appalachian Movement Press.

———. 1973c. *Songs for Southern Workers: 1937 Songbook of the Kentucky Workers Alliance.* Huntington, W.Va.: Appalachian Movement Press.

———. 1974. *O Mountaineers!* Huntington, W.Va.: Appalachian Press.

————. 1975a. "Interview with Don West, January 22, 1975," by Jacquelyn Hall and Ray Faherty. Southern Oral History Project. University of North Carolina at Chapel Hill.

————. 1975b. "Reminiscences of Don West: Interview by Dr. Alex Baskin." Stony Brook, N.Y. February 5.

————. 1979. "Hard Times Cotton Mill Girls." *Sing Out!* 27.3 (June–July): 11–13.

————. 1981. Personal interview by George Brosi. Berea, Ky. May 20.

————. 1982. *In a Land of Plenty.* Minneapolis: West End Press.

————. 1985. *In a Land of Plenty.* Reprint edition with additional poems. Los Angeles: West End Press.

————. 1986. "Harry Harrison Kroll: An Essay." *Appalachian Mountain Books News and Reviews* 2.2:18–21.

Wigginton, Eliot. 1992. *Refuse to Stand Silently By: An Oral History of Grass-roots Social Activism in America, 1921–1964.* New York: Doubleday.

Woodruff, Tom. 1970. Foreword to *A Time for Anger: Poems Selected from "The Road Is Rocky" and "Clods of Southern Earth."* Huntington, W.Va.: Appalachian Movement Press.

selected prose

Don West, October 1987.

clods of southern earth: introduction (1946)

Editors' Note: Drawing on his family background and longtime research on the "other history" of the Mountain South, West's essay "intends to tell about these people with rough hands, big feet, and hard bodies; about the real men and women of the South." A shorter, slightly different version of this introduction to Clods of Southern Earth *appeared earlier in* Toil and Hunger *(1940).*

Once upon a time, not too long ago, authors wrote mainly about kings and nobles—the aristocracy. Many stories and poems were filled with debauchery and intrigues. Writers occupied themselves in turning out tales about the purity of lovely ladies and the daring of gallant gentlemen who never did a useful day's work in their lives.

The fact that systems of kings and nobles, of aristocratic ladies and useless gentlemen, were always reared upon the misery of masses of peasants, slaves, or workers, was carefully omitted from most books. The idea that these same peasants, slaves, or workers might themselves be fit material for literature would have been heresy.

You may think this is a strange sort of way to begin an introduction to a group of poems. You may be one of those Americans who say you don't like poetry anyhow. No one can blame you for that. I've often felt that way, too. Maybe it's because too many poets write in the old tradition. Using an obscure and "subtle" private language, they write only for the little clique of the "highly literate" elite. But in spite of their high and mighty intellectual snobbery, one finds them, after all, concerned mostly with minor themes. Such literary gentlemen, writing only for the "elite" ten percent, spurn the "crude" and "vulgar" masses. They still have their eyes full of star dust. They see neither the dirt and misery nor the beauty and heroism of common folk life.

You say you want a poem with its roots in the earth; a poem that finds beauty in the lives of common people, and perhaps a poem that may sometimes show the reasons for the heartache and sorrow of the plain folks and sometimes point the way ahead. I don't blame you. I sort of feel that way, too.

Does this sound like a strange notion about poetry? Maybe it is. Some people say I have strange notions anyhow. I don't know. Lots of things I don't know. I've been a preacher, and I've preached the working-man, Jesus, who had some strange notions himself about the poor and rich and the slaves. I've been a coal miner in Kentucky's Cumberlands[1] and a textile worker in Carolina. I've been a radio commentator in Georgia and a deck hand on a Mississippi River steamboat. I've been a sailor, a farm owner, and farmer. I am now a school Superintendent. And I've wondered why it always seems that the folks who work less get more and those who work more get less. That puzzles me some. I've a notion it shouldn't be that way, and some say I have strange notions.

Maybe it's because of family background. You know, some people go in for that family stuff. I do come from an old Southern family. You've heard that one before, yes? Well, I don't mean what you think. Mine is a real old Southern family. Oh, I'm no sprig off the decadent tree of some bourbon, aristocratic, blue-blood family of the notorious slave-master tradition.

That's what is usually meant. You know—the professional Southerners who claim to be kind to Negroes—the tuxedoed gentlemen, the silk underweared, lace-dressed ladies coyly peeping from behind scented fans. No, I don't mean that. I'm more Southern than that. That represents only the small minority. My folks were the men who wore jean pants and the women who wore linsey petticoats. They had nothing to do with the genteel tradition. Some were the first white settlers of Georgia, and some were already settled when the white ones came.

Yes, on one limb of my family tree hangs a bunch of ex-jailbirds. They were good, honest (I hope, but it doesn't make a lot of difference now) working people in the old country. They were thrown in jails there because they were unemployed and couldn't raise money to pay their debts.

How in the devil a man is expected to pay a debt while lying in prison is hard to see. Maybe it satisfied the creditors to take it out on their hides. Anyhow, there they were, hundreds of them, and a man named Oglethorpe,[2] who had a big warm heart and a real feeling for folks, asked the old king to let him take a group of these prisoners to the new land.

The king didn't warm up to the idea much at first, but finally he was convinced. These outcasts would make a nice buffer protection for the more blue-blooded settlers of the other colonies, against the Indians and Spanish. The place later to be known as Georgia was just the spot. The colonies warmed right up to the idea, too. Nice to have a gang of tough jailbirds known as "arrow-fodder" between them and the Indians. So, you see, Georgia was started. The plan worked.

Some Southerners love to boast about their families. And I reckon I do too, a little. At least none of mine ever made his living by driving slaves. There's nary a slave owner up my family tree. The old story that we don't look too closely for fear of finding a "horse thief" is commonplace, of course. Indeed, wouldn't it be shameful to find one of our grand-paws doing such a petty theft? Who could be proud of a great-grand-daddy with ambition no higher than stealing a horse? B'gad, we Americans go in for big stuff! Steal a horse? No! But steal a continent, a nation; steal the lives and labor of thousands of black men and women in slavery; steal the wages of underpaid workers; steal a railroad, a bank, a million dollars—oh boy, now you're talking! That's the real class. Those are the ancestors America's blue-bloods worship. But steal a horse—aw, heck, the guy might have been hanged for that!

Guess I'd better tell you about that other limb on my family tree now. From what I can uncover, it had just two main branches with a few sprigs sprouting off. A forked sort of bush, you know. On that other fork hangs a white slave (indentured servant) in Carolina and a kind hearted old Indian of the Cherokees in north Georgia. To make a long story short—though I think it is a beautiful, if tragic one—this white slave girl and her lover ran away from their master in the Carolina tidewater country. The girl was pregnant, but the master had been forcing his attentions on her and that was more than her lover could stand. They set out toward the Indian country of north Georgia. Hearing the pursuers close behind, the man stopped, telling the girl to keep going and he'd overtake her if he got a lucky shot. He never overtook her. She went on and finally, weary and near death, reached the Indian settlement around Tallulah Falls in north Georgia. The Indians put her to bed and cared for her. The baby, a boy, was born. The child grew up as an Indian, married into the tribe, and had other children.

This, then, is the other limb of our family tree.

Do you think I'm telling about this tree just because it's mine? You're partly right. But the main reason is that, to a greater or lesser degree, it represents the great majority of Southern whites. And their real story has never yet been adequately told. Some day I intend to do it, to tell about these people with rough hands, big feet, and hard bodies; about the real men and women of the South.

That old Southern family stuff that you've heard so much about, always meaning the aristocratic, slave-owning tradition, is worn about as thin as the blood of those families today. Our people, the real Southern mass majority of whites, are the ones the Negroes were taught to call "pore white trash." And we, in turn, were taught the hateful word "nigger." Nice little trick, isn't it? Hitler used it, too. And it is still being used today, by the whites from the big houses, who engineer lynchings and make it seem that the responsibility is the white workers'.

Our people, and the Negroes, made up about 98 percent of the Southern population before the Civil War.

In addition to all this, I'm a "hill-billy." My folks were mountain people. We lived on Turkey Creek. And what a place that is!

Turkey Creek gushes in white little splashes around the foot of Burnt Mountain and down to the Cartecay. The Cartecay crawls and gurgles—sometimes lazily, sometimes stormily—down the valleys and hollows between the hills to Ellijay. Over the cataracts and through the fords these waters have gone on since nobody knows when—except that summer when the drought saw sands scorching dry, and the river bed looked like a pided moccasin[3] turned on its back to die in the sun.

Mountain houses are scattered along the banks of Cartecay. Mountain people live there, plain people to whom it is natural to ask a stranger to stay all night. They have lived there for generations—since the first white man pushed through the Tallulah gorge, and others came up from the lowlands to escape the slave system. Indians have also lived on the Cartecay. It was once their hunting grounds. But most of them were rounded up and marched west toward the setting sun. Mountain men on Cartecay have gone west too, in search of opportunity, but some have stayed.

The men who first settled the mountains of the South were fearless and freedom loving. Many, in addition to the prisoners, came to escape persecution in the old country. They had been outspoken in opposition to oppression and denial of liberties. Some came later into the friendly mountains seeking a few rocky acres they could till and call their own. They fled from the ever-encroaching wave of slave-holding planters in the lowlands. The "poor whites" in slavery days found themselves burdened down with slave labor competition. Their lot in many instances was very little better than that of the slave. In the lowlands of the planters they were considered a blight upon the community. They were pushed off the desirable lands. Left to them were the submarginal, undesirable ridges or swamps. Many, therefore, fled to the great mountain ranges of north Georgia and other states, where freedom of a sort was to be had. Disease, starvation, and illiteracy were the lot of tens of thousands of these "poor whites" who were forced to live in the hard, infertile regions of the South prior to the Civil War.

Now you may have thought, as I once did, that the old South was divided simply into whites and blacks—slave and master—and that everybody supported slavery from the beginning. I was taught that in school, from the history books, about my own state. But I'm going to let you in on a little secret that I didn't learn from the school text books. Here it is: Oglethorpe and the first settlers of Georgia were bitterly opposed to the whole institution of slavery. They fought resolutely against slavery ever coming to Georgia.

I dug this up from some old dusty records. Here is what Oglethorpe himself wrote in a letter to Granville Sharpe,[4] October 13, 1776: "My friends and I settled the Colony of Georgia. . . . We determined not to suffer slavery there. But the slave merchants and their adherents occasioned us not only much trouble, but at last got the then government to favor them. we would not suffer slavery . . . to be authorized under our authority; we refused, as trustees, to make a law permitting such a horrid crime. . . ."

But this isn't all. How deeply this idea of freedom and justice was planted in these early Georgians is further shown by a resolution passed January 12, 1775, endorsing the proceedings of the first American Congress, by "the Representatives of the extensive District of Darien,[5] in the Colony of Georgia." It said:

> 5. To show the world that we are not influenced by any contracted or interested motives, but a general philanthropy for all mankind, of whatever climate, language or complexion, we hereby declare our disapprobation and abhorrence of the unnatural practice of slavery in America . . . a practice founded in injustice and cruelty, and highly dangerous to our liberties (as well as lives), debasing part of our fellow-creatures below men, and corrupting the virtues and morals of the rest; and laying the basis of the liberty we contended for . . . upon a very wrong foundation. We, therefore, resolve, at all times, to use our utmost endeavors for the manumission of slaves in this Colony. . . .

There it is! These were men who indeed did not fit into a system of power and privilege for a few. But eventually their opposition was beaten down (though never destroyed). There went on a general infiltration of the bluebloods who wanted slaves to do their work. Finally there was a civilization, a "culture," an aristocracy reared upon the institution of slavery, built upon the bent backs of human beings bought and sold like cattle, and upon the misery of the overwhelming majority of non-slave-holding Southern whites.

This, then, is the so-called and much lamented "culture" of the "lost cause"! The basis of wealth and privilege was the ownership of slaves. This privilege was concentrated in a very few hands. The total population of the South prior to the Civil War was about nine million. There was about four and a half million slaves, over four million non-slave-owning whites, and, at the most, not more than three hundred thousand actual slave owners.

Culture, education, and wealth were limited to this narrow oligarchy of a few hundred families. Since the overwhelming majority of Southern whites owned no slaves whatsoever, they had little voice in government. The local and state governments were virtually executive committees for the slave masters. For lack of free schools, ignorance and illiteracy were the lot of the poor whites who were bowed down under the heavy burden of taxation of a slave-master government.

And so there grew up in these Southern mountains, communities of non-slave-holding farmers, scratching a bare livelihood from the stubborn new-ground hillside patches. They hated the slave system and the slave masters. Many of them refused to fight for the "lost cause" in the Civil War. They reasoned: Why fight for a system that oppresses us as well as the black slaves?

Yes, these were my people. I come from the Devil's Hollow region close by Turkey Creek at the foot of Burnt Mountain in north Georgia. Earliest memories are woven around the struggles of my Dad and Mother to dig a living from our little mountain farm. Life always seemed hard—like an iron fist mauling them in the face, knocking them down every time they tried to get up. But they wanted their kids to go to school, get educated. We went, the whole bunch of us. There were nine kids, three now dead. All of the survivors today are progressive thinkers, working for a better South.

Yes, I got something in schools—Vanderbilt, Chicago University, Columbia, Oglethorpe, University of Georgia, in European schools. But my best education has not been from classrooms and formal professors. My real education has been beaten into me by the everlasting toil and hunger I've seen, by the struggles in textile and coal mining centers, where our people were lured down from the hills with false promises of a better life; by the hunger I have seen in the faces of sharecropper kids; by my own sister, wife of a sharecropper, dying young from overwork and worry. It is this education of life—of prisons and jails for innocent men—that caused a determination never to seek to rise upon the shoulders of others; to rise only when the great mass of plain people can also have a richer life. And some day we will!

I love the South. Like hundreds of other Southerners, I dislike some things about its customs and ways. But our folks have lived and died there. Our roots are sunk deeply from generations back. My own Dad died young—toil and hunger, too much work, and too little of the right kind of food are the only honest reasons any doctor could have given.

We had big hopes when we left the mountains to become sharecroppers in the cotton lowlands. But those hopes were dead long before we buried Dad in Hickory Grove Church Yard.

So I pass these poems on to you who may care enough to read. They are little pieces of life—and death—picked up along the way. May they help to kindle little sparks that will grow into big flames!

the first jew i ever met and the devil's den (1985)

Editors' Note: Looking back on his life as a farm boy and his earliest encounters with a Jewish peddler, as well as the reality of anti-Semitism in the South, West wrote this essay as a chapter in his uncompleted autobiography. It appeared in Jewish Currents *magazine, December 1985, when West was eighty-one years old. During the late 1950s and early 1960s, West taught at a rabbinical academy in Baltimore, Maryland.*

He was a pack-peddler, a small stooped man. He carried a large oil-cloth bundle on his bent back. He had no buggy, no mule to ride. There were no automobiles and the closest train station was 16 miles away. He always came walking, often on the short-cut woods trails. There were no hotels, motels, or restaurants. He spent the nights and ate with mountain families.

Our home was a regular. It was a one room log cabin with a lean-to kitchen and eating place. Mama fixed a pallet on the floor by the hearth for him to sleep. Years later I ran onto him in Atlanta. He was running a pawn shop on Decatur Street. He was one of those small Jewish business men who helped us with the Herndon defense in 1932.

(It was the great depression time. Millions were unemployed. Angelo Herndon, a 19-year-old black man, led a group of some 2,000 hungry black and white workers down the streets of Atlanta to ask city officials for relief. City officials had said no one in Atlanta was hungry. If they were they should come and tell them. This was Herndon's purpose, food for hungry people. He was sentenced to 20 years on a Georgia chain gang. It took us two years to get him freed from Fulton Tower prison. Many black and poor white workers helped. And a number of small Jewish shop keepers made contributions. The ex-pack-peddler was one.)

As we came home from school we had to climb over the rail fence by the big beech tree below the house. From atop the rails we could see the front porch. Whenever we spied the large black pack leaning against the porch logs we were excited. The pack-peddler was there! We loved his visits.

We kids never did know his name. He was simply "the pack-peddler," and a lot of fun. He was kind, friendly. He talked with us, told of the strange world over the mountains. We thought it must be a lot different. He was different. Even his accent didn't sound like ours. He was interesting. We liked him.

He was so small. We wondered at him carrying such a passel of things rolled up in the big black bag. Our mountains were steep. Trails were rocky and crooked. He must get awful tired. Houses were far apart. Our closest neighbor was at least a mile. That was Roxy Reece.

She was a widow woman with three kids, Ivory, Mamie, and Price. Her man got killed. He had hauled a covered wagon load of apples the 100 miles to peddle in Atlanta. The elevator caught his arm and dragged him to a crushed pulp. We had no idea of what an elevator was. We just knew it was a contraption that went up. Some times when we cut a grapevine to make a swing out over the hill we called it our elevator.

Price, the red head, was Roxy's baby. She got no compensation for her man's death. She raised her kids by farming patches on Turkey Creek. She went to the fields, between the plow handles, like a man, as most mountain women did.

About half way between our house and Roxy's was the Devil's Den Hollow. The Devil's Den itself was about 200 yards up from where the trail crossed the hollow. It was a monster-sized hole in the ground. Looked like a big house top sunk upside down. Must have been made by a lime sink[6] or underground stream causing the earth to give way. At one end there was a great hole leading like a cave. That was the Devil's Door. For us kids it was an awesome thing. Rumors and folk tales had made it so. Years long past there were tales of folk disappearing never to be seen again.

For us kids to walk the trail across Devil's Hollow in daylight was scary. At night it was fantastically frightening. Even when I walked there with Dad I pressed close against him for security. When Price Reece rode his Betty mule by that hollow at night he always sang, whistled, or gave possum hunting yells at the top of his voice. And his Betty mule was always laying hoof to gravel at a pert pace. Price, who was in his teens when I was only nine, said his Betty mule could outrun any horse or mule in the country. She could outrun the Devil, too. Said he sang to let the Devil know he was not afraid.

Once the pack-peddler came after dark. Walked the trail right by the Devil's Den. We kids marveled at his daring. We asked if he wasn't afraid. We asked if he saw or heard anything of the Devil as he walked there.

"No," he said. "I'm not afraid of that kind of Devil. I'm more afraid of the kind that wears men's pants and has no horns you can see. The Devil does not exist within himself. He is the creation of fear. He is made on purpose to scare poor people. His big red horns are harmless. Do you less bother than your Daddy's old bull's horns."

He didn't seem to be a bit scared. We kids talked about it and wondered. Auburn Reece said Jews didn't like Jesus. Maybe they were friends for the Devil. But he had never had the pack-peddler stay a night in his home. I often spent a night in Auburn's home and liked the food his mother cooked on coals in the fireplace in a big iron oven. I thought the pack-peddler would like it too. And then Auburn wouldn't think he was the Devil's friend. I knew he wasn't. How could a friend of the Devil be so kind, so friendly? Wasn't the Devil mean? Didn't he have ugly horns to do his devilment?

The pack-peddler always unrolled his big black pack. He spread out the many varicolored shining items in the middle of the floor. It was exciting. Folks in furren[7] places must live a gay life we thought. We never had money to buy that kind of stuff. He always gave Mama something. Usually a red scarf or "fascinator" as we called it.

Mama prized it. Only wore it to church. Kept it carefully folded in the wall shelf. When neighbor women visited she took it down to show. She herself made more beautiful and creative hand-crafted quilts from scraps left over from making our clothes. But the fascinator was a thing of whole cloth from far off, strange places. Nothing like it was made in our mountains.

Once the pack-peddler came at nearly dark. Mama called me aside and asked me to run over to Roxy's and borrow a little bucket of flour for breakfast biscuits. Borrowing in emergencies was common with mountain people. We usually ate corn bread three times a day. We raised the corn and had it ground for meal at Larkin Kennemur's mill on Turkey Creek. We didn't have money to buy biscuit flour. It was not considered proper hospitality to set a visitor down to corn bread at breakfast. Biscuits were the proper fare.

I was not eager to walk that trail by the Devil's Den to Roxy's after dark. I told Mama. She said maybe my sister, Elsie, might go with me. I said: "No, what if I have to run, and Elsie can't keep up?"

"Didn' ye hear what the pack-peddler said about the Devil?" she asked.

"Yeah, I heared, but I ain't got away from bein' afeered," I said. "I'll go though." I went running down the trail toward Roxy's.

I remembered how Price always sang, whistled, or gave the possum hunter yells as he rode his Betty mule by at night. I'd do the same thing. Maybe if there was a Devil he'd think I wasn't scared. I also tried to think about all the pack-peddler said about the Devil. It helped.

Walking the foot-log across Turkey Creek I began singing "Pretty Saro" at the top of my voice. It lasted a hundred yards to the hollow. I then gave a couple of possum hunter yells and began singing "Single Life."[8] That was a girl's song. Maybe it might confuse the Devil. But I didn't hear or see a thing except a slick tailed old possum waddling across the trail. No Devil.

While Roxy filled my bucket with flour, Price asked if I wasn't scared to walk by the Devil's Hollow alone. I told him I sang so loud I couldn't hear anything else. Price told me to sing "Ain't got nobody, ain't nobody got me" on the way back. Maybe the Devil would think I was too hard to get.

I tried that song and was about in the middle of it as I crossed the stream. There was no foot-log on the branch. We just stepped on rocks. About midway a rock turned under my foot. I splashed right down in the water. Flour spilled, went drifting down toward Turkey Creek. I was dripping wet and upset. Mama expected me to bring biscuit flour for the pack-peddler's breakfast. With wet flour sticking to my shirt and pants I streaked back toward Roxy's. I'd borrow another bucket.

Price kidded me. Said I must have wrestled with the Devil. Said I ought to sing, "I Ain't Got No Flour Cause It's All Smeared Over Me." Said the Devil would likely have his own breakfast biscuits from that flour. He could scoop it right up out of the branch with his long nailed fingers. Oh, the Devil was pretty personal with us kids on Turkey Creek.

The more we heard the pack-peddler talk the less personal the Devil became. Fear began to lessen. Didn't quite go away but curiosity was stirred. Even a little daring. One day I had a fantastic notion. The next time neighbors' kids came to spend a Sunday with us I'd dare them to visit the Devil's Den, go right smack up to it. Among the kids I was one who sometimes made crazy suggestions like that. That Sunday Bill Morris and Elmer, Auburn Reece, Mandy and Mattie Mealer and a few others came.

"Tell you what let's do," I ventured. "Let's go see the Devil's Den. Let's go right up the hollow and look over the edge. I dare you all." I'd been there once with Papa in daytime.

It was a fearsome proposal. They looked at me like I was a wild thing. But it was a bright sunny day. Only the majestic white oaks, beech trees, and spruce pines cast gentle shadows on the hollow. A few kids took me up. Then others said they'd go part way and wait to see if we came back.

We went trekking up the hollow. It was quiet. Wind was low. Leaves were still. Only a rabbit jumped up from behind a bush and went streaking into the big hole at the bottom of the Den. Auburn said it might be one of the Devil's children. We'd better take distance. Others of us thought it was just a natural rabbit running for safety.

A wild fox grapevine twisted up into the limbs of a giant white oak right on the Den's edge. We frequently made swings by cutting off such vines near the ground. I saw that if this vine was cut we could swing out across the Den and back, holding on with our hands. Old Santa had left me a barlow knife Christmas. It was always in my pocket. I whittled the vine off and asked who wanted to try a swing.

"It will take you right out over the Den and bring you back if you hold on tight," I said.

None wanted to. I was scared myself, but determined. I'd try. Clutching the vine I backed up and made a running takeoff. It swung me all the way across and back, gaining my feet again. It was a thrill. I did it a couple more times and asked who wanted to try. First Elsie, my sister, who always thought she could do anything I did, said she'd do it. Then Auburn, followed by Mandy and the other girls, Before long the whole gang had made the swing.

We became brave, audaciously unafraid, even of the old Devil. As we swung out over the windless chasm of the great hole we began to yell a challenge at the Devil: "Come out, come out, old Devil. We're here, come out." One of the girls made up a jingle:

"Old Devil, old Devil
have ye heered
we all come to see ye
an' we ain't afeered."

As the sun began to crawl down behind the tall spruce pines, shadows crept up the hollow. Our bravery wilted a bit. Our eyes turned back down the hollow. Soon we wended our way back across the Turkey Creek foot-log on the trail toward home. But never again was the Devil's Den such a frightful fear. In later years it helped me to realize that many other fears were just as unrooted. Fear, prejudice, discrimination are cultivated crops. The harvest is measured in hopeless hurt.

People may fear the strange, the unknown. Anti-Semitism is an example. In 1913 Mary Phagan was murdered in Atlanta. Leo Frank, a Jew, was accused, tried, and sentenced to death. Before the execution a lynch mob broke into the Millidgeville State Prison, took him to Marietta, and hanged him in front of the Phagan home.

I remember it well, though I was only nine. It bothered me. I thought Frank might be a lot like the little Jew pack-peddler. A popular ballad, "Little Mary Phagan," gave the gory details. Tom Watson[9] and that song did much to kindle the lynching flames. Later I knew an old man who boasted that he stomped Leo Frank's face to a pulp with his hob-nailed boots. And later Frank was proven to be innocent.

I never forgot the little pack peddler. He taught some of us kids a lot. He cultivated our young curiosity and fertilized it with human concern. Years later when I taught at an Orthodox rabbinical institution in Baltimore, I would remember the little hump-backed man and his pack, the first Jew I ever met!

hard times cotton mill girls (1979)

Editors' Note: A frequent contributor to the New York–based folk song magazine Sing Out! *West often related the longtime role of music in his family and its dynamic in chronicling the history of the region. This article appeared in* Sing Out! *volume 27, number 3, in 1979. A year earlier, in volume 26, number 5, 1978,* Sing Out! *published a profile on West's mother, Lillie West, "No Fiddle in My Home," written by West's daughter Hedy, a national recording artist and folk singer. A transcription of the song by Hedy West appeared in* Sing Out! *volume 6, 1962.*

> She was singing:
> Hard times cotton mill girls
> Hard times cotton mill girls
> Hard times everywhere.

The voice was a high soprano. The sound drifted through the log cracks of the cotton house where I played at the edge of the cockle-burr patch. My Aunt Mattie sang as she washed dishes. Our people always sing. The clatter of plates and forks was an undertone to the high clear voice.

My Aunt Mattie was a spinner at the Atco Cotton Mill. It was a Goodyear plant. Our Grandpa Bud West moved his family from the north Georgia mountains to the foothills of Cartersville in 1915. My own family still lived back in the mountains. We dug a hard-scrabble living from the steep hill patches. Corn and beans and collards and tomatoes. A cow, a few sheep, chickens, yearlings, pigs, a few bee gums, and a pair of wiry-legged mules.

We peeled tanbark or hewed crossties and hauled them 15 miles to Ellijay where the railroad ran. We got $3 or $4 for a load. It took all day, from before daylight till after dark. There were no driving lights. Knowing mules kept the wagon on the single-track road. Sometimes it rained and we were stuck. My Dad would hunt a pole or fence rail. We pried and pushed and the mules finally pulled out.

We took lunch of home-made rye bread or wheat biscuits. Once grandpa

Kim Mulkey gave me a dime to buy lunch. I got some loose soda crackers and cheese at Sebe Burrel's store. That was plumb different.

Now we were visiting Grandpa Bud West. Back in the mountains Dad had hitched the mules to a covered wagon. Kids piled in on top of quilts and mule fodder. Rough roads made a three-day trip. We camped along. Some slept in the wagon; others made a pallet underneath.

I listened to the singing. It was about work time. Aunt Mattie would hitch the big iron-grey Woodrow horse to the buggy and drive six miles to the mill. It was a twelve-hour night shift and she had to get going.

"Cotton Mill Girls" was her favorite song. She sang just like she was making it up out of her own self. Like it was her story being told. I listened. I listened a lot of times and learned it. After the sound of Old Woodrow's iron-shod feet and buggy tires on gravel died down I tried singing it. I wanted to sound just like Aunt Mattie:

> Worked in the cotton mill all my life
> Ain't got nothing but a barlow knife
> Hard times cotton mill girls
> Hard times everywhere

It sounded right good, almost like Aunt Mattie. And I went on:

> When I die don't bury me a-tall
> Hang me up on the spinning room wall
> Pickle my bones in alcohol
> Hard times everywhere

Thought I did pretty good on that one, too, raising voice in the sad tragic humor of it.

Then I repeated the part about the barlow knife. That I could understand better. Once old Santa made me about the proudest kid in the mountains when he left a barlow with the usual peppermint stick and orange in my Christmas stocking. The barlow was the poor man's knife. It cost only a dime. It still tempts me. Every time I see a knife with a Barlow label on a counter I want to buy. Reckon I've given Hedy at least a half dozen.

But the stanza that fetched up the most vivid imagery was about the body on the spinning room wall and bones in a pickle barrel. I shut my eyes and leaned back on the cotton pile. I saw it plain as the sun-ball coming up over old Stover Mountain on a summer morning. A girl's body hung on a wall. Under it was a big wooden barrel just like Grandma used for kraut or pickle beans. The body and bones were my Aunt Mattie who had just gone down the road lickety-split in a buggy behind old Woodrow.

Thinking on it made me sad. But I sang it again at the top of my voice there in the old cotton house. The more I sang the sadder I got. I loved my Aunt Mattie and the thoughts of her hanging on a wall, in a pickle barrel, brought tears.

Why should this be? So beautifully young, so kind and understanding to a young mountain kid? Hung on a wall and pickled in a big wooden barrel. I got real mad!

Our family was close, loyal. An injury to one gave pain to all. The kid knew something was wrong. The song told it. Some of Aunt Mattie's hurt was there. Maybe injustice was sensed, tragedy. She worked a sixty-hour week for $4.

I liked that song. I sang it again, all the way through.

Years ago I learned a little more about folksongs, how they may ease pent-up feelings or ease the pain and bear the hope of a people. But "Cotton Mill Girls" still has a special place. I never hear or sing it without that haunting feeling. It is always my beautiful Aunt Mattie, now long dead after fast-fading young years in the mill. It is her singing again, her body on a wall and her bones in a big oak-staved pickle barrel.

When I taught "Cotton Mill Girls" to Hedy she worked it over a bit with family history and used it on one of her albums. It got scattered around in the great "folk revival" of this century. Others sang it.

As I write this I am in the New York home of Harry and Rachel Berkowitz. So warm, so generous, so like our own friendly mountain folk. They make every effort for my comfort. They know I love folk music. Rachel plays a passel of folk albums. One is a Folkways selection of international folksongs by the Pennywhistlers, a woman's singing group. The American song on the album is "Cotton Mill Girls."

I sit here listening. Remembering my Aunt Mattie and the Atco Mill in Georgia. That is her song, always her song to me—even when Hedy sings it. I still see the hanging body and pickle barrel. I wonder what the song means to the Pennywhistlers who may never have seen the inside of a cotton mill. And I recall Richard Dyer-Bennett's[10] distinction between the folk singer and singer of folk songs.

Rachel and Harry are Jews. In the mountains the only Jew we kids ever knew was the pack peddler. He came every year. There were no hotels or cafes. He slept and ate in mountain homes. Ours was always a stopping place. Coming in from cornhoeing we saw the big black oil cloth pack leaning against the logs on the piazza. We knew it meant an exciting evening. He would open the ponderous pack, spread out the vari-colored items before our eager eyes. I don't recall my parents ever buying anything. We had no cash money. But the peddler left my Mother a scarf. We called it a "fascinator," and she carefully folded and packed it away in the clothes shelf on the wall. When neighbor women came she took it out to show. She made lovely piece-work quilts far more beautiful. But this "fascinator" was a thing of whole cloth from strange places off yonder beyond the mountains.

The pack peddler brought news, too. We had no newspaper. Cotton mills were being built in the foothills, he said. Even women and girls got jobs with cash money for pay.

This was talked in many a mountain home. The eternal struggle to dig a living from stingy hillside patches caused the talk to spread. The notion was that it might be better to leave the mountains for the cotton mill jobs. My Grandpa Bud had six growing-up kids. He decided to leave Cartecay and go down to the mill at Atco. I remember it. Everything was packed in the covered wagon. In Bartow County he moved on a few farm patch acres. He would raise some cotton and truck crops. Grandma would peddle them on the streets of Cartersville. The bigger kids could work in the mill. That might make it a little easier.

But my parents always said they didn't want their kids to go to the mills. My Mother said she would take in washing, scrub, wear her knuckles to the bone to keep us out of the mills. In 1918 we left the mountains to become share-croppers in the lowland cotton fields.

As I grew up I learned more about struggle—and folk songs. I learned how Yankee corporations from Lowell, Falls River, and other places came South looking for hungry people and cheap labor. Part of it was when Grandpa Bud had to leave his truck patches and go to the mill. He died working there at $5 a week. We didn't know the name "brown lung" then. And in the 1934 period I saw log chains stretched across the gate at Atco with armed guards to keep out flying pickets. Like most Southern cotton mills, Atco is still open shop. J. P. Stevens doesn't have a monopoly on that.[11]

But the most poignant learning was in seeing my Aunt Mattie's vivacious youth wilt. In a few years from a lovely girl to a burned out, shriveled shell. And this for $4 a week.

Like thousands of other southern mountain women dragged down from the hills by false promises—at Gastonia and Marion in North Carolina, Elizabethton and Happy Valley in East Tennessee, and the Cabbage Patch in Atlanta[12]—the mill got her. It filled her lungs with dirty lint. It hung her up on the spinning room wall. It pickled her bones.

It buried her under Georgia's red clay dirt.

harry harrison kroll:
an essay (1986)

Editors' Note: In this essay, West notes the critical role of Harry Kroll, an English professor at Lincoln Memorial University, in the shaping of his own literary work and vision. Kroll was the author of over twenty novels and nonfiction books, including the memoir I Was a Sharecropper. *This essay, one of West's last publications, appeared in 1986 in* Appalachian Mountain Books, *volume 2, number 2, a combination of catalog and review of regional literature published in the 1980s by George Brosi, from Berea, Kentucky.*

He was a southern sharecropper. His parents were sharecroppers. They might have been the Jeeters in Caldwell's *Tobacco Road*.[13] He never got a high school diploma. He wrote novels about sharecroppers. Unlike Caldwell's Jeeters, Kroll's characters had dignity, self-respect. He was one of the three best teachers I ever had. One of the other two was Dr. Alva Taylor who later edited *Mountain Life and Work* magazine. The other was a shy little 17-year-old girl who taught the one room school where I finished sixth grade. Her name was Nina Reece. We called her "Miss Ninnie." But I'll write of them later. This is about Harry Harrison Kroll. He also taught James Still and Jesse Stuart.[14] We were students together at L.M.U.

Sharecropper, public school teacher, professor, novelist, warm human being, Harry Harrison Kroll was all of them. The first time I met him stands out in memory. It was on the Lincoln Memorial University campus. I had been expelled from a Georgia mountain missionary school that Henry Ford put millions into.[15] Opposing the showing of the movie *Birth of a Nation,* which I felt glorified the Ku Klux Klan, made me "out of harmony" with the administration. For several months I worked for Southern Bell Telephone Company climbing poles and stringing wires in the Georgia mountains. I wanted to go to college and hoped to get in by taking an entrance exam. I hoped to work to pay expenses. Money earned stringing wires I had sent to my Dad to pay his fertilizer and food bills.

It had taken two days to hitch-hike from Georgia. I slept in the Cumberland Gap Railroad tunnel the night before going on campus.[16] My blue bib overalls and shirt were in need of laundering. My six feet three inches so dressed made me look more like a hobo than a prospective student. But I was going to try.

The first person I saw was a lanky character ambling across campus in a typical sharecropper stride. I thought it might be a janitor. No doubt he noted my disheveled appearance and lost look. He spoke to me in a friendly tone:

"You looking for something, young man?"

"Yeah, the office."

"I'll show you." He turned and reversed his direction.

"Can a feller work to pay for his schoolin' here?" I asked.

"How much you got to start on?" he asked.

"Total of $1.65. I counted it after the last sandwich this morning."

"That's slim pickins. Depends on how willing, how tough, and how hungry you are."

"I'm right willin' and maybe pretty tough and always hungry. Worked last few months for Southern Bell stringing wires."

"If you worked why didn't you have some wages?"

"I did, but my Dad is a sharecropper and needed money for his fertilizer and food. I sent it to him."

"Your folks are sharecroppers? I know what being a sharecropper's like," he said, sympathetically. "I'll be talking with you." He turned and walked off in the direction he was going when he turned to show me the office.

A student bystander asked: "Do you know what that man is?"

I didn't.

"That's Harry Harrison Kroll. Head of English. Teaches literature and writing. He writes books."

"Writes books! I thought he might be a janitor."

"An honest janitor rates as high with Kroll as the university president. If you stay around here you'll find out," the student said.

And I did find out. I know of no other writer about southern people who surpasses him in understanding and sympathy for the poor.

I came to know Harry Kroll quite well. We became close friends. He was fired at the University the same year I was expelled as a senior for student strike activity in 1929.

One of his major books is titled *I Was a Sharecropper.* He was intimately acquainted with that life and its hardships. His own life is a dramatic story of struggle and sympathy for the underdog. His early years were filled with bitter, disappointing experiences. For a while he and his brother were itinerant photographers. Eventually he passed the exam to get a third grade teacher certificate. He and Olivia, his wife, got jobs in a rural school. When they taught at Pinecrest, Tennessee, Harry described it as "a school at the backdoor of one of the richest summer colonies in the South. . . . I wanted to make a model school . . . for enriching the lives of sharecroppers and white trash children."

His efforts for better education for poor whites and blacks were thwarted by big landlords. "Negroes and white sharecroppers were kept in hand by well-tried methods," he wrote. "It was mostly the credit and debt method. There is a code in the plantation region of the deep South . . . which forbids the tenant to leave the land so long as he is in debt to the land owner. . . . The bigger planters kept them in debt and generally controlled them."

No other major writer about the South has given as understanding a portrayal of the poor white and black. "I visited white and black cabins alike," he wrote.

His first novel had been a beginner's effort that attracted little notice under the title of *Mountainy Singer*. His first big success was a novel called *A Cabin in the Cotton*. In the early thirties it was the story of white and black sharecroppers uniting to steal cotton from the landlords who had stolen it from them. Hollywood made it into an outstanding movie at a time when they did do more relevant things than the "Rambos."

Richard Barthelmess and Bette Davis had the lead roles. It was a shocker to Harry. He had been fired from the Tennessee College. He was scraping along the bare edge of poverty. With his wife and kids he lived in a tenant house some 50 miles east of Nashville. I was then a Vanderbilt student and frequently made weekend visits. I remember so well the poverty of his family there. When Olivia set the table, we might be eating from a bowl, saucer, or tin bucket with just a spoon or knife.

That Sunday as I drove into the yard Harry came running out of the house waving a piece of paper:

"Hey, Don, look at this! By damn (that was his one cuss word). I'm gonna buy me a Hudson, rent a decent house and get some eating dishes."

I looked at the paper. It was a check for $20,000.00 for movie rights on *Cabin in the Cotton*! That was the early 1930's.

After that I never saw Harry again until 1945. It came about in a rather peculiar unintended way. I had been a public school superintendent in the Georgia mountains. My work there attracted some attention. I was given a Rosenwald fellowship for further study and was studying at Columbia in New York. One day a man called me. Said he owned a shirt factory in Tennessee. The union was starting to organize. He wanted me to go to Martin, Tennessee, and teach his workers there the principles of trade-unionism. Wanted to contract for three months. Word had spread that I knew a little about unions. I agreed to go after finishing the fellowship study.

Martin was just a small west Tennessee town. I knew that Harry was teaching there in a small junior college. Looked forward to seeing him again after the several years.

We visited and talked. We talked about southern writing and Harry's own books. He strongly retained his sympathy for the sharecropper and resentment of the big landlord. In one of his books titled *The Usurper,* Harry had portrayed a poor white with the temerity to assume the perogative of equality.

"And by damn, Don," Harry would say, "that's every man's right. There's something about the struggle for it that lends dignity."

I agreed.

Not long after that, Harry died.

knott county, kentucky: a study (1932)

Editors' Note: These excerpts are taken from the thesis submitted by West to the faculty of the Vanderbilt School of Religion for the degree of Bachelor of Divinity on May 14, 1932. West's thesis advisor was Dr. Alva Taylor, a Disciples of Christ minister and a leading figure in the Social Gospel movement, who also chaired the Church Emergency Relief Committee.

Knott County is one of the most remote and isolated of all the mountain counties. It is not different in many ways from many other of the highland counties, and it is very different in many other ways. My purpose in this thesis is to present the various phases of the county's life frankly, as clearly as possible and without any prejudice. Many ills and unfavorable conditions have been uncovered which I am not able to offer a remedy for.

Knott County lies almost in the extreme south-eastern corner of Kentucky. It is in the heart of Kentucky's famous mountains—famous for their lofty peaks, chopped ridges, scenic beauty, "moonshine licker," razor-backed hogs, hard working women, and feuds.

. . . .

Knott County is chopped up into scarred ridges and rock-strewn mountains, with fresh clear streams gurgling down the narrow valleys between. Few of the valleys are of sufficient breadth to afford any profitable cultivation. Most of the farming is done on the hill sides. In this county, as in many other of the highland counties, water courses are quite significant and very important. Communities, educational and magisterial divisions have been decided by the course of these creeks and branches. The inhabitants, by cause of necessity and convenience, have settled, built their homes and communities along the banks of the streams. Mountain water ways have been the backbone of mountain civilization. They have not only served the people for drink, both man and beast, but have furnished power to turn the creaking mill wheels to grind the corn into meal for bread, and have been the only high ways. They have furnished a natural, though rough and difficult, road over which the jolt wagons have driven for provisions, and communications from the outside world have been received. Creek beds have been, in many instances, the high ways of progress in the mountains. The old circuit rider must have had ample time to think upon the wonders of nature and work up his sermon while listening to the ever recurrent monotone of the gurgling waters, and the splash of his horse's hoofs as the tired animal faithfully plunged through one cataract after another, bearing his master to the little mountain church where he was to bring spiritual food to a hungry people.

• • • •

There is little doubt about the influence of geography upon the life and nature of a people. If we should go thoroughly into the mountain situation we would find geography wielding a tremendous influence. The mountains of Knott County have locked the people in and pushed progress out. At least, the so-called material progress, over which America has gone wild, but which I am not at all content to call such. The mountain people are essentially no different from other people. They have lived their isolated lives there among the hills, and in many ways the hills have shaped their lives. In a sense they have become a part of the hills and the hills a part of them. Many of the Knott County people have moved west, stayed a year or two years, and then returned to the hills from which they went. The only dentist in Hindman[17] is a man of high intellectual capacity, a graduate from a standard medical school. In his early life this dentist moved to Oklahoma, set up his profession and was doing well, but he did not stay. He returned to Hindman, where he may possibly get three dollars of work a week. This man told me that "the plains were too straight and level, the people were nice, but not like the people here. And anyhow, I just wanted some mountains to look at."

• • • •

The people of Knott County have all the good and bad qualities of the other mountain sections. Hindman was once the scene of desperate feuds and clannish wars. Bad John Wright, who died last year with 28 notches on his gun (the character, Devil Judd, in John Fox Jr.'s book, *The Trail of the Lonesome Pine*), once haunted the creeks and trails of Knott County.[18] I have seen the house from which he and his clan fought it out to the finish with Boggs and Hays. But such a character as Bad John was an exception, even of the olden days, and practically none of them exist today. Nowhere have I met a people who are so hospitable and kind at heart. Their home life is simple and frugal, even to the point of hardship and poverty. Many nights while making the survey of the county or at other times, I have ridden up to a one room log cabin at dusk, I, a stranger, but they asked me to get down and stay all night. The food would be simple, but I ate their sow belly, gravy, and corn bread, talked around the open fire, and then went to bed in the same room with the whole family. Young and old women, men and boys slept in the same room in which I would be sleeping with some of the boys. One particular instance I remember quite well when the fire was still blazing rather high. We were all in the same room and went to go to bed. I should not have done it, but because of my contact with the outside world, I had taken on some of its sophistication and felt embarrassed when bed time came; I remember quite well how I got under the quilts and then pulled my clothes off trying to keep from creaking the bed while doing it.

This is one picture of life in Knott County mountains. Many times I've wondered why such people, many of them of keen intellectual capacity, continue to live back where the dark summit lines of the mountains limit their horizons and shuts them off from the world with all the modern fineries and pleasures. There must be a reason why many of these people continue to cling to the bare hills and try to wrest a livelihood from their exhausted soil. There must be a reason, even greater than the mere shiftlessness which many superficial observers attribute to the mountain dwellers.

· · · ·

There is a reason, perhaps a sentimental reason, why the mountaineer clings doggedly on to some little hillside farm which he must cultivate with a hoe and then barely makes a living. Many such farms are too steep for a horse or mule to be used for plowing and all the cultivation is done with a hoe. Knott County is practically free from tenantry. The mountain man owns his little farm, with perhaps only a log cabin for a home, but still it is a home, and the mountaineer has maintained what a great part of America has lost—the sanctity of home life. It would be hard to conceive of a more dissatisfied group of people than a group of mountaineers taken from the hills and forced to live in rented apartments in Chicago or New York City. That would simply not be home life to them, and they could never quite fit into such surroundings.

Because mountain people do still preserve this regard for home life, and because there is a certain sentiment for the mountains which could not be replaced by the glamour of city life, we can begin to understand why so many are still living back in the coves and hollows. "They allus long fer mountains to strike their eyes agin."

· · · ·

It has been said and written by many so-called authorities that the mountain people are sentimental with a strong trend toward emotional unfixity. Writers like John Fox Jr. and Lucy Furman have painted their characters in this man-ner.[19] But these writers have not given true pictures. The mountain people are not sentimental in the way they have shown them to be in their books. Lucy Furman and Fox wrote of Knott County twenty years to thirty years ago. Their work, of course, was novels, and they simply gave the reading public something it was looking for and expected already in the type of mountain character. Their books are shot through with sentimentalism. The mountain people about which Furman wrote make fun of her books. It is easy for them to see the fallacy of what the outside world has swallowed as true mountain portraits.

.   .   .   .

The stranger or "furriner" never sees the real heart of the highland people. They come into the mountains, praise their beauty and grandeur with high flung words, and the highlander can't see just why they should run on that way. To the mountain man the mountains are a matter of course. They are a part of him in a sense. He feels them and lives with them. He is not unappreciative as some have said. But the mountains may have a grip on his soul that would give vent to such an expression as:

> You are mine,
> you chopped ridges,
> you scarred and ragged hills!
> I am a part of you,
> you are a part of me.
>
> Do you know that a mountain man
> has gone from you?
> You mountains,
> silhouette against
> a fading sun-down sky.
> Did you feel the surge
> of my pulse beat
> when I flung myself
> on your breast
> and sifted your porous soil
> through my fingers?
> Did you know that
> a human soul was there
> in stark nakedness
> where cold stars shone down
> above Troublesome?[20]

Did it mean anything to you
the thing you had done to me?
Do you know that you
have set me free
and made a slave of me?
You Cumberlands,
tender and terrible!
You give men life and beauty,
take life and leave desolation!
Lying motionless
in the misty moonlight,
fringed by a gloaming
sylvan green,
streaked by streams of
silver song.

. . . .

This large percentage of home owners connects with my former explanation of why the mountain man loves the hills and stays there. Most of them own their homes and it has come to have great significance to them. But what the new generation is going to do is not known. Certainly the new blood will not carry on in the same old way. Modern machinery and methods are coming in to replace many of the old customs which were really not bad after all. The mountains have been rich in a culture, natural and fine, all of their own. The new day will demolish and destroy this culture along with other worthy things. And the mountain man will probably be all the worse off, as he has been wherever the moderns have come into his country with factories and coal mines. It's a joke to talk of taking civilization into the mountains with industry. Our modern industry has never seen civilization, and only enters the hills to rant and tear at the throats of a people who have lived their independent lives for years alone. The story of coal swindlers in the mountains of Kentucky is one long black and bloody disgrace.

Of course there is much that is unlovely in the marital relations of these pioneer people. The women become passive and disappointed with sex life and experiences. The men know nothing other than the physical satisfaction of their own desires. They have never been taught better, perhaps a few learn, but the great mass go on torturing their wives and leaving them unsatisfied and longing for a real experience.

. . . .

26

Due to the fact (and other reasons) that these people are sadly bound togeth-er by common ancestry, and other relations, it is entirely possible that some day they may work out their own salvation along with that of the common man of all other places. If they can ever be moved to see the advantages of cooperation—Socialism—they would form an irresistible force to hurl at the present inhuman system which is grinding out the blood of the people in ev-ery section. Their religion, church, and other prejudices will hold them back for some time to come yet, but the proper leadership coming from their own ranks will gradually lead them out of that intolerable darkness. I have no de-sire to see anything done for them. I want them to do it themselves, and they will be perfectly capable of doing that if they can in some way be awakened to their responsibilities. For years they have accepted the lot of circumstances without a murmur. They have been missionarized, pauperized, and sentimen-talized, but there's still good blood and courage in these common, plain, un-sophisticated people. My ambition and desire for them is perhaps expressed best in a poetic form—

> *Mountain Boy*
> You are more than a dirty child
> In patched overalls.
> You mountain boy . . . !
> The hills are yours,
> The fragrant forests,
> The silver rivers
> Are your heritage.
>
> Dreamers. Thinkers.
>
> Rise up, young hillmen
> Sing your ballads,
> Dream your future.
> Up and down the valleys,
> Over the ridge-roads.
> Climb your jagged mountains.
> Gaze into blue space . . .
> Turn your thoughts free.
> Nourish your imagination.
>
> What will you do for your hills,
> You mountain boy?
>
> Love the soil.
> Your father's blood

Made it rich.
His sweat has caused fruit to grow.
Sift the coarse soil
Between your fingers.
Exult when its runs between your toes
Through brogan shoes[21]
As you follow the plow.
Yours is the poet's life.
You rhyme the soil,
Dig and plant
And watch the corn grow.
You are the heart of a nation—
Even America.

O farmer boy,
Rise up!
Sing your songs,
Live your life
Even as you know how!

sweatshops in the schools
(1933)

Editors' Note: This letter by West appeared in the New Republic *on October 4, 1933, after work-study students at the Berry School in Rome, Georgia, including one of West's younger cousins, decided to organize a union and go on strike. The essay underscores West's concern for educational reform and labor rights.*

Recently there has been a significant student strike in the Berry Schools, at Rome, Georgia. Berry is a school for poor whites which parades itself as a great philanthropic and humanitarian institution. The students pay their tuition by working during the four summer months. Before the depression they were paid from sixteen to eighteen cents an hour, working from ten to twelve hours a day at manual labor of the hardest sort, some of it semi-skilled. This summer, however, the authorities reduced the working students to the disgracefully low wage of ten to twelve cents an hour, while tuition remained the same as before and the prices in the school store, where students must buy their supplies, were raised considerably. Resenting this injustice, the students went out on strike, demanding enough out of four months' work to pay eight months' tuition, and a reduction in the school-store prices. The strike was ended when officials promised to endeavor to meet the demands and not to expel students for striking.

Since they returned to work, students report that the authorities are holding the club of expulsion over their heads. I am an alumnus of Berry and know too well the reality that lies behind their fine story of helping "poor mountain boys and girls." I think the public should be told the nature of this and other missionary institutions with which the South is cursed.

Don West, Monteagle, Tenn.

georgia wanted me dead or alive (1934)

Editors' Note: In 1934, West was working in Atlanta on behalf of a defense committee for Angelo Herndon, a Communist activist imprisoned for leading a hunger protest. A warrant for West's arrest was sought that summer under the same 1866 anti-insurrection laws applied to Herndon. West fled Atlanta in the back of a car, hidden under sacks. Upon arriving in New York City, West recounted his experience in an article published on June 26, 1934, in the New Masses, *a prominent political and literary journal of the American Left in the 1930s.*

> Thy star-crowned hills and valley sweet,
> Georgia land, my Georgia land!

The little school house at the foot of Burnt Mountain rang with the music of our voices. Thirty mountaineer children proudly lifted our state song up through the cracks in the roof. Echoes resounded from the sides of Burnt Mountain. They mingled with the dark thicket of Devil's Hollow. A farmer across the valley on the mountain stopped his mule. The song floated up through the fodder blades. Two of his grand-kids were in that school! He smiled. The last verse climbed up from the valley.

Old Kim Mulkey[22] clucked to his mule. The plow tore through crab grass roots, hung on a sour wood stump. He jerked it loose, plunged it into the dark loam soil. Old Kim had a feeling of satisfaction. He was the most respected citizen in the Burnt Mountain neighborhood. For years he had been justice of the peace. He "rived" the boards from white-oak trees to cover the single room school house at the mouth of Devil's Hollow. He had never gone to school. Reading and writing had been learned by candle light around an open fireplace in the evenings. But he wanted better things for his grandchildren. They must be good, educated citizens!

Kim Mulkey was my grandfather.

A one-room log cabin stood on the ridge above Devil's Hollow. Down below Turkey Creek sang and split its sides against the rocky banks. The Hollow was dark and foreboding. Children dreaded to pass there after dark. Up in the new ground field, above the cabin, corn stalks bent to the winds. Southern breezes softly whispered as they crept through their blades. Crickets chirped. Katydids chattered like a bunch of old women at a quilting. Jim West[23] held his plow handles sidewise to keep it up in the next row. Roots jerked at the plow point. The mule was contrary. It was an all-day grind—"Gee, haw. Giddap." The mule was interested in a bunch of grass.

Below the plowman a young woman dug at the crab grass and sour-wood sprouts. From early morning till noon she toiled. An hour off to cook a meal of corn bread, sow belly, and turnip greens. Then back to the corn rows again . . . till dusk spread a sleepy spell over the hills and valleys. She was Jim's wife. These two were my parents.

These are my earliest memories. My folks had always lived in the southern mountains. We were Scotch-Irish with a little Cherokee Indian blood. Dad fought the rocky hillsides for a living. Mother just faithfully followed his plow, digging crab grass and sprouts from the corn rows. My job was to "tend the baby." Down by the creek under a huge weeping willow we played and fought—quarreled, made up, and loved. (Today that baby sister is a grown woman, and a Communist organizer in the Deep South. I never see her any more.) Later there were six other kids added to our family. The living got harder. But mountain families are always large. Life is bitter.

In the school house my grandfather built we kids sang patriotic songs and learned about the wonders of Georgia. There were the mountains, foothills, piedmont, and plains. There were cotton, corn, vegetables, turpentine, and timber; the rich deposits of minerals, the coast line, and fishing. The varieties of climate were unsurpassed. We saw the rolling hills, the creek and valley. The grand summit of old Burnt Mountain stood like an eternal sentinel watching our lives—the suffering and hates, the joys and sorrows of Georgia mountaineers! I remember how I thrilled with pride! Georgia! Surely there was no other place like Georgia!

> Thy star-crowned hills and valleys sweet,
> Georgia land, my Georgia land!

Later I grew up and left the hills to seek an education. Mountaineers often try to better themselves by getting educated. But it is a hard grind. I worked as a telephone lineman. I worked in steel mills, came to Philadelphia to spend six months in a radio factory, dug ditches, plowed fields, shoveled coal, and dozens of other jobs. Anything honest to help get an education. My parents sacrificed my services at home so I could work my way through school. At sixteen I went away, a long-legged green mountain boy. It didn't occur to me that I was leaving the hills for good. They had always been our home place.

Many times, I recall, I've gone away from Georgia for a few months—once for two years to Europe—always eager to come back. As the train pulled out of Chattanooga over the Blue Ridge into Georgia, I've eagerly watched for the first sign of her red clay hills. I loved Georgia. It makes no difference where a mountaineer goes, he "allus has a-hankering" to go back to the hills—his homeplace. I have yet to see the mountain man who has gone out and doesn't somewhere have a longing to return to the hills. I was that way. The mountain people were mine. I loved them. For years I stumbled around trying to find a way to help them. Three years were spent getting educated to be a preacher. I entered the church only to find that when I preached sermons against the exploitation of mill workers in the factory town where the church was, I found myself no longer wanted. I lost the job. I was a school teacher and worked in a mountain missionary school. But all these efforts were so futile. It seemed like painting a rotten apple red. I learned that there were two classes. I organized for the Socialist Party in the South. But "Jim Crow" locals were only one of many things that showed me the bankruptcy of the Socialist program! One day a *Daily Worker*[24] came to my hands. It was news! In the South the Reds were hard to find because of the illegal situation. I talked with Socialist leaders— Clarence Senior, Norman Thomas.[25] It was no use! But I still had hopes in the Socialist Party. I rode a motorcycle from Atlanta to New York to see Clarence Hathaway.[26] He was the only real Communist I knew anything about. Four days I stayed with him. He was considerate, kind, the most human person I thought I'd ever seen. How different from the tales we heard in the South about long-haired Bolsheviks with a knife between their teeth and a bomb in each pocket ready to cut loose on the first person they met!

I returned to the South to be state organizer of Georgia for the Communist Party!

Today I write this article in an East Side New York coffee shop. I think of Georgia, the long past, the recent weeks. I am a fugitive from Georgia! Ruling-class justice demands my arrest. It threatens me with the electric chair or a long term chain-gang sentence! It brags what it did to Angelo Herndon—18 to 20 years! "Ought to be lynched, the damned nigger, though! Nigger lovers ought to be killed, too. Reds ought to be sent back to Roosia where they all come from! Burn Communism out of Georgia! Georgia is a hundred percent American. Pure old Anglo-Saxon blood. No room fer them furriners, them Roosian Reds!"

"One hundred percenters!" I think about my people. The first to settle the Georgia mountains. And the Cherokees, the real "one hundred percenters!"

The Georgia rulers brand me as a dangerous criminal! A Roosian Red! They threatened to get me "dead or alive." I have committed the unforgivable crime of organizing Negro and white workers together to struggle for better living conditions! It is the same "crime" for which they are sending Angelo Herndon to the chain gang for 18 to 20 years. I, a native white Southerner, a one hundred percenter, took up the job Angelo Herndon had to drop! But these ignoramuses still jabber about "Roosian Reds"!

The world finds welcome at thy door,
Georgia land, my Georgia land!

My old motorcycle went sputtering down out of Tennessee into the hills. Again I was returning home, to Georgia. That was last summer after leaving Clarence Hathaway. I had found what I had so long been feeling for. I had a different program, a new vision. I wondered what kind of welcome I was to receive.

That old school song rings in my ears. Our teacher was honest. She did the best she knew, perhaps. I don't even hate her now for whipping me once till the blood ran down my legs. But I no longer wonder about the welcome of the Georgia ruling-class. Georgia has a welcome to offer her own sons who have opinions differing from the ruling-class! Such persons are welcomed on the chain gang or in the electric chair!

Three weeks ago the Georgia Supreme Court handed down its decision on the Herndon case. It condemned him to a slow, agonizing death! No man in Herndon's position, under all the brutality John Spivak so truly pictured in *Georgia Nigger*,[27] could hope for more than a few painful years! With the Herndon decision the authorities launched a merciless reign of terror against the Atlanta workers. The Assistant Solicitor General, Rev. John Hudson, with his famous "Red Squad," haunted the working-class sections for days. They raided private homes, tore into closets, trunks, in search of "radical literature." All books, papers, magazines, dealing with workers' problems or organization were seized or destroyed. News stands were forbidden to sell the *Daily Worker, The New Masses, Liberator, Labor Defender*,[28] or other working-class publications. Workers were forbidden to receive these publications by mail on threat of the same fate that they settled on Angelo Herndon! They got a warrant for me, charging "inciting to insurrection." They threaten to get me, "dead or alive." Georgia's famous old slave insurrection law makes it possible for the ruling-class to suppress all workers' activities and attempts to organize legally. Hitler's brutal fascist dictatorship in Germany, where all pretense to democracy has been abandoned, is hardly more effective in destroying workers' freedom than are the rulers of Georgia. But Georgia is still a state of the United States of America, supposedly a nation of "freedom and Democracy"!

Georgia land, my Georgia land!

Even Olin Montgomery, one of the nine condemned Scottsboro boys,[29] was taught to sing that song!

let freedom ring
(1936)

Editors' Note: This theater review by West originally appeared in the Daily Work-er, *the newspaper of the Communist Party, on November 18, 1935. It was also published in 1936 as the foreword to the publication of Albert Bein's* Let Freedom Ring: A Play in Three Acts, *which was based on* To Make My Bread *(1932). This novel by Grace Lumpkin dealt with the Gastonia, North Carolina, textile strike in 1929.*

Cruel, vicious, vivid reality! Sorrow and death, struggle and new hope. I sat lost in its perfect portrayal. The mountain cabin. Little pinch-bellied John and Bonnie. Old Grandpap, the mother, kinfolks and neighbors.

I lived again back when I was a kid—before my people left the mountains for the textile mills. That first scene—old Grandpap, how like old Kim Mul-key my own Grandpap who so reluctantly left the mountains with the exodus of our clan to the low lands and cotton mills. How like our neighbors and kin folks—even the familiar pack-peddler!

Let Freedom Ring did not bring tears to my eye. Why should I shed tears over seeing the picture of what I've known all my life? From that first scene back in the mountains to the magnificent and triumphant close, with the death of their leader spurring them on with greater determination to grimmer struggle, this play rings true.

Anxiously, I'd waited to see *Let Freedom Ring*. So many things are written of the South. So seldom has the true South been pictured. I had become super-skeptical of writers on the southern situation. I saw Caldwell's *Tobacco Road* and it made me curse. I saw Langston Hughes' *Mulatto* and regretted its one-sidedness.[30] But I am enthusiastic over *Let Freedom Ring!* I am happy that at last an artist has produced a play that bores right into the core of Southern life.

With keen and discriminating understanding, with sensitive and sympa-thetic strokes, Albert Bein paints this picture of an awakening South, of a youthful and gigantic proletariat testing its strength, of the unity of black and white workers being wielded over prejudice and lies by a common interest. And there is the Southern mill owner, his sheriffs and gun thugs—brutality, terror, murder—How truly they all fit in.

Albert Bein takes his play from Grace Lumpkin's novel, *To Make My Bread.*[31] No better basis or source could have been found outside of actually living, eating, starving, struggling with the Southern workers themselves. But it takes a master to so thoroughly absorb the spirit and contents of a book and then reproduce the original scene so perfectly as Bein has done.

I make no pretense to being a literary critic, but I do know the South about which *Let Freedom Ring* tells, and I know it's as true as if those characters were living in Gastonia, North Carolina, instead of acting a part in the Broadhurst Theatre.

If thus to picture the hopes and struggles, misery and loves, hates and fears—the whole life of a suffering, poverty-ridden people, so that they live on the stage, is great, then *Let Freedom Ring* is a great play. I know of no other standards by which to judge. I think it is a great play. It has a broader base than anything I've seen on the South. It is one of the most significant things yet to be produced about the South.

No person today who is interested in the South, where the class struggle is sharpest, where misery rides heaviest and ruling class brutality is most blunt, can afford to miss seeing *Let Freedom Ring*. Every class-conscious worker should see it. Writers, who want to see how one artist has created a perfect picture, should see it.

How I wish it could be brought to the South! How truly would the Southern workers see their own lives reflected and be stirred to greater struggles. But if it cannot be brought to the South, it can be kept alive here. It will serve to lessen the misunderstanding of the southern situation. Such a play is one of the greatest literary needs today. Albert Bein has done a splendid job. I take off my hat to him as one of the very few writers who know how to write about the South.

thoughts of a kentucky miner (1936)

Editors' Note: This short story first appeared in 1936 in Mountain Life and Work, *the magazine of the Council of the Southern Mountains, an organization that, from 1913 until the 1980s, brought together professionals and community workers in the Mountain South region. The story was later reprinted in West's collection* In a Land of Plenty *(1982). According to West: "When I wrote it I had been in a Kentucky jail for several weeks. I used the pen name because I knew the magazine would print nothing under my name then." Although the editors in 1936 were not sympathetic to West or his work on behalf of the National Miner's Union, he did subsequently publish poems and articles under his own name there.*

Lame Shoat Gap looks like an old house sunk upside down in the mountain. Smears of dawn daub the east, filter through murky fog, and rest above Dark Hollow. Scrub oak bushes are silhouettes on the rock cliffs; look like corn shucks full of sausages hanging from the rafters. Everything is quiet, like a farm before roosters start crowing.

Down below, Dark Hollow lies snoring. Huge folds of dusk wrap her up in black blankets. Here and there lights flicker out from a miner's shack, like spikes of gold half-hammered into the dark. Dark Hollow's where we live. It's just like the name. Darkness loves that hollow; comes early and stays late.

We slope downward on the other side of Lame Shoat, trudge along to the creek trace; then start up Razor Back to Greasy Gap and down to the mines. Brown beech leaves carpet the dirt. They hide rocks and dead limbs. We stumble. The leaves rustle apart and back together like ripples on a mill pond. Withy beech limbs claw at our faces. They slap and sting with the sharp December morning. Carbide lights sputter. A sudden breeze snatches the blaze and is gone.

We are six brothers, all six feet. Never been to school. We just know the strength of six feet of muscles. Our shoulders are bent, hunched forward as if trying to fend a blow. When we walk our long arms dangle down 'most to the knee. We are not as good to look at as we used to be. We mine coal. Miles back into the bowels of the mountain we burrow, like a wild animal clawing its hole for hibernation. Our days are lived in the dark, bent in a strained crouch like you've seen a football team before the kickoff. Our heads set well back between the shoulders; necks bent sort of like a goose-necked hoe. That makes a large Adam's apple. Our eyes curve upward as if we study the weather. The mine is full of treacherous horse-backs—slate flakes that drop without warning. They leave a hole the shape of a horse's back, and crush whatever they fall on. We're always looking upward.

We are sleepy. Getting up at three o'clock every morning, tramping over Lame Shoat to the mines, is tough. Even for muscles like seasoned hickory, warped in the sun. We've done this since we were big enough to lift a chunk of black coal.

We are a solemn group. Never know what to expect next. Maybe a gas explosion. Maybe a horse-back. One brother is minus an arm. A horse-back got him. Knocked his carbide light out. He was working in an isolated room. For half a day he lay there in the dark with half a ton of slate rock crushing his arm. We missed him at night and went a-looking. His arm was ground up in a bloody mess. We managed to drag him out to the drift mouth.[32] The doctor was gone. The arm stayed that way till next day. But he loads ten tons of black coal now. He loads ten tons with the one long arm.

Mostly we stumble on toward the mines in silence. Now and then a limb slaps back. One curses. Another grunts. His foot plunges into a hole. A round rock turns an ankle. One falls and grabs with his hands. We slide down bluffs, catch slim hickory saplings to hold us back. Dark traces across the mountains, worn by stumbling feet. Dark entry, jet as the coal that lines its side. Hard black coal down in the ruts of the earth. Bodies as black as spit, black spit.[33] Our lives are dark. Our minds are cramped.

Occasionally there are scant snatches of conversation. Mostly it's about our conditions, our kids. Down there in Dark Hollow where we never see daylight except on Sundays, where blackness likes to hover like a smothering cloud, shut out from the light of decent learning, our kids are struggling to grow up.

But this is America! We are part of her. Our fathers hewed the wilderness and fought the Revolution. Our fathers were dangerous men. They believed in right. They took their guns and went barefooted with Washington. They made a revolution. And there may come a time when we are dangerous men, even the one-armed brother. For every day we look and say: "God, must our children follow our stumbling feet! Is there no sunshine of new life, of intelligent learning, ideas that will penetrate even the dismal depths of Dark Hollow?"

Our kids, they're all that matter, now.

tobe-boy (1940)

Editors' Note: This short story, dealing with a Georgia mountain farmer's hard-scrabble life, first appeared in Mountain Life and Work, *winter 1940. West also reprinted the story in his fledgling* New Southerner *newspaper in the summer 1956 issue. While West worked intermittently for years on an unfinished novel, tentatively titled "No Lonesome Road," he published very little short fiction.*

Old Shug Cantrell stooped his shoulders to the plow handles. Red Georgia dirt crumbled up and dribbled down under the plow beam. Little clods tumbled out of the furrow like brown field mice stirred out of their nest. Dead ragweeds snapped and lay down under fresh soil.

Furrow on furrow the man and the old mule stumbled around the mountain side. A bunch of dominecker hens scrounged into the row, snatching greedily for bugs and grub worms.

At the end of each furrow of stubble, Shug kicked the lever that loosed the turner wing. The wing flopped over and was turned down the hill for the back furrow. Shug plowed with a hillside turner—a contrary plow. Sweat ran down into his eyes. It dripped from the mule's belly in little dirty streams.

Down the swag below, his woman grubbed at the sourwood and locust sprouts. She swung an old grubbing mattock. Her long arms reached high overhead in rhythmic circles—the motions of a fiddle bow at a square dance. Now and then a thorny locust sprout slapped back against the woman's body. She stopped and raised her dress tail. Carefully she pulled the sharp thorns from the white flesh of her thigh. Soft April winds felt good blowing against the smarting scratches. They wafted the scent of peach blossoms from the big plantation across the road.

Come dusk, Shug unhitched the trace chains, tied the lines to the gears, and led the mule down to the branch for water. Almost caressingly he smoothed the ruffled hairs where the chains had rubbed. He patted the old mule's nose and picked a few cockle-burrs from his tail.

The mule had tromped the furrows of many plowing seasons. His ear muscles had long since ceased to function; the big ears flopped down like the drooping leaves of a tropical plant. His hip bones stuck up as if made for hat racks. One eye was blind. Most of his teeth were gone. The old man fed him on corn meal dough.

"Whoa, Tobe-boy. Take it easy." Shug was currying him down with a corncob. He talked to the mule as he would to a man-person. "Take it easy, Tobe-boy. Curryin's half feed they say. Got to plow a crop with you, Tobe-boy. Many a row we'll tromp this summer. Thought I wasn't going to have no mule. But you're a mule awright, Tobe-boy. Shore, you're a mule!"

The old man pulled the bridle over the flopped ears. The animal staggered into the stable, rubbing a high hip bone against the door facing. Shug heaved a deep sigh. The new mule, it seemed, could pull a plow. Didn't look so handsome, but he could "shake a plow stock awright!"—as much as Shug could stand anyhow.

His other mule had died this spring. Old age and the hard winter had finished him. He just lay down in the stable and passed out. Things looked pow'ful tough for a while. Shug still had four small kids at home to feed. The few acres of rented hill-side was all their living. He had swapped his onliest milk cow and the seven laying hens for the old plug mule. The kids needed cow's milk, but the cow didn't plow. Crops must be plowed.

Shug turned from the stable door, dragged out a double-foot cultivator from the shed and tightened its handles. He picked up a dull-pointed bull-tongue plow. Holding it on the old piece of railroad track, he hammered the point to a sharp edge with the back of a poll ax. These were his working tools. Sap was up; frogs were croaking. Spring was here and that meant plowing.

Dark had already settled when the woman called from the house that supper was on the table. Shug picked up the slop bucket by the pig pen and stumbled up the rocky foot-path.

The feeble flicker of a kerosene lamp lit the room. Kids crowded around on the slab bench that ran along one side of the table. Shug sank down in a wire-bottomed chair on the other side, both arms resting on the table. Fatback with turnip "sallet" tasted mighty good after a day between the plow handles.

Shug hardly heard the roar of the auto motor stopping in the yard. He didn't know the sheriff and Mr. Harper, the landlord from the big plantation across the road, were there till Lump Blalock called out: "Hey, Shug, come out here. Want to see about that mule yuh got."

"Mule!" A cold shiver ran down Shug's backbone.

"Got a fifa (a lien) agin' that mule, Shug," the sheriff said. "Chig Padgett owed Mr. Harper here twenty-three dollars and fifty cents. The mule stood good. Mr. Harper must be protected."

"Fifa! But I swapped Chig Padgett my cow and seven layin' hens for this mule. He's mine—all I got to make a crop with. I can't—"

"Too bad, Shug. But it can't be helped." Sheriff Blalock's voice was smooth and ingratiating. "Jestice is jestice, yuh know. Mr. Harper must have his jest dues. We'll give yuh till tomorrow—either raise cash money or we'll jest be obleeged to take the mule. Mr. Harper shouldn't ort to lose his jest dues. He must be protected."

"Cash—cash!—why, we swapped our cow, our onliest cow—"

Shug stumbled around for the words to explain.

"Can't help that, Shug. Mr. Harper here must be protected. Jestice is jestice, yuh know. Course he got Padgett's cow, but that don't nigh pay the debt. Here's a notice from the court. We'll see yuh tomorrow." The sheriff handed Shug a piece of paper with some writing on it. The old man wadded it between his crooked fingers.

Sleep didn't come to the cabin that night for Shug and his old woman. They sat before the fire, staring into the red embers, and long after the embers had died down they sat there glumly slumped on the hearth stones.

Shug missed his oldest boy, Reef, who'd gone off looking for work. He wished Reef was there. Reef'd know something to do. He'd allus helped. He bought them the cow Shug traded for the mule. Reef said it was so the least ones wouldn't be rickety in the legs like Lourindy Mealer's younguns; their legs were bowed so they couldn't hem a shoat in a ditch.[34]

They hadn't heard from Reef now in a long spell—not since rumors were narrated through the hills of a mine explosion where Reef worked. That had been a pow'ful botherment to Shug and his old woman.

The old man sat there with toes stuck in the ashes. He remembered his oldest boy as a little tad. Back in the mountains where they'd lived before moving to the cotton country, little Reef would clamber a-straddle of the mule's back behind Shug. All day long they would ride through the mountains looking for strayed yearlings, or shoats turned out on the mast. Shug was strong then. He had a young mare mule, too. Name was Allafair, and no better ever struck hoof to grave. The two, the man and the mule, would turn their furrows against the best in the mountains.

Come daybreak the old man bestirred himself. Dawn flickered in the east; then flamed like a burning brush heap. Dusk clung for a little while around the swamp edge. Then the sun-ball rose up clean and round, looking like a big new-ground punkin cut half in two and stuck up in the sky.

Chickens cootered around the door steps. The pig squealed and rooted at the pen poles. Down at the barn the old mule brayed and pawed the stable door.

"Dad burn it! That mule!" Why did he have to start pawing and braying the first thing? Shug would have liked to make himself think he'd had a bad dream.

Ten o'clock and Sheriff Lump Blalock. Old Shug sagged down on the wagon tongue. He saw them halter Tobe-boy and lead him from the stable. He watched his tail swish the air as he ambled off up the road, his big ears flopping back and forth. Tobe-boy turned his head toward the house as they led him up. He blinked the good eye and switched his tail up over the hat-rack hip bones. The old woman sat on the door steps. Her eyes were bleary.

Shug got up from the wagon tongue and stumbled against the double-foot cultivator. Then his toe struck the sharp point of the bull-tongue plow. Over across the branch he saw the hill-side turner standing on the furrow.

He stogged off down a cotton row. His foot kicked the dead stalks and they snapped off at the ground. Frogs were croaking. Sap was up. It was April, spring—and cropping time.

dreams (1944)

Editors' Note: Dealing with West's thoughts on the "American Dream," this essay first appeared as one of his "Superintendent's Columns" in the March 1944 issue of the Monthly Scrapper, *the Lula-Bellton high school newspaper. From 1942 until 1945, West served as the superintendent of the public school in Lula, Georgia. Along with local distribution, West sent the* Scrapper *to other educators, writers, and activists on a nationwide mailing list, drawing considerable interest and support.* Mountain Life and Work *republished the essay in its summer 1944 issue.*

Childhood memories last longer and sometimes influence us more than we think. That's why it's so important that children have proper environment and training in those formative periods.

I remember a certain old fellow back in the north Georgia mountains where I was brought up who termed himself a "practical man." "The Devil," he said, "is a practical man, too, but God is a dreamer." He explained the evil and misery of the world that way. And, in our parts, it seemed a pretty good explanation, for the affairs of evil seemed to go forward with great efficiency while the cause of the righteous seemed often to stumble and progress was hard to see.

Old Kim Mulkey, my grand-dad, had a different idea, though. He was even then an old man and I was a little boy, but he talked to me like I was a grown person—or maybe he was young like me. He talked to me about dreaming. He said man could never cease dreaming, and he urged me to dream, for then, he said, I would never grow old.

He said there wasn't much we'd ever done with our hands that hadn't existed first as a dream. Storytellers, he said, had spun tales and created legends of men in bird-like movement through space for generations. Man dreamed of imitating the birds for ages before the Wright brothers finally managed to lift their crude contraption off the ground.

My grand-father said dreaming was different from thinking. No man can really shake a dream out of his head, and he wanted me, little boy that I was, to see the universe as a wondrous and unfinished vision. For once a man has a dream, his eyes will try to find it or his hands to fashion it. Nothing can stop him. He can't stop himself. The hungry man dreams of food, and man hungers not alone for food. The sick dream of cures, the slave dreams of freedom and young people dream of love.

Out of our pain, and needs and longings come the visions we strive to put together with our hands, or pound out of life with our labor. Man's dominant dream for centuries, my grand-father said, has been one of an abundant, free and friendly society. In every generation this dream has driven man to the cross, the dungeon, the stake, or the jail.

America—lusty, youthful, daring—dreamed well and worked vigorously for that dream. We founded a democracy and opened a frontier that attracted all the dreamers of the world. Men do not pull up roots and cross an ocean to a wild and uncharted land unless they are capable of great dreams. Each came with grim determination to create in living reality the vision in his heart.

We ripped up forests, cleared farms, raised cities, dug mines, dammed rivers, tied the East to the West with railroad tracks and strung it with wires carrying the human voice from New York to California. We produced a George Washington, Thomas Jefferson, Tom Paine, and Abe Lincoln. We freed the slaves and united a nation torn asunder by bloody civil war.

The dream was always here. The American dream is strong, vigorous. It is not easily crushed or discouraged, for it was born from the brains of strong men and women—revolutionists and pioneers. It has come down from generation to generation. It is a composite of all the fire and courage and laughter in history. It is sure and relentless.

This American dream is bigger even than big America. It is the hope of all humanity everywhere for a decent, friendly society, where a man can live and work and laugh and be free and have friends. It is not something merely to hope for. It is a thing we can plan and build. All these troubles of war and fascist intrigue, all these petty native demagogues with their two-bit plans for establishing fascism here—these cannot thwart the American dream.

Troubles, conflicts, wars, toil, and sacrifice are fires in which the American dream is forged. It will be made a reality. There is still a Delaware to cross, a frontier to conquer—but that's all right, we'll do it!

Yes, we'll cross that Delaware, and we'll sew up the cut places in the body of this old world. Wounds will heal over on bodies and in hearts. Only the red scars will remain to remind future generations of the depths to which the American dream has sunk its roots.

But I'm glad my grand-father used to talk to me. I'm proud of the words of old Kim Mulkey.

georgia crisis (1947)

Editors' Note: This radio speech by West was transmitted in Atlanta over WATL radio on February 6, 1947, in response to one of the most bizarre events in Georgia politics. When the governor-elect Eugene Talmadge suddenly died on December 21, 1946, three men claimed the post. A raucous assembly of the Georgia legislature abruptly appointed Talmadge's son, Herman, the governor, despite protests. After ruling the state for sixty-seven days, repealing various election laws, Talmadge was removed from office by the Supreme Court, which ruled that Lieutenant Governor M. E. Thompson should serve as the acting governor. West's speech was later published as a pamphlet by Rev. Claude Williams on behalf of his organization, the People's Institute of Applied Religion, in Birmingham, Alabama.

Fellow Georgians:

I speak to you as one of many thousands who have been stirred by the startling recent developments in our state. I am moved to speak up as a native Georgian who realizes that these are times when no public spirited citizen can afford to keep quiet.

We have witnessed recently, and are witnessing, no ordinary squabble of politicians, no ordinary stealing of an election in our state. And although Georgia has become the brunt of many radio and stage jokes, what is happening here is certainly no joking matter. The next few days may determine whether our great state will continue onward along the road of progress it has begun to travel under the leadership of former Governor Ellis Arnall or whether it will become the first spot in which the creeping disease of fascism takes its roots and begins to spread.

Just What Has Happened?

First, may we ask, just what has happened to us in Georgia? Simply this: in the recent period we have witnessed an attempted nazi-like seizure of power in our state by the Talmadge forces. In 1932 I was a student traveling in Europe and I heard Hitler make a speech one day. The similarity of Hitler's program and what is now being advocated for Georgia by the Talmadge-Harris[35] forces causes me to shiver with cold fear for the future of Georgia. Not only does this concern Georgians, but every freedom-loving citizen in the entire United States.

Hitler's speeches in 1932 put forth the same ideas against the Jews as the Talmadge–Roy Harris machine now puts forth against the Negro people in Georgia. Because I do not want to see my state and my people end up in the same manner as Germany, I urge that you think soberly and act with both wisdom and speed to prevent it.

Neither Hitler nor Talmadge had a majority of votes. Both used thugs and force to take power away from the people. Both used prejudice and hatred to split in order to divide and conquer. What has actually happened in Georgia is an attempted nazi-like putsch or seizure of power by force. I want to warn you, my fellow Georgians, that unless we alert ourselves to the tremendous importance of what goes on, we too, will be the victims of an open fascist dictatorship!

The Fascist Nature of White Primary

Already we see the fruits of this attempted dictatorial seizure of power in the proposed white primary bill, a nazi tactic to maintain power by those who illegally claim it. The result of this bill would be to turn the most important election in our state over to a little clique of power-mad politicians. It would result in disfranchising, first of all, the Negro people, and at the same time, large sections of the white people of Georgia. It already carries with it the threat of re-introducing the poll tax, the proceeds of which would go into the coffers of a corrupt political machine closely resembling the Hitler pattern.

Hitler first attacked organized labor, then the Jews, the Catholics, and Protestants—all people who failed to bow to the nazi yoke. In Georgia the Talmadge forces direct their first attack against the Negro people. They do so under the banner of the Hitler race theory.

They want to deprive the Negro people of their constitutional right to vote, a right that has been won by the sacrifice and struggle of the Negro people on behalf of American democracy in both peace and war. Thousands of Negro soldiers and sailors fought and died bravely and gallantly to defeat Hitlerism and to maintain democracy in this land.

Is their reward now to be a denial of their fundamental rights as American citizens to vote? The conscience of the people of Georgia will not, must not, permit this to happen.

White Primary Strikes at Whites and Negroes

The Talmadge–Roy Harris machine claims that they only attack the Negro, that the white primary is to the interest of the white people. But let us not forget that Hitler made similar claims about the Jews in Germany. The truth is that the white primary will also steal the right to vote from the majority of white Georgians as well and will place political power in the hands of a fascist-minded machine controlled by Talmadge and Harris. Many thousands of the white people of Georgia oppose this Harris white primary bill because they simply understand that it will take the right to vote away from them. This is not only true of this particular white primary bill but is true of any and all such bills regardless of their form.

Defeat All Forms of White Primary

Therefore, the only way open for the white people of Georgia to defend their democratic rights is to guarantee that all people, including Negro people, have the right to vote. For, we must realize the basic truth that democracy, like peace, is indivisible. If we choke off the democratic rights of one section of our population this will inevitably result in strangling these rights for the rest of the population. The German people learned that—but too late!

That is why, in addition to simple justice and Christian morality, it is in their own direct and immediate interest that the democratically minded white people of Georgia must take the leadership in resisting and defeating any effort to deny the Negro people the right to vote—whether by this particular Roy Harris white primary or any other type of white primary or poll tax legislation.

As one who was born and brought up in Georgia, and whose ancestors have been here from the time Oglethorpe and the original colonists landed on our eastern shore, I am thoroughly convinced that the more Georgians who vote the better state we will have, and that any form of restriction in voting weakens our forward march of progress and threatens the very foundation upon which General James Oglethorpe and our early fathers established this state.

The experience of all nations under fascist dictatorships has taught me that any attack upon a minority group endangers the entire people. The world paid for that lesson at the cost of 20 million human lives in the recent war against Hitlerism. We must not sit idly by now and permit the same sort of thing to be foisted upon our own great state.

Unity for a Better Life

And what does all this mean in terms of bread and butter, of bettering living standards? In 1932 the German people might have asked the same thing about Hitler's program. The Talmadge machine again, after the Hitler pattern, offers no real program for raising the standards of living of our people. Again, like Hitler, a minority group is dragged out as a scapegoat, and there is certainly an implied threat against labor. But I tell you, the enemy of the White People of Georgia is not the Negro people. On the contrary, in the fight for a freer and better life, the Negro people have been and are, the best allies of the democratically minded white people. The enemy of the people of Georgia is the Talmadge–Roy Harris machine and the Wall Street backers and Georgia corporations it represents.

Not the "Wool Hat" but the Silk Hat Boys!

We hear a lot of twaddle about the "wool hat boys" as backers of Talmadge.[36] But I want to say the real enemy of the Negro people is not the common laboring white man whether worker or farmer. This phrase "wool hat" is used to pull the wool over all of our eyes. The real enemies of the Negro people, as well as the whites, are the silk hat boys. Don't forget that. The entire economic life of the South is strangled by Wall Street corporation control. While the Talmadge cohorts rail against the "outsiders," the Yankees, and the "furriners," they themselves serve the interest of the real outside enemy by raising false issues, by splitting and dividing our people. This weakens our march of progress and permits the railroads, the utilities, the textile interests, and the Wall Street banks to continue to suck the life blood out of our state.

The late President Roosevelt, honorary citizen and beloved friend of Georgia, put forward a program which offered hope for our people. Ellis Arnall implemented and expanded this program, leading our state to some of its greatest achievements.[37] The people of Georgia must still continue to work for and demand the expansion of these beginnings from both state and federal legislators. Such a program can be realized only by the greatest harmony, mutual goodwill, and common effort of all people, both Negro and white. Such peaceful, positive, constructive progress cannot be made by preaching hatred and prejudice against any section of our population. It demands the fullest unity of all democratically minded citizens regardless of creed, race, color, or political belief.

A Peoples' Program for Georgia

It is my conviction that such a program will include the building of better schools with well paid and well trained teachers so that every Georgia child—without discrimination—will have educational advantages equal to any in the nation. It will include housing so that every family can live in decency, comfort, and security—and a special housing program for the veterans. It will guarantee jobs and living wages with collective bargaining rights for all laborers. It will begin to wipe out the wide-scale farm tenancy and sharecropping which create rural slums. It will make farm ownership a reality for all those who till the soil.

These objectives most certainly are not created by attacking the Negro people, by sowing prejudice and hatred. As a matter of fact they can only be achieved by guaranteeing them for all without discrimination against any section of the people.

Wall Street Backs Talmadge

But the Wall Street backers of Talmadge know very well that such a positive program can never be achieved as long as the negative ideas of destroying our democratic election laws are posed as the main issue.

This is why the Talmadge–Roy Harris gang would rather talk about the white primary. They would rather throw the dust of prejudice in our eyes while leading us down a blind alley to our own destruction. Hitler so raised such false issues in Germany and led the German people to disaster.

We Georgians have a great and glorious heritage. Our founding fathers fought and died for the basic principles of freedom and human decency. We are proud to be a part of that section of the nation that has produced so many stalwart defenders of human rights and freedom. But never since the day Thomas Jefferson signed that immortal document, the Declaration of Independence, has freedom in our state and nation been so dangerously threatened. And freedom, like peace and security, involves eternal vigilance against every restriction upon the rights of any section of the people. If we permit prejudice and hate to rob anyone of his democratic rights, all freedom—yes, all democracy—is threatened. Our fathers defeated the efforts of King George, and in our own day we have defeated the Hitler efforts, to destroy this freedom from the outside. Now this Talmadge machine seeks to do from the inside what King George and Hitler failed to do from the outside.

It's Up to All of Us

So what can we as citizens do in this critical hour? We certainly cannot afford to be disinterested. And there are things to be done, things every citizen can do. First, you can continue your organized protest against this forcible seizure of power. You can get your organizations to take action—your club, church, lodge, union. You can insist that the legally elected candidate be seated as governor and that Herman Talmadge be ousted from the office which he is attempting to seize illegally. You can express your opposition to any and every white primary bill and insist that your legislators vote against such bills.

We people of Georgia don't want to work against the Constitution and Bill of Rights of the USA. We don't want to let our state become a proving ground for American fascism! Then we must play our role as loyal Georgians and true Americans by immediately stamping out this nazi effort to conquer our state!

speaking of the poet
(1951)

Editors' Note: This essay, addressing West's view of the poet's role in society, appeared as an introduction to his sixth collection, The Road Is Rocky. *This volume of poetry was published by New York–based New Christian Books in 1951.*

Speaking of the poet—is he not a double man? Is he not a man of two selves, who lives with the people and of the people, and the man who lives alone?

Refining, developing, hammering out inside himself the thing he sees in the people, the poet brings out its beauty, or he makes it ugly. It's the thing inside the people the poet brings out.

How can the poet speak when he has not walked with the people, when he has not been inside their hearts? And how can the poet sing whose own heart has not been broken?

Poetry will come from the South—and songs to sing. Our land is more than materialism and greed! It will come—up from the sub-soil of folk life, from the broken lives and hearts and troubled souls.

And the poet himself will move among the broken pieces scattered in the darkness, and his voice will call—in trouble—not always sure, except of hope, of faith and hope.

The poet will piece the torn old scraps together, and there'll be beauty, there'll be hope and a way toward the future. No dark voice of despair is the people's poet!

Even the twisted old pieces will shed beauty, the beauty of human dignity, of being part of a person.

But how can the poet speak if he has not been inside the heart of the people, if he has not lived there, if his own heart has not been broken?

For the poet takes upon himself the hurt of other men, the ache of other hearts.

west answers vfw's letter
(1955)

Editors' Note: This essay, West's reply to a questionnaire by the Dalton, Georgia, chapter of the Veterans of Foreign Wars in 1955, underscores his view of citizenship and patriotism. During this period, West had been serving as the editor of The Southerner *newspaper, a weekly tabloid published by the Union Assembly of God church in Dalton.* The Southerner *supported a strike by chenille workers in the local textile mills. The two Dalton newspapers hounded West for his past political affiliations; the* Dalton Citizen *even printed a special "Don West supplement." This essay appeared in the* Dalton Citizen *on September 1, 1955, and was reprinted in* The Southerner. *Under extremely volatile conditions, West resigned from* The Southerner *in January 1956 after refusing to cooperate with a grand jury and take a "loyalty oath."*

Mr. Harry Campbell of the Veterans of Foreign Wars has written an open letter in which he questions my political beliefs.

That any man or group should set themselves up as an "inquisitorial body," assuming the authority to call citizens in question relative to religious or political beliefs is a violation of the spirit and principle upon which this nation was founded.

Through the dark ages of struggle and sacrifice the human race has at least partially freed itself from the bondage once imposed by a Pope or political dictator. The whole Protestant movement under Martin Luther was a fight against the evil powers which sought to impose a hard and fast political and religious control. The "protesters" of that period were persecuted and killed. They upheld the belief that there was one Mediator between God and Man, Jesus Christ, and each man should have a free choice to choose in those sacred matters of personal beliefs.

Our American heritage stems in part from that struggle. Our fathers came here seeking religious and political liberty. Many of them were of persecuted minorities. Our Constitution with its Bill of Rights expresses their determination that this should truly be land of free men. The First and Fifth Amendments particularly, go back to Magna Charter, back to the dark days when powerful inquisitorial rulers used force, violence, and physical torture to compel "confessions," even from innocent men.

Therefore, it is a major violation of this American principle to answer any question as to personal beliefs on demand. No Pope, no President, no dictator of any kind, and no group in the United States has the right to set themselves up as "Father Confessor," demanding that free-born citizens make confession to them in such matters. Every true citizen of this nation thanks God, and our far-sighted forefathers for that.

Personally, I have many times, by spoken word, in my books or in our newspaper, made voluntary statements on the matters raised by Mr. Campbell. But as a free-born citizen of the USA, whose ancestors were with James Edward Oglethorpe, and whose whole adult life has been devoted to upholding the contract and spirit of the Declaration of Independence, Constitution, and Bill of Rights, it would be nothing less than traitorous for me to accede to the demands of any group in matters of conscience, whether it be President, Pope, or even a little voluntary McCarthy Committee.[38]

Now Mr. Campbell who writes me the letter may be a good, honest, well intentioned man. I do not know him personally. He and his group may think they act as a loyal citizens. I do not question that. Nor do I condemn them as individuals or citizens. I think many well-meaning citizens today are confused. Under the spell of hysteria once fostered and fed by Sen. Joseph McCarthy, now utterly discredited even among his own fellow senators, many citizens have been led to do things for which they will later be sorry. But I simply cannot assent to the proposition that anybody has any "inquisitor's" right to demand answers from any citizen relative to his political or religious beliefs. To do so is to violate a basic principle of our Constitution. And I uphold that Document in the fullest confidence that history will further prove our ancestors who produced it were right.

On the other hand, for the benefit of many honest citizens who may be confused by what they've heard or read, I will restate a number of things about myself which I have hitherto voluntarily stated either vocally or in writing.

To consider the "Communist" accusation: That word means different things to many people. To Mr. Harry Campbell a Communist "is one who advocates the overthrow of our government by violence."

I will restate again what I have voluntarily said hitherto, that I have most certainly never in all my life been a member of such a party. Nor have I ever advocated the violent overthrow of our government. I do not believe in such a philosophy.

But there are other interpretations. Senator Joseph McCarthy might call a good Democrat a Communist. In fact, he implied as much about the whole Democratic Party in his "twenty years of treason" reference. Franklin D. Roosevelt was labeled with that term by the McCarthy type men.

And to some big mill owners, intent upon squeezing every possible penny out of the sweat and toil of their workers, and to their servile editors, any man who works for the organization of the unorganized workers is a Communist, any man who wants to see chenille workers and mill workers of the South organized and getting a decent living wage is a Communist. And to some people, any man who advocates the Democratic rights of man, his right to be judged by his work, his deeds—his fruit—and not by smearing propaganda, is a Communist. I heard a union organizer say just this week that he had been organizing workers in Southern cotton mills and other industries for 32 years, and he had never once gone into a town to begin an organizing drive unless he had been called a Communist. That is an old and almost worn-out company tactic.

Yes, I believe in justice and mercy. I believe in and advocate the rights of all workers to organize into a union of their own choice. I believe in a living wage and decent working conditions of all who labor. If they call that being a Communist, then I could be called one along with many millions of other Americans!

One thing is certain, I've never been a good actor. I cannot pretend to be a thing unless I am genuinely for it. Even on a college debate team I refused to debate in favor of a proposition I did not believe in. In my writings and public speeches I have often indicated my intense love for peace and quiet. I don't like loud noises, loud voices, or violence of any sort. Though raised on a Georgia farm, I could never quite bring myself to kill a chicken or pig without a feeling of hurt inside. Violence has just simply never been in my system. I have never knowingly or intentionally hurt a human being in all my life, and the idea of violence against my fellow man is, of all things, the most repugnant. This is why I have many times stated my deep aversion to all forms of violence, whether between nations or the overthrow of governments. To suggest that I would ever advocate the violent overthrow of any government is preposterous. I believe the Bible teaching: "Thou shalt not kill," and "Blessed are the peace makers," can help make men live like brothers.

Back in the depression 1930s, I saw many hungry children. I saw the beginnings of the CIO,[39] and I worked with the union of the unemployed and WPA workers, called the Workers Alliance. I've stated before that anyone who worked with labor in those days would perhaps have worked with some Communists. The Communist Party was, and still is, a legal party in the USA. In the last World War our soldiers fought side by side with Russian soldiers against the Nazis and Fascists. Eisenhower and Zhukhov[40] were very good friends. Guilt by association, or guilt by kinship, are certainly not a part of the American spirit.

My position is that I do not probe into a man's politics or his religion. That is none of my business. Nor do I consider it anybody's business what mine are. What people have said about me, considered me, or written about me is another matter. Regardless of where it has been written or said, I do not assume responsibility for what others say or write. And if a man is working for a good cause, I don't need an FBI file on the background of his personal religious or political beliefs before I work with him.

Those who read *The Southerner* or have heard me speak, know my public and voluntary statements that I am NOT a Communist. They also know that I have said saying this will not keep someone from calling me one. But doesn't it seem strange that in 1948 when I backed Henry Wallace's candidacy for President,[41] the Atlanta Communist leader was as bitter in his attacks upon me as were the Ku Klux and other kindred elements?[42]

But frankly, all these attacks never make too much difference. A man, after all, must live with his own conscience. That is a matter between himself and his God.

Now as for Mr. Harry Campbell's statement that "each member" of his organization is willing to answer the questions he raises, I wish to state that I have absolutely not the slightest interest in what "each member" believes as to his politics or religion. As far a I'm concerned they can be a Roman Catholic, or a Buddhist, a Baptist, Methodist, or a Mohammedan, an infidel, or a Socialist, Democrat, Communist, or Republican. I don't feel impelled to call any of them into account as to his personal beliefs. That is each citizen's privilege and right. It is none of my business. I wouldn't even inquire into their private attitudes relative to whether they uphold the Supreme Court—the supreme law body of our government—in its integrated school ruling.[43] For I have no desire to arrogate to myself the authority of the inquisitor, to call any citizen in question on matters concerning his conscience.

Again I say, I am not the issue. The real issue in the Dalton area is the rights of workers to organize and bargain collectively. The attack on me is only to confuse the issues. I do not believe the working people will allow this maneuver to succeed.

In closing I want to say that I am an ordained minister in the Church of God of the Union Assembly and a 100 percent American!

we southerners have a rendezvous with destiny (1956)

Editors' Note: Subtitled "A Ruminating, Reflective, Rambling Editorial," this essay draws on a journey West made in the South in 1956. It appeared in the summer 1956 issue of the New Southerner, *a newspaper West launched after leaving Dalton, Georgia. The newspaper's banner proclaimed it to be the voice of "truth, hope, love, brotherhood, non-violence, simplicity." Printed by Aubrey Williams's Southern Farmer operations in Montgomery, Alabama, West intended his newspaper to be "an independent, liberal voice for the rights and liberties of both Negroes and whites in the best American tradition." Unable to raise sufficient funds, West had to abandon the paper within a short time.*

Twenty years ago Franklin D. Roosevelt said: "If I worked in a factory the first thing I would do would be to join a union." He said that because he believed unions were good not only for the working man but for the country as a whole. The past 20 years have proved FDR to be right. No honest, and informed person can deny the good that labor unions have done by raising wages and the standard of living, by helping to achieve social legislation and social security, and in general bringing about more democracy for the people of our country.

Nothing More Powerful Than an Idea Whose Time Has Come

There are times in the life of a people, or a region, in which an idea becomes more powerful than a mighty army. We believe that time has come, and unionization of southern workers is just such an idea. The South stands at the threshold of a new era of mechanization—automation in industry and agriculture, the potential of peaceful use of atomic energy.

"Better a Dinner of Herbs Where Love Is . . ."[44]

This belief was confirmed by extensive travel over the South in the past few weeks. In the East Tennessee mountains we drove up a winding, rocky, rutted trail to a one room cabin home. We spent the night with warm-hearted, friendly people. Love, hospitality, friendship and hope lived there. The Southern mountaineer, humble and often isolated, has traditionally been devoted to independence and freedom. We can't forget that he turned the tide of the revolution at King's Mountain.[45] In every war volunteers from the mountains have been greater in proportion than any other part of the nation.

Courage, Friendliness, Hospitality, and Patriotism Are the Mark of the Mountain Man

Another day we drove to Bristol, Virginia, and spent the night in the home of a businessman. The place was spacious, with many rooms. It was so different from the single room mountain home of the night before—all except the same kind of genuinely warm, friendly welcome, an eagerness to discuss southern problems, and hope for our future.

Later we drove through the TVA area in Tennessee and Georgia. It is easy to see the benefits of new industry and aid to farmers that Roosevelt's vision has accomplished here. No wonder Estes Kefauver is such an ardent champion of the TVA![46] We visited Atlanta, Macon, and South Georgia. We spent three weeks in Florida and saw a state going through an industrial revolution! We believe more is happening in Florida today than in any other previous time in history. We visited a town whose headlines have reached around the world—Montgomery.[47] We visited western North Carolina and stopped, as we have many times before, to talk with the Indians at Cherokee.[48] The sore plight of the Indians, the most original of all Americans, and in our humble opinion the most generally oppressed and forgotten, deserves not only a full length editorial but a wide campaign of publicity. Back up the creeks and hollows, in cabins along the steep rugged sides of the great Smokies many a humble Indian family may have literally only a "dinner of herbs," but our experience causes us to know that love, a long memory, and proud spirit are also there. The Indians deserve better from America. They deserve the right to a life of decency and plenty, and to rebuild and preserve their own cultures.

Factories Now Grow on Once Eroded Sand Hills

But the thing that strikes us most in recent travels over the South is that it is becoming ever more industrialized. And not only by run-away textiles and clothing plants, but chemicals, plastics, synthetic fibres, paper and pulp products, light and heavy metal manufacturing, and factories and mills of every description. In Orlando, Florida, we were told that some of the big engineering firms were locating there.

In areas of Alabama, Tennessee, and Georgia where only a year ago we looked at eroded sand hills and marginal land, factories have sprung up. In South Georgia a farmer told us an average tractor does the work of six to eight men. Some of the displaced farmers, tenants, and croppers find work in the new mills. Others may join the endless stream of migratory farm workers, gathering the crops from one end of the land to the others. In this area with its turn from cotton to cattle raising, we saw many empty, dilapidated share-cropper shacks. We also saw evidence of the new mills in the towns.

A Once Militant Georgia Farmer Leader

At Thomaston in Central Georgia we stopped at the Court House. This area was the birth place in Georgia of the once powerful Farmers Union of some 50 years ago. At this Court House Charlie Barrett, a local citizen who served for 22 years as national president of the Farmers Union, addressed working dirt farmers in the early beginnings.[49] Those were times of threats and violence. Once when Barrett was advertised to speak in that Court House the officials locked the door. They had arrested a Farmers Union organizer from Texas and had him in jail. They said Barrett could not speak in the Court House. But Charlie Barrett, who had the reputation of not being afraid to fight a circle saw, said if they didn't open up he'd bust in with an ax. The officials opened and the meeting was held. Later the national office of the Farmers Union was established at Union City, Georgia, a few miles out of Atlanta and remained there for many years.

We wondered as we drove along through the warm Georgia countryside with the languorous air and blazing sun, does not the spirit of the old Charlie Barrett and the younger Tom Watson, the spirit of the Populists once so vigorously alive here, still live in the hearts and minds of their children who work in the neighboring mills and factories or on the farms?[50]

Some Like 75 Cents an Hour Wages

We ran onto a curious story by a bus driver in Blue Ridge of North Georgia. He said that everyone in town, led by the mayor, was working to get a new factory built there. That is, everyone but one man, the largest land and tim-ber owner in that and the adjoining county. He was against a new factory be-cause he didn't believe in paying more than 75 cents an hour wages! In con-trast to this was the story told us by Lowell Kirby, a very intelligent young man from that county who now works at the Lockheed Plant near Marietta, Geor-gia. Mr. Kirby, an ex-GI, who plans to study journalism at the University of Georgia night school in Atlanta, is earning $1.92\frac{1}{2}$ an hour. About 15,000 are employed at Lockheed, a little over 10 percent being Negroes, many are em-ployed in the scientific and professional divisions, they have risen to the highest skilled ratings in both the mechanical and the assembly line divisions. The vast majority of the Lockheed workers are members of the International Associa-tion of Machinists. The union has won wage increases up to $1.50 an hour min-imum, health insurance, and other benefits.

Unions in Lockheed and other plants in the South are proving in practice the benefits they bring the workers which no demagoguery can for long cover up. Such actual benefits are the strongest possible argument for unions.

Great Enemy of the South

We do not pretend to say that it is easy to organize the South. Perhaps noth-ing good ever comes easy. We know from experience that the employers and their political whipping boys are dead set against labor unions. And we are aware of the greatest threat to democracy and unionism in the South, the White Citizens Councils.[51] It is interesting to note that these Citizens Councils did not start out first as openly anti-labor. Organized by big planters in Missis-sippi as a new form of Ku Kluxism against the Supreme Court's school deseg-regation ruling, the Councils have spread throughout many parts of the South. They now have many members and the backing of open-shop employers. The Citizens Councils have become the main weapon against labor unions in the South. In Chattanooga, Memphis, Birmingham, Montgomery, Atlanta, Augus-ta, in some towns of North and South Carolina, and elsewhere they pour forth hate-filled racist propaganda. They are trying to split up the labor movement and the workers, and hope for a new "secession" of Southern labor from the great body of 15 million workers in the AFL-CIO. To our mind such Councils, built on hatred and fear, are a menace to the general welfare of the South. We would not underestimate them, but we do not believe they will be able to stop the growing spirit of unity among southern people.

Brotherhood, Fellowship

Faith may be "the substance of things hoped for," but "Faith without works is dead."[52]

The labor unions of this land were established in faith and hope. The Bible says "the fruit of the spirit is love, joy, faith," and it speaks of "the unity of faith." We have deep faith in the working men and women of the South, and in the southern people generally. That faith has been reinforced by talks with many people over the South lately. Particularly are we impressed by what is happening in some of the churches and the attitude of certain religious leaders. There is a growing emphasis upon giving "substance" to faith, upon practicing fellowship and brotherhood. More southerners see the meaning of the violence and racist propaganda of the Citizens Councils and political demagogues. In South Georgia's black belt,[53] for example, we recently visited, spent the night and ate with Rev. Clarence Jordon.[54] In the common dining hall of the integrated cooperative farm of which he is director, we enjoyed a unique fellowship. Rev. Jordon, a native Baptist, graduate of the University of Georgia and Louisville Seminary, gives faith the works that make it breathe a vigorous life. "There is no segregation problem if you practice the Gospel of Jesus," he said. It is as simple as that. The practice of real Christianity means brotherhood, not segregation, and he sees that day coming for the whole South and nation. His Christian sentiment is fully shared by the 60 other members of that Fellowship Farm.

Devotion and Courage

The devotion, courage, and achievements of the union men and women in the railroad and telephone strikes, of the Sugar workers of Louisiana and the hotel workers of Miami have left an indelible imprint on Southern workers.

Five Million Potential Union Members

There are some five million southern workers in the varied chemical, textile, coal, and other industries that can be organized in the South. We believe the great body of organized labor, the AFL-CIO, can, must, and will do this job in the months and years ahead. They will receive the unstinting help of the some two million already organized Southern workers as well as of a large section of the unorganized workers and many other Southerners of varied background. And they will receive the blessings of all who love the South and our nation. The job will require great patience, skillful, varied tactics with no single blue print as the answer. And this job is not alone the responsibility of labor and the unions. It is the job for every Southerner who loves the South, regardless of class or politics, or race or religion—for everyone who is concerned for the South's future welfare.

For a unionized South will mean an end to the wage differential, and a rise in the Southern standard of living.[55] It will bring a genuine New Deal for the South with an end to widespread poverty, prejudice, and political demagoguery. It will mean a South of economic security, of progress and brotherhood in this coming era of atomic energy, of automation and the factory farm.

"There Is No Fear In Love; but Perfect Love Casteth Out Fear"[56]

The job ahead is not easy. But it can and must be done. Let us not forget the words of FDR, the true and great friend of the South. He spoke out of a heart and spirit in tune with the above Bible truth when he said: "We have nothing to fear but fear itself." Let us go forward then with the spirit that casts out fear, with confidence and faith to finish the task ahead. Let all who love the South, and our nation, lend whatever aid or sympathy possible to unionize our beloved Southland!

the death of old major
(1966)

Editors' Note: This story is a tribute to a family horse and a way of life. It appeared in the fall/winter 1966 issue of the Appalachian South, *a magazine West and his daughter, Ann Williams, launched after he founded the Appalachian South Folklife Center in Pipestem, West Virginia. Whether it was intended or not, the title bears an interesting reference to the character of the workhorse in George Orwell's novel* Animal Farm *(1954), about a revolution gone awry.*

I braked the pickup to a quick stop. It was past midnight. The trip to town had been longer than expected. I was in a hurry, but there in the middle of the dirt road just off the highway stood Old Major, our stallion. The headlights glistened on his sleek hair and sparkled when the glow caught his eyes.

His head was not held high now in the usual proud way. It drooped low. He stood headed toward the barn holding his left hind leg up. A cold chill ran up my spine. I knew something bad was wrong.

I got out of the pickup. Major raised his head and nickered feebly. Seemed that he wanted to say he had been waiting for me. I saw at a glance what had happened. Across the highway the pasture gate was open. Careless city hunters must have left it open. Major had walked out on the speedway. When a big trailer truck hit him, knocking him into the ditch, he had struggled out, hobbled as far as he could, and waited.

He nickered again and winced as I passed my hand over the bloody leg. Both bones were broken about a foot above the hoof and the hip was smashed. One could move the leg back and forth, limber as a rag. I knew that this was the end of old Major.

Major wasn't really old. We said "old" only because we loved him. He was only five years. His full name was Ideal's Major Allen. That's the way the registration papers read. He was sired by champion Beau Ideal, and was himself already a prize winner. Hedy, our younger daughter, and her sister Ann had raised him from a gawky colt. They were as proud of him as he seemed to be of himself. Hedy taught him to shake hands, to lie down for her to mount, and other tricks. She had watched him grow to be a big stallion with white stockings who walked as if there were springs in his hoofs. He was a Tennessee Walker.

Major was indeed the family pet, our favorite of all the colts and mares on the place. Proud, full of fire, he seemed to have more sense than any animal on the farm. He even seemed to know about children and how to treat them. He actually seemed to love them. Hedy would ride him standing up or even standing on her head on his back, child-like, to show off. When little Judy Hall, our neighbor's four-year-old, wanted to ride, Major would plod along like an old workhorse. Once the toddler lost her balance and came up on his neck. As she clung to his mane, Major lowered his head and let her slide to the ground unhurt. But when I mounted his head went up, his eyes sparkled, and he was off like the wind.

He was a big tease, too. If one of us went into the pasture where he grazed, he would come galloping full speed straight at us. When almost upon us he would suddenly stiffen his legs and skid to a stop. At such times his big brown eyes would twinkle as if he wanted to say: "You thought I was going to run you down, didn't you?" Then his nose would nuzzle our pockets for carrots or apples. He dearly loved both, and seemed to think our sole purpose should be to carry pockets full of them around for him.

But there on the side road old Major whinnied feebly and let his head drop low. Somehow I could hardly believe this was the end. Only that morning I had felt his powerful muscles under me as I rode him over the road in a vigorous workout. I was thinking how I would write Hedy and Ann about it. They were away in college. How could I tell them that a truck hit Major and we had to put him out of his misery. For I knew he had to be killed, but I couldn't do it. It would be too much like killing one of the family. I went to get the vet.

The half-wakened vet rubbed his sleepy eyes. It was on the morning side of midnight now, but Claude, the feed mill operator, came along. I was glad, for I didn't feel like helping with the job.

Old Major was standing in the same tracks on the dirt road. He really looked old now. It may have been my imagination, but his eyes held a despondent look as I looked at his low-hung head and heard the familiar nicker.

I walked away into the darkness. I didn't want to see Major fall. I didn't want to see his body lying by the roadside ditch, cold and stiffening. Come daylight I would get John Hall to take the tractor and drag him away. I wanted to remember old Major as he used to dash across the green sod, head high, mane flying, ears back and that impish twinkle in his eyes.

jesus, the quiet revolutionary (1967)

Editors' Note: This essay underscores the connections West made between religion and politics. A graduate of the Vanderbilt Divinity School and an ordained Congregational minister, West preached at churches throughout his life. This essay appeared in 1967 in Orion Magazine, *a periodical that focuses on questions of faith and society.*

Personally, I like the plain Jesus, the carpenter-working-man Jesus, concerned for and close to the poor and common people. That Jesus was hard as nails used in the building of houses, but gentle as a child in a feeling for human needs. Pompous efforts to fasten him up in stained glass windows of costly cathedrals or confine him to solemn assemblies with ceremonial ritual have never impressed me.

Empty, pious phrase-mongering unrelated to human need leaves me cold. Likewise I have scant concern for priestly religious garb . . . robes, frills, back-turned collars, and such. Much of my work can be done in a pair of blue-bibbed overalls. I do not condemn those who feel a need for status symbols, phrases, special clothing, or ceremony. It just happens that I feel no need for such.

For I see Jesus as a simple (not simple-minded), down-to-earth revolutionary who sought to change an evil system based on competitive violence and greed for material wealth to a structure centered around human values and need. He was a plain, quiet revolutionary who sought no outer display of beads, religious robes, ceremony, or credentials. Nor did he resort to long-winded rigmarole of pious phrases to vindicate the truth. He was not given to the use of wordy theological cant so dear to the hearts of some religious officials then and now. I think he must have been as impatient with such as was the old prophet Amos.[57] His own language was extremely simple and earthy: "Go feed my sheep" were the people's own words.

This quiet, plain-spoken Jesus had most of his trouble with the leaders of organized religion, who were then, as so often since, lackeys of the political status quo, who upheld a system of aggrandizement and violent greed. Jesus gave priority to love and human concern. This was a radical departure from the existing socio-religious form . . . then and now. It was simple, though, and easily understood by the poor and the common people. First priority he gave to love . . . "love one another." When human life is cheap, this is indeed a revolutionary priority.

The hungry masses of all ages have aspired, hoped, and worked for a time when their bellies can be filled, their backs clothed, and decent shelter shield them from the raw elements. They have longed for the time when men can live and love and laugh in security and at peace with their fellows. They dream, love, and hope. Jesus knew . . . and He was no "opiate of the people." This is attested to by the way he was received in gladness by the poor, but with anger and violence by the rich and powerful.

He recognized . . . and condemned . . . the evil of riches possessed by the few while the many go hungry. It was no piously phrased cant when he said: "hardly shall they that have riches enter the Kingdom," and, "It is easier for a camel to go through a needle's eye than for a rich man to enter the Kingdom."[58] Nor was he repeating pious phrases when he labeled the Pharisees "hypocrites" who observed a lot of religious ceremony with great show but "omitted the weightier matters" of justice. They were "blind guides that strain at a gnat and swallow a camel."[59]

How simple, how plain, how real and earthy—in the people's own language. Jesus was always like that—so much like the people. He was different only when being different made a difference. In modern terminology he was so "square" that they couldn't tell him from the people. He moved among the people like fish swim in the open waters. To me, this is the test of a true revolutionary, and not that he wears beads and braids or sports an outlandishly different hair-do or face. This kind of outer appearance "rebellion" is for adolescents, and so often practiced by affluent youths of our time in a sort of papa-mama protest. The real revolutionary affects no style or manner, dress or language that may set him apart from the people or erect barriers to communication. He may at times find it convenient to lose himself among the people. Jesus did on a number of occasions.

It happened once after he made a revolutionary speech in the Nazareth Synagogue. (He said His purpose was "to preach the gospel to the poor . . . heal the broken-hearted . . . deliver the captives . . . set at liberty those who are bruised." These objectives were shockingly un–status quo.) There he faced an angry, lynch-spirited gang of religious fanatics who sought to cast him head-long over a bluff to his destruction. But Jesus, obviously so indistinguishable from the people, managed to lose himself in their midst. The Bible says: "Passing through the midst of them," He went His way.[60]

At another time, following a temple speech in the area of the Mount of

Olives, Jesus had exposed the hypocrisy of scribes and Pharisees regarding the stoning of a poor woman taken "in the very act" of adultery. Again, He was in a hot spot. His enemies were taking up stones to cast at him: "But Jesus hid himself" (among the people again) and went out of the temple, going "through the midst" of the people. Only the man who looks like the people can lose himself among them.

This, incidentally, is a lesson some youths who associate with what they call "the movement" might well learn today. Often they seem to be talking to themselves, vying with each other in proving their "revolutionary radicalism" by mouthing many four-letter words and affecting strange manners of speech, dress, and hair styles that can only erect barriers of communication and set them apart from the people. It sows confusion, misunderstanding, and hinders essential unity of the people. Maybe this is a reason why the power structure hucksters take up and market the wares of these "revolutionaries." But this may be an infantile sickness that maturity will eventually cure—if it isn't too late.

But there is always the "stooge," the "fink"—even in small working class groups. We had them back when we were building the miner's union in Appalachia. They infested the civil rights and Black people's movement. Paul Crouch, Harvey Matusow, and many lesser known creatures did yeoman service by lying about honest men and labor organizations. (Crouch, incidentally, died of cancer of the tongue.) But the "fink," the paid "witness," the "informer" were not created by Senator Joseph McCarthy or Eastland of Mississippi,[61] though Crouch, Matusow, and others served such men. Every people's movement from the beginning of time has had them. Spartacus contended with traitors.[62] So did Jesus. Even his little select group of twelve men had its Judas! Judas, the false witness, the paid informer.

We will note here two things about the incident of paid witness Judas's betrayal. First, those who accompanied Judas with swords and other weapons were from chief priests and elders—organized religion, which played lackey to the political power. Second, the incident witnesses again to Jesus's oneness with the people. Else why should informer Judas need to come along to point him out to the enemy? Judas had the agreement that "Whomsoever I shall kiss, the same is he; hold him fast."

Jesus, the quiet son of Man, exemplifying the revolutionary quality of love in action, was so much like the people that, as the song goes about Lincoln, "They couldn't quite tell where the people left off and Abe Lincoln began."

The enemy always needs Judas when the true revolutionary is involved.

romantic appalachia;
or, poverty pays if you ain't poor
(1969)

Editors' Note: This essay expresses West's devotion to the ingenuity of mountain-eers and his growing dismay at outside intervention. It originally appeared in a slightly different version in the West Virginia Hillbilly *on March 29, 1969. This influential Appalachian tabloid, which hailed itself as a "weakly" publication, was edited by the author and chronicler Jim Comstock, a lifelong resident of Richwood, West Virginia. The Appalachian Movement Press, launched in West Virginia by the former student activists Tom Woodruff and Danny Stewart, reprinted the essay in their series of pamphlets in the early 1970s. West also included the essay in his collection* In a Land of Plenty *(1982).*

Almost every day we get letters from those wanting to come to Appalachia to "fight poverty." They've read about the Southern Mountaineers. They've seen movies, comic strips, or TV (Lil' Abner, Beverly Hillbillies).

It's not that there's no poverty in New York, Philadelphia, Baltimore, Chicago, and other parts. There is. But Southern Appalachia has that "romantic" appeal.

Just a few years ago it was the southern Negro, and dedicated (or adventure seeking) young "yankees" came trouping to the South on freedom rides, marches, and such. Not that racism, segregation, and even riots didn't exist in the North. They did. But since the Black militants kicked the whites out, suggesting they go organize their own kind, the next most romantic thing seems to be the Appalachian South.

So we are "discovered" again. It's happened every generation, sometimes more often, since the Civil War. After a few people in the North, following Lincoln's awareness, realized how the mountain South played a strategic role in defeating the Confederacy, there was a twinge of stricken conscience. First came the religious "missionaries" from New England and other parts North to lift us up and save our "hillbilly" souls. They brought along their "superior" religion to do it—and were closely followed by corporation emissaries buying up mineral rights for 25 cents to 50 cents an acre.

The Union General Howard, marching through the Cumberland Gap, had been so deeply impressed by the friendly spirit, aid, and support given his soldiers by the mountain people that he communicated it to President Lincoln. Lincoln himself vowed that after the war something should be done for "the loyal mountaineers of the South." One eventual result was Lincoln Memorial University at Cumberland Gap.[63] (We have degrees from that school.)

Subsequently a whole passel of mountain missionary schools sprang up. The loyalty of the southern mountaineer, his anti-slavery sentiment and action, and the plight of the poor little mountain boys and girls in isolated Appalachia were told in lurid details in the North. Many missionaries were New England women who, some of the romantic fables held, were disappointed in love. They came to the mountains to lose themselves. Nonetheless, they had "uplift" in their eyes. A few even married hill men. We reckoned maybe that was part of the "uplift" too.

I attended one of these mountain missionary high schools. I remember so well how the New England "Pilgrims" used to come down each year. A special train brought them on a siding to the campus. All of us little "hillbillies" were lined up with candles lighted on each side of the dirt road for half a mile with carefully coached greeting smiles. It was a "great day." We were supposed to be cheered when the "Pilgrims" told us how we were "the last remnants of the pure old Anglo-Saxons" who, of course, were the most superior of all peoples. This, maybe, ought to have made us feel good and "superior" in spite of our poverty. And we did have poverty then. It's nothing new in the mountains.

Our biggest show was reserved for the Henry Ford visits. The old oxen were yoked to a wagon loaded with wood to amble all the campus roads, managing to meet the Ford procession on numerous occasions. (Henry might give us a flivver, you see.) Oh, but we really got to do our stuff then, including the old mountain dances with Mrs. Ford and Henry. That, we learned, was Henry's favorite dancing, and he gave the school more than a flivver, too. Ford put millions into that school. He also gave jobs to graduates in his non-union Detroit Plant which, he vowed, would never sign a union contract. Though we walked out of Appalachian poverty through the slums of Detroit, Henry would protect us from all the union evils.

Ford, we learned, was a tight-lipped guy. He never bored us with speeches as others did. He was the "silent but strong" type. He also doted on our supposedly "pure old Anglo-Saxon" heritage. And we learned he had no use for the "money-grubbing Jew." (Ford later financed the organization of the "Anglo-Saxon Federation"—and a virulent "Hate-the-Jew" campaign that taught Hitler lessons. His newspaper, the *Dearborn Independent,* printed the "Protocols of the Learned Elders of Zion," and he financed their printing in the hundreds of thousands of copies as a pamphlet. Purporting to be a sinister Jewish plot to rule the world, the "Protocols" were proven to be false and were so labeled by leading scholars. Only after a public boycott—by Christians, Jews, and others—of the Ford cars which brought near-bankruptcy to the Ford Motor Company did Ford apologize to the Jews and publicly repudiate the "Protocols." Henry Ford was a man greatly gifted mechanically, with a flair for finance, but ignorant about nearly everything else.)

When later at a mountain college (Lincoln Memorial) Henry and Mrs. Ford showed up, we sort of felt like old friends. Dancing the mountain folk dance with Mrs. Ford again, we could talk about back when Henry didn't confine his southern mountain interests to high school. He beckoned to "the best" in our colleges, too. We were inspired to "make a success," "get ahead," "be somebody," just like Henry had. The dollar mark was the standard, always.

Each time we are "discovered" a passel of new missionaries invades the mountains. Old clothes, surplus food, and such are made available and some temporary reforms may result—crumbs thrown to the poor who need whole loaves and some meat, too. Some stirring is stimulated. Hope flutters painfully to escape the lint-covered mill hills or dust-blackened shacks behind slate dumps[64] only to fall broken-winged in polluted air or rivers outside. The missionary effect is to dull the razor-edge thrust of the people toward human betterment. Appalachia's colonial status—the ownership, production, and distribution structure—is left intact, hardly shaken or questioned.

As the nation's awareness of the new "discovery" wanes and, despairing of saving our "hillbilly souls" anyhow, the "missionaries" begin to pull out again. In such manner went many Presbyterians, Congregationalists, and other religious cults years ago. More recently it was the Appalachian Volunteers, SCEF, VISTAs, some CAPS,[65] and other assorted conglomerates of poverty warriors. Shortly we may be forgotten again, until another generation "discovers" poverty in Appalachia.

Yes, the southern mountains have been missionarized, researched, studied, surveyed, romanticized, dramatized, hillbillyized, Dogpatchized,[66] and povertyized again. And some of us who are natives and have known this hard living all our lives and our grandpa's life before, marvel that our "missionary" friends discover us so often.

(Southern Appalachia is a colonial possession of Eastern-based industry. Like all exploited colonial areas, the "mother country" may make generous gestures now and then, send missionaries with uplift programs, "superior" religion, build churches, and sometimes schools. They'll do about everything— except get off the backs of the people, end the exploitative domination. That the people themselves must eventually see to. The latest "missionary" move is the "War on Poverty." It was never intended to end poverty. That would require a total reconstruction of the system of ownership, production, and distribution of wealth.)

This is not the first time in our lifetime that big city folk have come down to save and lift us up. I remember the 1929–1930s. Southern Appalachia was discovered then, too. Young "missionaries" were sowing their "radical wild oats" from the Black Belt of Alabama and Arkansas to Harlan County, Kentucky, and Paint and Cabin Creeks in West Virginia. They were mostly transients, as "missionaries" frequently are. I don't know a single one who remained. I do know quite a few who returned North and are now rich men, some multi-millionaires. It was a thrilling experience to be in romantic Appalachia or other parts South for a spell, but it was nice to have a rich papa up North to fall back on.

Not long ago, visiting in an affluent apartment house on Riverside Drive in New York, our hostess asked if I knew who owned that building. I didn't, of course. "Well," she said, "it is your old friend, Alex—, and this is just one of several he owns."

I remembered Alex very well. Once I drove his car from New York to Birmingham. He was a super activist, and articulate, as big city folk frequently are. He was sure he had the answers, too, about solving the problems of the poor. If you disagreed you were just no doggoned good, maybe an enemy of the poor. But I went to see him there in New York recently. He is not interested in the plight of the poor anymore. His time is given to looking after his multimillion dollar real estate business. He sowed his "radical wild oats" down South years ago.

There is a qualitatively different situation for those who come to fight poverty in Appalachia now and back in the 1930s. Then they came (Theodore Dreiser, the great American novelist, brought a passel to Pineville and Harlan, Kentucky[67]) on their own. There was no OEO,[68] no VISTA, no Appalachian Volunteers. Nobody was paid a good salary to fight poverty. They made their own way, shifted as best they could. It was depression times, too. Some did good work—helped to smooth the way for a future union and such. Some were murdered by thugs. Others were beaten, crippled. Issues were sharp and violence too common. There was more to it than writing songs, though songs were written. "Which Side Are You On?" came from Harlan, Kentucky, "Solidarity Forever" came from the Cabin Creek struggles.[69] There were underground papers, too, that didn't have an address or an editor's name. They were really underground, no romantic play-like. They who worked at organizing the poor had to keep a wary eye. The murder of the Yablonski[70] family is a throw-back, a reminder that the billionaire coal operator families always play rough, and for keeps, against effective opposition.

I remember a night on a mountain road above Harlan town in the 1930s. Six operator gun thugs with deputy badges and a young native organizer. Beaten to unconsciousness, thrown in the brush for dead, he came to hours later, crawling from the nightmare, stumbling down the mountainside to where a friendly old couple tended him in their humble cabin. A few nights later, in a fourth rate Hazard hotel, beyond sitting up, unable to pay for food or lodging, dirty, hungry, listening to every footstep in the hall outside with fearful uncertainty. Organizing the poor in the 1930s was risky and extremely uncertain. I speak from experience here.

But things are considerably different now. The young "missionary" in Appalachia has it comparatively easy. First, he is paid. He has food to eat regularly, a place to sleep. He goes to bed with scant fear of being murdered in his sleep. He holds meetings without slipping around secretly in the bushes or basements. His meetings are not liable to be broken up or machine-gunned by operator thugs with deputy badges. And in an area where tens of thousands of families live on less than $2,000 a year, poverty fighters may get much more. Some salaries are large—$10 thousand, $15 thousand, $20 or 25 thousand or more.

We know one poverty "consultant" who received $500.00 a day for his consulting. He was later hired by a poverty-fighting agency to work four days a month at $10 thousand a year salary. Others received similarly outrageous stipends. And some of the bright young "missionaries" who came down in one of the poverty-fighting brigades, perhaps despairing of saving our "hillbilly souls," certainly failing to organize the poor, now find money in poverty by setting up post office box corporations that receive lucrative OEO grants or contracts to train others to "fight poverty." If they failed to organize the poor themselves, they nonetheless can train others to go out and do likewise. They became "experts" in the process, and now get well paid for their "expertise."

Recently a new agency, a-burning to "change the image" poverty creates in our area, to be financed by OEO "seed money," proposed to pay its director $25 thousand a year with $16 a day per diem, the assistant to receive $20 thousand and so on. The claim is that such salaries are essential to get "qualified" personnel. Some of us who have seen the "missionaries" come and go over the years may think that such salary demands are indicative of precisely the kind of quality not needed.

From their affluent middle-class backgrounds, so many do-gooders who come into the mountains seldom grasp the fact that the poor are poor because of the nature of the system of ownership, production, and distribution. When the poor fail to accept their middle-class notions they may end up frustrated failures. Some put their frustrations into a book (like *Yesterday's People*[71]).

Others set up the post office box corporations to get in on the "benefits" of the system. Both have been done.

Their basic concern was not how they related to the mountains but how the mountains related to them and their notions. With their "superior" approach, they failed to understand or appreciate the historic struggles of broad sections of the mountain people against the workings of the system dating back beyond the 1930s: early Paint and Cabin Creek battles; the armed march with five to seven thousand miners camped at Marmet in the Kanawha Valley, marching toward Logan to help fellow miners against gun thug terrorism; the Battle of Blair Mountain, where the enemy dropped bombs from the air; the battles of Evarts, Harlan, and Bell in Kentucky; Gastonia, Marion, High Point in North Carolina; Elizabethton, Wilder, Coal Creek in Tennessee, and later Blue Ridge in Georgia and the Black Lung West Virginia Strike in 1969. And before that the mountain man's struggle against a slave system that oppressed both the poor white and Black slaves.

These modern "missionaries" (some, already "ex-missionaries"), despairing of us, may return home. Ten years from now—if the world still stands—they may look back from their affluence with nostalgia for the time when they sowed their "radical wild oats" in Appalachia.

The "missionaries"—religious or secular—had and have one thing in common: they didn't trust us hill folk to speak, plan, and act for ourselves. Bright, articulate, ambitious, well-intentioned, they became our spokesmen, our planners, our actors. And so they'll go again, leaving us and our poverty behind.

But is there a lesson to be learned from all these outside efforts that have failed to save us? I think so. If we native mountaineers can now determine to organize and save ourselves, save our mountains from the spoilers who tear them down, pollute our streams, and leave grotesque areas of ugliness, there is hope. The billionaire families behind the great corporations are also outsiders who sometimes claim they want to "save" us. It is time that we hill folk should understand and appreciate our heritage, stand up like those who were our ancestors, develop our own self-identity. It is time to realize that nobody from the outside is ever going to save us from bad conditions unless we make our own stand. We must learn to organize again, speak, plan, and act for ourselves. There are many potential allies with common problems—the poor of the great cities, the Indians, the Blacks who are also exploited. They need us. We need them. Solidarity is still crucial. If we learn this lesson from the outside "missionary" failures, then we are on our way.

people's cultural heritage in appalachia (1971)

Editors' Note: This essay deals with the longtime grassroots traditions of protest in the Mountain South. It first appeared under the title "The Heritage of Appalachian People" in the May–June 1971 issue of Mountain Life and Work. *It was reprinted as a pamphlet by the Appalachian Press in July 1971.*

Sometimes references to the cultural heritage in the Appalachian South mean merely the quaint mannerisms, Elizabethan word pronunciation, "old fellerism." Or our beautiful folk ballads, songs, music, tall tales, lore, quilt-making, and other arts and crafts may be included. All of these certainly are part of our heritage and should justly be considered. The folk songs, ballads, music, tales, and such grow out of the subsoil of folk living the hope and hurt, the sorrow and longing of our people. All of these are part of it, but not all.

We believe a true understanding of our history will help to explain not only our songs and music, but that understanding works both ways. Our songs and music help us to understand the heritage from which they sprang, our people, problems, why we developed differently from the rest of the South, and where we may be able to go in the future. Our purpose is toward a more meaningful appreciation that may help in solving current problems and enriching that culture.

Brief Background Pre–Civil War

The history of Southern Appalachia has a peculiar content and quality which, in so many ways, set it apart from the South and the rest of the nation. Some causes for this, no doubt, are due to the cultural origins of the original settlers. They came largely from a background of old country rebellion against repressive economic, social, political, and religious suppression. They were predominantly from Celtic origins.

Further influences grew from the nature of historical developments in relation to conditions and institutions in the New World. These conditioning influences in the Old World and developing events in the New created a Southern Mountains sub-culture, clearly distinguishing it from that prevailing in the old South of which it was a geographical part. These differences centered mainly around issues of political and religious independence, freedom, and slavery.

I will not here go into any great detail, but may I say that years of research in Southern Appalachia's history and cultural heritage have enabled me to document everything contained here, and much more. The purpose here is a brief index to what is meant by Southern Appalachia's peculiar role in American history.

Independence, self-government, the freedom of man have always more or less had a place in American ideology. Because of certain specific influences, it was in the Appalachian South that these issues were first most strongly raised and acted upon. The old Regulators of North Carolina at the Battle of the Alamance fought unsuccessfully against the exploitative taxes and dictatorial rule of the royal governor Tyron before the American Revolution. Taking refuge across the Smoky Mountains into what was later to be east Tennessee, they participated in setting up the first self-governing community in the New World. There at Watauga[72] was written and adopted the first constitution for self-government by American-born men. A little later, from these southern mountains, three "declarations of independence" were written and advocated for adoption before the eventual Jefferson document. It was here in this mountain South that the sharpest issues of slavery were joined, as the modern abolitionist movement was born and cradled in infancy, toward a growth leading to the Emancipation Proclamation and the freeing of four million Black chattels. Here the first newspaper in America wholly dedicated to abolishing slavery was published (*The Emancipator,* Jonesboro, Tennessee, 1820). William Lloyd Garrison of New England was only 10 years old when these southern Appalachians were organizing their manumission societies and launching the *Intelligencer* and *Emancipator.*[73]

And it was here in the mountain South that the gentle Lundy came (after the death of *Emancipator* editor Embree) to labor and sweat and shed his tears as he struggled to print his *Genius of Universal Emancipation* on the mountain abolitionist press. It was also Lundy who after three years in Jonesboro moved his operation to Baltimore to be more in the mainstream, and on a speaking trip to Boston met and influenced Garrison to become an active abolitionist. Garrison was then editing a temperance sheet. At Lundy's subsequent invitation, Garrison came to Baltimore to assist him. After a year in Baltimore, Garrison was jailed for editorial attacks on a local slave trader. When Lundy and friends managed to obtain Garrison's freedom, he returned to New England to start his *Liberator.*[74]

The relevant point here is that the movement to abolish slavery was not a New England–birthed thing with pesky "Yankees" meddling in the affairs of "Southerners" ("Southerners" meaning always, of course, the no more than three hundred thousand slaveholders, never the six million nonslaveholding whites nor the four million Black slaves).

It was in these mountains that the venerable Dr. Samuel Doak organized his freedom teaching academies—Washington and Tusculum—later to become Tusculum College, which is still in operation at Greeneville, Tennessee. Likewise, it was here that two native Kentuckians in 1865 organized and set on its way Berea as an integrated abolitionist institution to teach the principles of freedom to Black and white mountain youth. From here came the internationally known abolitionist leader, John Rankin. Educated by Dr. Doak at Tusculum, Rankin moved to Ripley, Ohio, where he kept an Underground Railroad station, wrote voluminously, and led a movement against slavery, particularly in the Presbyterian Church. Rankin sent nine sons to the Union Army. Garrison called himself a disciple of Rankin, and Beecher called Rankin the "Martin Luther" of the abolition cause. Many other noted men were educated by Sam Doak in east Tennessee, among them Charles Osborn,[75] who moved on to Indiana to lead an anti-slavery movement for which he was "read out" of the Quaker religious order, but never silenced. Another was Sam Houston.[76] His later decision not to sign the Texas ordinance of secession may well have been influenced by his Tennessee mountain education.

There are dozens and dozens of other mountain men who lived dangerously and worked ceaselessly and sometimes gave their lives in the struggle against chattel slavery. Two such from Appalachian Virginia were remarkable in their selfless devotion to human freedom. The first, John Fairfield, as a "conductor" on the Underground Railroad, seemed to live a charmed life. He went into every slave state to lead refugees over the shadowy trail up across Appalachia to Canada and freedom. The other, John Kagi, a Virginia school teacher, took two Black refugees with him when he went searching for John Brown at Lawrence, Kansas. Kagi became John Brown's close friend, right-hand man, and most trusted lieutenant. He died at Harper's Ferry. The fate of John Fairfield, who would "give the shirt off his back to a needy refugee," is unknown.

Even the mountains of Georgia and Alabama have their dramatic events and anti-slavery heroes. (Winston County, Alabama, and Dade County, Georgia, seceded from their respective states when those states seceded from the Union.)[77] Christopher Sheets, in the legislature from Winston County, led the fight in convention against William Yancey's secession drive. The preponderant slaveholder influence defeated Sheets' efforts, but he came back to north Alabama to organize mass meetings against secession and the evolving Confederacy. He was arrested and spent the Civil War years in a Montgomery prison. The Alabama mountains were hotbeds of anti-Confederate guerrilla activity. A similar condition prevailed in north Georgia.

In Alabama, Robert Tharin had been a law partner with William Yancey.[78] But he shared Christopher Sheets' anti-slavery sentiment and activity. In 1857, he proposed to publish a newspaper, the *Non-Slaveholder.* He also defended in court poor whites accused of associating with Blacks. Given a slaveholder kangaroo court trial, Tharin was sentenced to 39 lashes on the bare back and to exile. Going north via an Underground Railroad station kept at Cincinnati by Levi Coffin[79] (a Carolina mountain man sometimes called the father and president of the Underground Railroad), Tharin eventually joined the Union Army and in 1863 published a book which he dedicated to the "poor white trash of the South." It was a powerful appeal to the poor whites against slavery.

Tharin's book was quite similar in spirit and content to that of the North Carolina mountaineer Helper, whose book, *The Impending Crisis,* became one of the most controversial anti-slavery books ever written.[80] It was banned and burned in the South. Men were jailed for possessing or circulating it. At least two men were lynched, and Helper was forced to flee for his life to the North. But in 1860 it was reprinted and used as campaign literature to help elect Abraham Lincoln to the Presidency. These stories are not in the history books our mountain children study. They are just a few examples of southern mountaineers who, although unknown, ought to be schoolbook heroes for our mountain youth, to help inspire and restore dignity, self-respect, pride, and confidence. They sprang from our people and from a cultural heritage differing sharply from that of the old slaveholding South. History has been so twisted that often a distorted self-image is developed. And it is our belief that a people's self-image is most important; it determines what an individual or people try to do, and it greatly affects growth and development.

The Civil War

Then came the Civil War. And from a southern mountain point of view, it was a civil war, not a "war between the states." In that struggle, the Appalachian South continued to play a distinctive and strategic role. The area stretched down across nine states to Georgia and Alabama, seven hundred miles long and up to three hundred miles wide. Although geographically a part of the Confederacy, the Appalachian South sent some two hundred fifty thousand volunteers to the Union Army, more than would have been the draft quota had it been above the Mason and Dixon Line. They joined without inducements of bounty promises and with the almost certain knowledge that their homes would be devastated if the Confederacy had the opportunity. This certainly happened at least in areas of Tennessee around Knoxville.

After the Civil War

During the war, the mountain South was considered a dangerous threat to the Confederacy. The mountaineers were considered "traitors." At one point, a Confederate official complained that the mountain South represented a greater threat to the Confederacy than either army of the Union. And undoubtedly he was right. Had the two hundred fifty thousand southern volunteers been thrown on the other side, the history of America might well have been written differently.

After the war, there was a long period of stagnation in the mountain South. Roads and other internal improvements were neglected. Schools and education were worse. Men whose ancestors had been fairly well-educated grew up illiterate, signed their names with an X. Many of the long-form deeds[81] to "mineral rights" on mountain lands were thus signed. Then came new developments which were to change, destroy, and play havoc with much of our mountain heritage and culture: representatives of northern-based corporations buying up "mineral rights" at 25 cents to 50 cents an acre.

The long-form deed to "mineral rights" had a clause granting the owner the right to use whatever methods he felt were necessary to remove those minerals. This clause has been used in modern times to legalize the atrocity of stripmining.

With coal rights owned by outside corporations, mines were opened and the mountain man suddenly found himself in strangely new circumstances. He was no longer a free man. He lived in a company town where houses, store, church, school, streets, and roads were owned by the company. He was compelled to trade in the company store, live in a company house, send his kids to company schools, and go to a company church. Whether he wished to or not, he paid the preacher. Frequently the preacher's salary was checked out of the miner's wage before he received his check.

A mining village usually lay along a creek between two mountains. It had a single road that only led in and out. Often the company had an entrance gate across this road and an armed guard stationed there day and night. Strangers without a pass were not admitted. Add dangerous working conditions, low wages, and a constant fear of being fired and we have a virtual serf or slave-like situation. It went hard against the grain for a once-proud and independent people.

The spirit might writhe under such conditions, but fear muted voices of protest. If they were heard, it meant loss of a job. Eventually, though, a notion was born and began to grow: mutual aid, organization, union. These ideas were at first whispered, secret. A quiet word, a nod or an undercover handbill—a secret meeting, of necessity—in basements, out in the woods, even in a cave. For the company imported professional gunmen to terrorize, to brutalize, to kill; they did them all. Sometimes the most secret gathering would be discovered and men were murdered.

But the mountain spirit had been a free thing. "Mountaineers are always free" is not a meaningless motto for West Virginia. Great, dramatic, militant, and heroic struggle ensued—Coal Creek and Tracy City in Tennessee, Harlan and Bell Counties in Kentucky, Cabin and Paint Creeks in West Virginia with five thousand armed miners camped at Marmet, marching toward Logan to aid brother-miners brutalized by a reign of gun-thug terror, the battle of Blair Mountain with planes dropping crude bombs on the marching miners—memories of desperation.[82]

Long years of determined struggle against gun-thug terror finally won. The old freedom-loving independent spirit asserted itself. The longings for self-respect, human dignity, and food for their children survived even the worst brutalization. The miners organized. They won a contract with better working conditions, more safety, better wages. The locked gates with armed guards at mine village entrances were removed. The miners were no longer forced to trade in the company store.

Then the union was militant, democratic, with rank-and-file participation in the decision-making process. All seemed well, with future promise. Victory was good, and it seemed to be a lasting thing. Miners trusted their leaders, and this was their mistake. They forgot that the cost of liberty and human welfare is always eternal vigilance. They forgot that power corrupts and that great power corrupts greatly.

In the beginning, conditions were so bleak, violence and murder so commonplace, that John L. Lewis himself was compelled to lead militantly, to conduct a democratic organization. But Lewis lost sight of a union's function and purpose. He developed no rank-and-file education program. He did not see such understanding of the membership as essential. Lewis made the decisions. Lewis got drunk on power. He eventually consolidated that power into what became a virtual union dictatorship. It was passed on to Tony Boyle, who is currently and finally under federal indictment for his power misuse. (Appalachian Press Ed. note: After this essay was written, Boyle was finally convicted for the murder of the Yablonski family.) Lewis ruled by the strong-arm method. Those who questioned that rule wound up its victims. The fate of the Yablonski family[83] is the natural fruit of this violent heritage in coal. In the United Mine Workers Union, local districts were not permitted to elect their own officers. John L. Lewis appointed them, and after him Tony Boyle. The miners lost all voice in decision-making. When automation came, Lewis made no fight to protect the members. Tens of thousands of miners were replaced by machinery. Other tens of thousands are scattered through Appalachia, disabled, disillusioned, on welfare.

But again the mountaineer fights back. He is resilient—he may be bent, twisted, warped, but given the opportunity he comes up again. He stands straight like the man he was and is. Last year in West Virginia, the mines were solidly closed down and forty thousand miners marched on the state capitol demanding mine safety legislation. They kept the mines closed—against the national union leadership's orders, against the corporations, against the politicians in the state government—until a bill was passed.

robert tharin:
biography of a mountain abolitionist
(ca. 1970)

*Editors' Note: Since the 1940s, West had intended to write a full historical treat-
ment of the antislavery traditions in the Mountain South. This essay, which was
printed as an Appalachian Movement Press pamphlet in the 1970s, was one of
several chapters West had completed.*

He was a young man, idealistic, inclined to be serious, perhaps naive—at least,
inexperienced. He was not a slaveholder, nor the son of one. Nor was he a native
of Alabama when he hung out his shingle over a law office in Wetumpka in
1860. He was a newcomer from the South Carolina hills. Born on a farm Jan-
uary 10, 1830, he had by hard work and perseverance managed an A.B. degree
from the College of Charleston in March 1857. Going to Alabama where cer-
tain kinsmen lived in September of the same year, he continued work and study
and graduated with the University's A.M. degree in 1860. That was also the year
he set up law practice in partnership with William L. Yancey at Wetumpka.
Montgomery and Yancey's main offices were only a few miles away.

His name was Robert S. Tharin, A.B., A.M., and now a member of the Ala-
bama Bar, admitted in 1859. The oath administered on that occasion made a
deep impression on him. In it he swore allegiance to both the Constitutions
of Alabama and the United States, and further, it stated that never was he "for
considerations personal . . . to neglect the cause of the defenseless and op-
pressed."

Unlike many old South Carolina families whose ancestors had been To-
ries in the War of the Revolution, his grandfather had fought under the noted
(and hated) "Swamp Fox."[84] His father, a loyal Union man, had opposed Cal-
houn's secession sentiment as treasonable.[85] This was hardly the kind of
heritage calculated to bring peace of mind, personal welfare, comfort, or
security to a serious minded young southern mountaineer in Wetumpka,
Alabama, in the year 1860.

Nevertheless, he was there. And there never seems to be a limit to the au-
dacity or dreams of the idealistic young. He had already married a beautiful

Alabama girl and they had two children. How much a family can complicate and bring sorrow and hurt to such a one is only known to those who have themselves had the experience.

Space does not permit going into fuller detail on this at this point. We mention it as a factor in the background of a man who was destined to be an exile and refugee from the land of his birth because he challenged the despotic rule of its Slavocracy.

It was a time of trouble alright, the year 1860. Times were difficult, hard enough for the average man drugged by over-doses of racist oratory. But for the thinking, sensitive man of ideals, it was a time of spirit testing. As clouds got blacker tempers got hotter. Violence and disaster hovered about. Over the South frustration and confusion spread an intellectual black-out. From early times the slaveholder minority had ruled. For the past three decades it had dominated the national government in Washington. Boasting white superiority and a "superior" culture built upon slavery of the blacks, the oligarchy kept control by a constant appeal to prejudice and racial fears.

In this the slaveholders were realists. They knew that control over what they chose to call the "mean whites," or "white trash," must be as certain, was as important, as the control of slaves.

Edward Ruffin, Slavocracy's spokesman par excellence,[86] put it bluntly when he explained that they excluded all the "lower classes" from a voice in government, "whether slave or free, white or black." Ruffin declared that if these "mean whites," or property-less class, had the ballot they would use it to rob the rich of their property.

And hadn't the great Calhoun himself—patron saint and spiritual mentor for all true Confederates then or later—warned that free democracy ". . . would destroy our (Southern) system and destroy the South?"

Just a bare mention of the word "free" was itself sufficient to start frothing of editorial mouths. "Free" was an obnoxious, a mean and ugly word. It became a red flag, as "subversive" and as suspect as the word "peace" was to become in the mid-twentieth century.

The *Richmond Examiner*, to which George Fitzhugh[87] was a contributing editor, gave true voice to Slavocracy sentiment. "We have got to hating everything with the prefix free," it growled, "from free negroes down and up, through the whole category of abominations . . . free farms, free labor, free n . . . s, free society, free will, free thinking, free love, free wives, free children and free schools, all belong to the same breed of damnable isms whose mother is sin and whose daddy is the Devil." But most of all the *Examiner* "abominated" freedom "because the schools are free."

And the state of Louisiana, so sensitive to Slavocracy's every pulse beat, decided to eliminate free labor on its various upkeep and internal improvement jobs. The government of the state of Louisiana, in 1853, bought itself one hundred black slaves!

Oh, it was a great age in the Old South, a bright and wondrous glory with a culture we should look back on and whine because of its loss. The "dragon of democracy" was well nigh dead. If Slavocracy had its way it would be finished off in all the land. The *New Orleans Crescent* chirped gleefully on October 27, 1859, that ". . . the productive laboring element (white and black), having its teeth drawn (is) robbed of its ability to do harm by being in a state of bondage."

What glory! What grandeur! Only the mean and ugly, only the spokesmen of slaves and the great majority of southern whites would question it in the South. And they were the "niggers" and the "trash." But even "trash" can be bothersome. Hadn't spokesmen for the North Alabama "hillbillies" demanded that the ordinance of secession be submitted to popular vote?[88]

Such ideas were dangerous and "evil." And it looked like that ugly agitation to test the rule of the Slavocracy would never cease. For a long time abolitionist troublemakers had been spreading their pernicious doctrine. It all got started up there in the mountains of Tennessee and North Carolina. Those damned "hillbillies" again! They were everlastingly messing up tidewater and lowland affairs of the Cotton Kingdom. Hadn't they started the modern abolitionist movement? Hadn't the "hillbillies" printed the first abolitionist newspaper? And hadn't they kept messing around till they spread that infernal abolition doctrine to Garrison and New England?

Among the first Americans to see and understand the evils of slavery were such southern mountaineers as Samuel Doak, Elihu Embree, Charles Osborn, and John Rankin of Tennessee; Cassius M. Clay, John G. Fee, and James G. Birney of Kentucky; Christopher Sheets and Robert Tharin of Alabama; B. S. Hedrick, Daniel R. Goodloe,[89] and Hinton Helper of North Carolina. Even that old "Swamp Fox," Francis Marion, fighting the many Tories of South Carolina, had pointed up the evils of slavery. "The people of Carolina form two classes—the rich and the poor," he had said. "The poor are generally very poor, because not being necessary to the rich, who have slaves to do all their work . . ."

One of that hated number, Hinton Helper, ought to be hung and quartered. His *Impending Crisis* in 1857 had caused a Slavocracy heart spasm. Garrison and his gang up North were bad enough. But the Northerners mostly made sentimental talk about morality and the "nigger." And hadn't the Dred Scott decision settled that? Hadn't it shown that the black man had no right the master was compelled to respect, and that slavery was national while freedom was sectional? It was these Southern "renegades" with appeals to the "mean whites" who caused Slavocracy's big trembles. Helper's book dramatized and drove home the role of slavery in keeping the poor white, as well as the black man, down in want and squalor. The book showed how slavery destroyed all freedom and dirtied the dignity of labor.

There had always been Southerners who opposed slavery. The Negro himself was the strongest opponent. But as much, if not more, fearsome to slaveholders was the growth of understanding and antislavery sentiment among the poor whites. And the ever-present potential of slave–poor white unity was a grim spectre stalking the land, haunting the dreams of the oligarchy.

Thus abolition, begun in the South, had been well nigh suppressed by the 1840s. Many anti-slavery Southerners exiled at the North (or underground) helped concentrate opposition along sectional lines. The struggle looked like a sectional matter. But prior to 1840 abolition was mainly in the South. Berea College in Kentucky, founded by native leaders in the 1850s, was not only abolitionist but interracial—for poor mountain whites and blacks. Maryville College in Tennessee, another institution among the mountain people, developed along the same lines with about half its students becoming abolitionists before 1841.

An East Kentuckian, James G. Birney, left his law practice in Huntsville, Alabama, and came back to Kentucky to lead the anti-slavery movement and launch the *Philanthropist.* Forced to move across the river into Ohio, Birney continued his efforts. There he endeavored to arouse the whole country against the institution of slavery. He also sought to "politicize" the abolitionist movement, led in the organization of the Liberty Party, and became its first candidate for president in 1846.

The "peculiar institution" may have been a dying duck, but it fought back. To protect it, slaveholders everywhere were willing to sacrifice the principles of free speech, liberty, and the right of petition all over the land. Slavery could only be maintained at this sacrifice. To keep men in slavery it is necessary to keep them in ignorance, devoid of all knowledge of freedom. This they did by outlawing education for blacks and providing no public school system for the whites.

But more than these sacrifices were necessary—the spirit of open-mindedness and the search for truth in general must also be destroyed. And these also became conspicuously absent in the Old South. In 1856 the intellectual, Francis Lieber, was glad to leave South Carolina for an educational post at the North. The University of North Carolina fired B. S. Hedrick, because he voted for Fremont.[90] And the University of Virginia, proudly fathered by freethinker Thomas Jefferson, had difficulty finding a history professor though offering a very high salary. That old Jeffersonian tradition was completely repudiated. Qualified minds hesitated to accept a position where freedom of thought and expression were so circumscribed.

Of all these things the slaveholders of Wetumpka were not unmindful in

1860. Nor were they ignorant of the attitude of their own North Alabama "hill-billies" with the anti-slavery leader, Chris Sheets, who made the fight to submit secession to a popular vote, organized mass protest meetings against it—and was to lie in a Confederate prison throughout the Civil War.

But now here was Bob Tharin, defending poor whites in court against slave-holders, openly opposing slavery and secession, proposing to publish a newspaper to be called the *Non-Slaveholder*—and all within twenty miles of Montgomery! May the Lord preserve all true slaveholders! And what's the world coming to anyhow? The very idea of a newspaper for non-slaveholders. A paper spreads ideas. What could be more dangerous? Of what, above all else, can a despotism stand less? Hadn't they ruled by prohibiting thought—by drowning it in race propaganda, religion, and oratory?

It was a time for all good pen-prostitutes, preachers, and orators to come to the aid of their oligarchy. It was a time to be up and doing. And the Slavocracy had its willing servants. It had a full share of long talkers and little sayers. The poor whites, no less than slaves, must be kept in their place. Such mountain men as Helper, Sheets, Tharin, Clay, and many others were feared, hated, and hounded. In the 1850s Slavocracy's flunkies took to the stump.

George Fitzhugh, of the Virginia Tidewater, cynical, arrogant, shrewd, and cunning, boldly proclaimed the superior virtues of slavery. In his *Cannibals All* he argued those virtues and in favor of extending slavery over all the land. "Slavery, black or white, was right and necessary," he proclaimed.

Thornton Stringfellow's *Scriptural and Statistical Views in Defense of Slavery* had a fourth edition in 1856. And in 1858 Senator Robert Toombs of Georgia was shouting that "American slavery . . . would find its euthanasia in the general prostration of all labor."

William L. Yancey, Alabama's egocentric secession leader, carried the propaganda invasion to the North before Lee tried Gettysburg. In Cincinnati, October 24, 1860, Yancey made a "great" speech in which he sought to indoctrinate the laboring North with slaveholder racism. Warning them that freeing the slaves would result in a "mulatto government," Yancey proceeded to describe the terrible "nigger." "They will elbow you on the streets, in the workshops, on the roads, and in the fields. They will underbid you for every species of labor, for they have no wish beyond the satisfaction of today."

Yancey continued to describe the evil effects of the "rich man's nigger," free and in economic competition with the poor white blacksmith, bricklayer, wheelwright, carpenter, or agriculturist. "Are you willing, my hard-handed, hard-working countrymen of the North, to be placed on a level with the black man?" Yancey yelled. "Are you willing to get on the platform prepared for you by this fanatical (Republican) party at the North? Do you want to compete for your industrial pursuits with the black nigger?"

Three months and eighteen days after that speech Yancey stood up in the State Convention at Montgomery and voted for secession. He also voted against leaving it to the people for a ratification.

And Tharin asks, who were the delegates to that Secession Convention? "There was no non-slaveholder who helped frame that secession ordinance. There was no hard-handed mechanic, no hard-working non-slaveholder of the South in that traitor crew. . . ." Those secession framers ". . . were the representatives of slaveholders, slaveholders themselves."

The Rev. John H. Aughey, Mississippi Presbyterian minister, gave an example of Slavocracy oratory by a Colonel Drane, one of his church members at Choctaw, Mississippi, in 1860: "If the black Republicans carry their ticket," this Christian Colonel declaimed, not only would ". . . Our God-given rights to carry slavery into the common domain . . . (be) . . . wickedly taken from the South," but daughters of the poor white men would be compelled to mix with "buck-niggers." He complained that "Our rights are trampled on. Our slaves are spirited by thousands over the Underground Railroad to Canada. We have lost millions and are losing millions every year by the operation of the Underground Railroad."

Drane then struck out to prove Southern "superiority." "We are a more moral people than they are (Yankees). . . . Who originated Mormonism, Millerism, Spirit-Rappings, Abolitionism, Free-Loveism, and all the other abominable isms which curse the world? The reply is the North."[91]

Flowing on into the sweet and blissful dream of slavery producing undying love and devotion of slave to master, the orator explained the reason to be the slaveholder's nobility. They were a more moral race than the yankees. "Their servants hate them; ours love us; my niggers would fight for me and my family. If ever there comes a war, let us arm our trained servants and go forth with them to the battle. They hate the yankees as intensely as we do, and nothing could please our slaves better than to fight them. Ah, the perfidious yankees! I cordially hate a Yankee!"

Nor was Alabama to be outdone by Mississippi. Its Seventh District Congressman, Jabez L. M. Curry, speaking in Wetumpka, Tharin's own town, gravely informed his audience that, "As soon as Abe Lincoln takes the presidential chair, five hundred thousand Wide-Awakes, already drilling for the purpose, will rush over the borders, lay waste your fields, emancipate your negroes, and amalgamate the poor man's daughter with the rich man's buck-nigger before your very eyes!"

Now there you are again. Put that in your pipe and smoke it you poor-white non-slaveholder! Let that soak into your craw, and if you have any grit in your gizzard, where does your loyalty belong? The Congressman has spoken, and he "ought to know."

What about this guy, Bob Tharin, of your own town who opposes slavery and secession, who holds Union loyalty, defends a "Lincolnite" in court, and even now proposes to publish a paper called the *Non-Slaveholder*? Maybe Tharin wants his daughter "amalgamated," but do you want your own daughters forced into bed with a big black "buck-nigger"? What about it, you poor whites? Didn't he say it would be the "rich man's buck-nigger and the poor man's daughter"?

The excitement caused by such orations is inestimable. It was always the rich man's "buck-nigger" and the "poor man's daughter," never the rich man's daughter. The purpose is obvious. And it was by no means of slight effect. The question of poor white loyalty was basic. The politician slaveholders worked at it everlastingly. Who'd do their fighting if the poor white turned? Only by that loyalty could the Confederacy hope to wage meaningful war. And, ultimately, it was largely by lack of loyalty and defection, with many thousands joining the Union Army, that the Confederacy lost.

Such, then, is something of the background against which young Robert Tharin opened his law office in Wetumpka in 1860. "No sooner had I opened my law office in Wetumpka," he wrote, "than an opportunity occurred for me to risk something for the sake of my oath. One of the 'poor white trash,' was dragged down to the river, laid across a log and whipped, by a throng of black-guards (slaveholders). . . . They had charged him . . . with associating with negroes. He was ridden on a rail until his clothes were literally torn off his body. From the lintel of his own door he was repeatedly hanged until he was black in the face."

This poor, bedraggled victim of slaveholder ire sought the legal aid of Tharin. "He was a pitiable object. Fright and general bad usage had left their marks upon him." Though a native Southerner, this was a new experience for Tharin. It was still his "learning" time. "My eyes were not closed to conditions of the South even then," he wrote. "I had felt some very indignant emotions, when seeing the prostration of the many at the footstool of the few."

The mob victim's name was Franklin Vetch. He came to Tharin's office, seeking legal aid. He began to tell his story. ". . . Sometimes he would stand on one foot, sometimes on the other," Tharin wrote. "He sat down at my invitation, but the seat of his pants having been ridden off on the jagged fence-rail . . . the cold contact of the chair started him back to his feet. . . ."

"I felt humiliated," Tharin reported. "I approached the poor trembling victim of mobocracy. I looked with changed feeling upon him. Encouraged by my manner, he raised his eyes. Fear had added a gleam of almost insanity to their expression; but there was a ray of hopeful intelligence . . . which was very touching."

"Mr. Vetch," Tharin asked, "who sent you to me?"

"Mr. Hill."

"What do you want?"

"Fair play."

"Do you want my services as a lawyer?"

"Yes, sir."

"You are too much excited now—come to me next week."

"Will you take my case then?"

"Maybe so."

Tharin sensed danger here—to himself, to his family, and to their future. He hesitated. After all, he had a wife and two children. He was their sole support. He owned no property, held no slaves. For a new young lawyer to take the case of a poor white mobbed by the leading aristocracy of the area would be inviting trouble. It was unheard of. But Tharin remembered his oath. It had a clause about not neglecting the cause of the defenseless and oppressed for personal reasons. He remembered other victims he had known before becoming a lawyer, and he made further investigations. He found that "Vetch had been a victim of even more than that of which he complained." But he still hesitated.

"I almost hoped that Vetch would not come back," Tharin wrote. And ". . . as the time drew near I thought he had forgotten: but no! he came and asked me to take his case. He even urged me to take it for the sake of justice." Vetch knew well the wide-spread violence and intimidation practiced against the poor whites by the local aristocracy.

Tharin knew Vetch to be one of "the poor white trash," perhaps unreliable because of an environmental background of violence and fear. But he also recognized that if there ever had been a man "defenseless and oppressed," Vetch was one.

He was torn in conscience. He even felt resentment against the man, Vetch. It was Tharin's testing time. Vetch had come back.

"I felt a stranger anger against Vetch," he wrote. "I almost hated him for being 'defenseless' and for being 'oppressed' . . . but I took this case."

Then began a bitter experience, an ordeal for Tharin and his family which, ultimately, was to separate and drive them from their home as exiles in a strange land. The struggle began, ". . . a struggle that shook the whole community." Wetumpka had never witnessed anything like it. The local aristocrats had never seen a lawyer who stood up to challenge their right to do as they wished, even to mobbing a poor white whenever it suited them. And they were accustomed to having the poor whites knuckle under. Their resentment was against both Tharin and Vetch.

"The parties sued became more than ever unmerciful to Vetch," Tharin wrote. "They threatened to kill him if he did not leave the community. They offered him bribes." But Vetch was stubborn. He stuck to his guns, backed by other poor whites. "The poor whites of the community secretly encouraged him. . . ."

Tharin himself was threatened. Efforts were made to intimidate and cause him to withdraw from the case. But his own determination had grown when he saw how the poor brow-beaten Vetch was sticking. Then, on the day the case was to be called, "Vetch disappeared." Tharin appeared in court for his defense, but "no Vetch." The defendants produced a paper, purportedly signed with Vetch's mark, saying he pressed no charges. The case was dismissed. But Vetch himself was never seen again. The supposition was that he had been murdered and his body hidden. Such acts were not uncommon in the Old South.

The ring-leader of the local mob was a young man of an old family, "long residents, and endowed with negro property, that great passport to impunity" in many areas of the Old South.

Vetch was gone, but what about his lawyer? Tharin found himself "the most unpopular man in Wetumpka" among the slaveholding class. "Lies had been freely circulated" before the trial. "With a sudden unpleasant awakening," he found himself in a "modern Sodom," and felt his blood curdle at the thought that as long as he could remember the "class to which Vetch belonged" had been growing more "oppressed" and more "defenseless." "In my native South Carolina I had been too young to note the workings of aristocracy upon the oppressed poor."

Later, a refugee and exile, Tharin was to write: "There are many Franklin Vetches in the South. . . . The leaders of the conspiracy are loud in their ex-clamations for States rights; but their whole scheme is based upon the destruction of State and personal rights. They pretend to Southern independence, but ignore the personal independence of the white people of the South; they shout Southern rights, yet they have completely annihilated Southern rights. Mine, alas! Where?"

Nothing Tharin did seemed to please the slaveholders. In the *Wetumpka Enquirer* he had earlier run a series of articles advocating the establishment of small farms for the landless and "the use of water-power of the falls and rapids" of the Coosa River which runs through the village. His article pointed out the "injurious effects" of large "overgrown plantations" upon the greater population. "I was never popular with the slaveholders after that," he wrote. "Small farms would benefit 'the masses,'" and that the slaveholders did not want.

But he kept working. He tried to organize a Union Party in the area, and continued to make pro-Union, anti-secession speeches. While the response was good among the non-slaveholders, they had no funds to finance organization, and all their efforts were closely watched by the powerful and violent slave-holders. Threats, intimidation, mob action were common. "Disgraceful scenes would often occur when . . . I would launch a fiery denunciation at the head of Yancey, with whom my law partnership had been some time at an end," Tharin wrote.

To those history writers, or teachers, who so glibly lump the Old South together—non-slaveholders and slaveholders—before the Civil War, as one united "the South," Tharin has a correction. Speaking at Buckville, a few miles from Wetumpka, he gave a realistic analysis of "the South," using the 1850 census. "I will attempt to define the term 'South,'" he said. "The 'South,' when applied to the slaveholding section of the United States, signifies six millions of whites and three millions of black inhabitants . . . the number of slaveholders in the South (and elsewhere in the Union) is three hundred and forty-seven thousand . . . while the white population in the South is six million one hundred and eighty-four thousand. . . . The non-slaveholders of the South are at least twelve times as numerous as the slaveholders. If we take Alabama herself . . . there are over fourteen persons who have no negroes to one who does. . . . If Alabama be divided into fifteen cities, about the size of Mobile, the non-slaveholders will have fourteen of them, the slaveholders only one!"

But this small minority "South"—some three hundred thousand slaveholders—"held all the offices of profit or of trust and dominated over them (the majority) with an iron hand!"

Tharin felt keenly about this matter of just what or who was "the South." Again and again he hammered on it, trying to get across the idea that there was not a united South with unanimous support for a slave system. In an article in the *London* (England) *Daily News* for November 27, 1861, he comes back to it again. This time he was discussing the term "South" as used by men such as Yancey. ". . . Whenever such men as William L. Yancey speak of the South, they never mean the non-slaveholders who represent the numerical proportion of fifteen to one as compared with the planters or slave holders. . . ."

He went ahead to explain further that "the non-slaveholders are, by far, the most important class, yet, on account of the skillful agitation of the slavery (and race) question, the slaveholders have obtained a despotic mastery, and allude exclusively to themselves and their property, when they use the expression 'the South,' 'Southern interests,' etc."

Tharin didn't know it, but his words were a prophesy of the way history was largely to be written, taught, and read, about "the South" a hundred years later. The Yanceys, Jeff Davis, the Toombs, and the Stephenses, set the pattern for a latter day history writing.[92]

In the *London News* article Tharin further defined the role this Southern slaveholder minority which, ". . . possessing all the implements of power, this diabolical mob stifled every breath of remonstrance, and almost every thought of resistance. Some of the oppressed . . . Unionists (myself among the number), openly opposed the reign of terror, which was studiously produced by Yancey and his colleagues. False imprisonments, murders, expatriation, 'cruel and unusual punishment'—the torture of cowhide, tar and feathers, and fence-rails, public and private confiscations—these were the coercives which ensued . . ." and were widely used in the slaveholder bid to rule at all cost.

In 1858, as the election of delegates to the Alabama State Convention neared, Tharin had announced as the "UNION CANDIDATE." He very nearly won, and wrote, "I would have been triumphantly returned from Coosa County, had it not been for the contemptible tricks of the Wetumpka branch of the 'Secret League of United Southerners,' of which the main Society at Montgomery was presided over by the notorious William Lowndes Yancey."

Threats, intimidation, violence—the typical Old South (and "New" South) method of keeping control in the hands of a few—were used. A non-slaveholder could not be permitted. Even at that early period they had sensed Tharin's sentiment as to slaveholders and poor whites. "While I despised the insolent usurpations of the cotton nobility, I loved, while I pitied, the non-slaveholding whites, whose only hope in the world was the overthrow of King Cotton," he wrote. "I knew that never, in Congress, in state legislatures, in conventions—whether political or commercial, State, sectional, or national—has the non-slaveholder, as a class, had any—the slightest—representation. On the contrary, by the aggressive usurpations of the planters, we had been doomed to a condition, as a class, but little, if any, above" the slaves themselves. "The dominant class, possessing unshared legislative sway, easily excluded these, the people of the South—under the insulting epithet 'poor white trash'—from educational and social advantages, until the mere mechanical operation of choosing which slaveholder or cotton planter, should misrepresent us, was all that was left us."

The Breckenridge Club was active in Wetumpka in 1860.[93] Its job was to line up and keep the poor whites under control. Terror and fear, threats and intimidations, were commonly used. Unionists—and there were a considerable number—were tarred and feathered, ridden on rails, hanged, shot, or "accidentally committed suicide." A small shop keeper and non-slaveholder named William S. Middlebrooks, accused of being a "Lincolnite," was mobbed, dragged through the streets by slaveholders, and thrown in jail. While in prison they tore down his fences, raided his house, insulted his wife, and would have wrecked the house, but the wife "gave them to understand that she could and would shoot," and "the terrified young rebels" fled. Defending this "Lincolnite" only added to Tharin's troubles. But he did it. The results were, of course, what might be expected. Middlebrooks was ruined, his business destroyed, and he was left destitute. Thus did the "gentle" aristocrats of the glorious Old South tradition dispose of opposition.

Tharin's determination was strengthened constantly by the knowledge that many thousands of non-slaveholders over the South shared his sentiment and, to some extent, his plight. They were the inarticulate ones whose views have generally been lost to history. Often confused by deliberate slaveholder racist type propaganda, kept in ignorance for lack of public schools, under the spell of fear, they often acted to hurt themselves. Tharin, an educated poor hill white, gave them some articulation. Had it not been for these few the sentiment and views of the Old South non-slaveholder might be entirely lost. True, Tharin became more of the spokesman for the lowland whites, and most of the anti-slavery, pro-Union sentiment was centered in the Southern Mountains. But for the scrappy findings here and there, most of that has been lost also.

Ruth Scarborough, in a Ph.D. thesis study of opposition to slavery in Georgia prior to 1860, calls attention to this wide-spread attitude there. And again, most of it was in the mountains. She writes:

"In extreme North Georgia dwelt the mountaineers. . . . They were devoted to the Union and would have supported emancipation if it had been attempted. . . . The mountaineers were anti-slavery in sentiment. They were an inarticulate element and their views have usually been lost. . . ."

More articulate than many of his kind, Tharin's views are more than his own, more significant than just the opinions of a single man. To some extent he provides a mirror reflecting a much wider scope. He gives us a tiny peep, though not entirely satisfying, at the non-slaveholding lowlander of the Old South. "I never envied the planters of Wetumpka or, indeed of any part of the South," he wrote. "My dislike to them arose from their contemptible meanness, their utter disregard to common decency, their supercilious arrogance, and their daily usurpation of powers and privileges at variance with my rights and the rights of my class. . . ."

Tharin was even then conscious of speaking for more than just himself. He spoke for his "class." Such an attitude, of course, must "bear its fruits." And while we say he spoke for more than himself, we must also credit the courage of the man as a person. It takes a particular kind of courage to speak up for those who have no voice, for the inarticulate. And there is never any hope for reward, other than the silent gratitude of those for whom such a one speaks. The hurt of the inarticulate cannot, of course, fend off the blows of the evil and powerful. Tharin's ordeal had just begun. His actions were to bear their fruits—a bitter-sweet tasting stuff.

On a lovely day in January 1860, Tharin was looking out his kitchen window at a view of meadow and low-lying hills in the distance. Wetumpka has a particular beauty in its own surroundings of rich, fertile soil and a variety of vegetation produced by a mild climate. But on that day there was a knock on his door. Visitors?

"Mr. Tharin . . . we have been appointed by the vigilance committee to request your presence before them."

There it was, the widely feared vigilance committee! That committee was not official, but nontheless powerful. It ruled by secrecy and fear—and the fact that its members were well armed and could shoot with impunity. Charges had been placed against Tharin by the vigilance committee. But he, never the one to admit the legality of the illegal, nor to accept a thing as right because it held guns, questioned on this occasion: "By what authority does a vigilance committee summons a freeborn citizen . . . before them to answer charges?" he wanted to know. "By their own authority!" was the fierce and insulting reply.

They dragged him away to the meeting place. As they approached the gathering, "a barbaric scene" burst upon their view. About two hundred and fifty planters, many belonging to the "first families," were congregated around the building. A voice from among them shouted: "Have you got the d—m rascal?" "Got him! I reckon we have," came the reply.

Tharin's conduct before this committee of mobsters was one of showing utter disdain. He did not deem it necessary to defend himself. He had done no wrong. In the time-honored tradition of those who have stood for decency and liberty against evil and overwhelming odds, his words were an indictment of the mobsters and their slave system. His speech on that occasion gives further index to the quality of the man, as he flung indictments at the very ones who held him, with the power of life or death, in their hands.

"When all the dearest privileges and time-honored rights of Americans are . . . denied; when 'taxation without representation' oppresses God's poor, for the benefit of the rich, in every state in this union, and the non-slaveholder of my native section, although a very large majority of the population, are compelled to pay their tribute into the treasury for the benefit of the cotton-planters, who monopolize, as their own, all the offices, honors, emoluments of government, in direct violation . . . of the Constitution. . . ." It was indeed a sad time.

Frequently interrupted by loud and vulgar jeers, Tharin continued: "I have lived to see mobs usurp the function of the outraged law, and imprison and even execute innocent persons without a trial, judge, or jury!" On the ashes of democracy, trampled into the dust by mockery, "Aristocracy has reared a throne . . . upon whose downy summit reclines a despot . . . ! 'King Cotton' is his terrible name. He flourishes his bloody scepter," not only over three million black slaves, but also over "the 'poor white trash' who encumbers the soil sacred to the patent leathers of the 'patriarchs' of the peculiar institution.'"

"Why, he's a damned abolitionist," a voice shouted.

Continuing a stinging indictment of "that aristocratic class, to which you, sirs, affect to belong," Tharin charged that the "crime" for which he had been dragged before that illegal body was his "attempt to restore my down-trodden fellow citizens to their just rights. Born a free man, I shall ever remain a free man! I come not here to answer, but to make charges—grave charges . . . I charge you with trampling upon law and liberty; with violating all the most sacred provisions of the Constitutions of your own state and of the United States. . . ."

But that illegal vigilance committee made its own charges against Tharin, regardless. They were three in number:

1. He had "conversed with several non-slaveholders in the neighborhood" concerning their rights.
2. He planned a newspaper, to be called the *Non-Slaveholder.*
3. He "was organizing the people into secret associations" against the secession ordinance.

The verdict was, of course, "guilty." His punishment was set in typical slaveholder spirit:

1. "He shall receive thirty-nine lashes . . ." laid on the bare back.
2. He shall "be escorted by a committee . . . to Benton, and placed in the charge of the captain of the first boat" that stopped there, and shipped out.
3. "Shall he ever return to this community, he shall be hanged."
4. "Proceeds of this meeting" to be published in the *Montgomery Advertiser and Post.*

The fourth part of this sentence was a blow at Tharin's wife who, sick in bed, driven to distraction by fear for his safety, had almost gone insane. She, from a "respectable" family, had been a "sheltered daughter." Only her love for Tharin and an understanding of what he stood for prevented a total breakdown. However, Tharin philosophized, "This was but the fate of hundreds, thousands! of Unionists in the South."

It was indeed the fate of other thousands. But regardless of this fact, it is always a hard row for each one of them. Idealistic, hopers with faith, dreamers about man's greater good and ultimate potential though they may be, each act of cruelty carries a keen stab, evokes a sensitive response. With a sick wife and an invalid child, who can measure the feeling of or the cost to such a one under those conditions? But that was not all. Lashed and beaten into a semi-insensible state, dragged along by a heavily armed crew of slaveholding ruffians to be put aboard a boat with a death penalty if he ever returned, the thought and feeling of such a one are beyond describing. To add to the "disgrace" and "embarrassment," they forced Tharin to ride a scrawny stubborn old mule. Thus, this Southern Mountaineer, whose "crime" had been to uphold justice,

in the Old South, was driven from his home leaving there a sick wife and in-
valid child.

Thus Tharin was separated from his family and exiled to a strange land. It
meant many things, including a new beginning with problems multiplied
manifold. But somehow the man stood it. But at times, midst all the persecu-
tion and violence—maybe partly because of it—these native Southern loyal-
ists seemed to have had a prophetic clarity in advance of that held by the Fed-
eral leaders of the day. This seems particularly true as regards the use of slaves
in the Union Army, and protecting the rights of Southern Unionists. Tharin,
like Aughey of Mississippi, argued that the Federal Government ". . . owes to
Unionists everywhere, protection," just as Federal prisoners of war were pro-
tected.

And from the "Military Dungeon, Tupelo, Mississippi, July 11, 1862," lying
in prison with some hundred other local loyalists, awaiting the execution of
his own death sentence, John H. Aughey managed to smuggle a letter out to
Seward in which he concurred in Tharin's view.[94]

"A large number of citizens of Mississippi," Aughey wrote Seward, "hold-
ing Union sentiments . . . are confined in a filthy prison, swarming with ver-
min, and are famished from hunger . . . We are separated from our families,
and suffered to hold no communications with them . . . Our property is confis-
cated and our families left destitute . . . all they have, yea, all their living being
seized upon by the Confederates and converted to their own use. Heavy fet-
ters are placed upon our limbs and daily some of us are led to the scaffold, or
to death by shooting . . . These evils are intolerable, and we ask protection,
through you, from the United States Government. The Federal Government
may not be able to release us, but we ask the protection which the Federal
prisoners receive."

Aughey felt, with Tharin, that if the Federal Government let it be known
that a rebel prisoner would suffer death for every loyal Southern prisoner killed
by the rebels, it would stop the mass killings by the Confederacy. He pointed
out in his letter to Seward that ". . . loyal Mississippians deserve protection as
much as the loyal citizens of Massachusetts." He urged further that Confed-
erate sympathizers behind Union lines be arrested and "held as hostages for
the safety of Union men . . . who are in prison in Tupelo and elsewhere." If
that were done, ". . . the rebels would not dare put another Union man to
death" in the South, he felt.

Of such were the thoughts of Tharin and other Southerners in the 1860s.
But Robert Tharin was not an abolitionist in the Garrisonian sense. He did
not quite hold with the racial attitude of his fellow-Southerner, John Fairfield,
of Virginia. His main concern was for the poor whites, victimized by the ig-
norance and prejudice perpetrated upon them by a slave system. For his time

and place, Tharin had some excellent understanding, a sensitive feeling for the oppressed, and an unfailing courage.

There is much more to the Tharin tale than time and space here allow. It is a long tale of temerity in the face of overwhelming odds, of dramatic episodes on the trail to free-soil where, at Cincinnati, in February 1861, the home of Levi Coffin afforded the exile an asylum. At one time or another, Coffin's home became "an asylum" for many Southerners, both black and white.

Tharin's story is a continued and consistent tale of another anti-slavery Mountain Southerner dedicated to liberty and loyal to the United States at a time when aristocrats pursued the course of treason in an effort to overthrow that government and expand their slave system. It includes accounts of his family, finally rescued from the Confederacy, come to join him at the North. And there, settled in the Quaker city of Richmond, Indiana, they thought of quiet and study and a job to provide a living and educate their children.

But a war was on. The Slavocracy had fired upon Sumpter. Tharin's young wife, "delicate in health, shattered in constitution . . . a stranger in a strange land . . . chilled by the hard, cold, icy manners of the ladies of the North . . . (and with) an invalid boy," still shared her husband's courage. She agreed that he should join the Union Army—to fight for what they both believed in. Stranded as they were in a "strange land," financially broke, Tharin joined the Army as a private with wages woefully inadequate to support a family.

His is part of the story of the Old South, long neglected. Years ago I promised to try one day to tell more of that tale—the tale of men in jeans pants and women who wore linsey petticoats, "they who had nothing to do with the genteel tradition." They were the "real Southern mass majority of whites" whom the blacks were taught to call "poor white trash" and they, in turn, were taught the hateful word "nigger." Robert Tharin understood too well (for his own personal safety) how the slaveholding aristocrats despised and misused both the slave and the white non-slaveholder. He understood how they used the brave non-slaveholders, whom they had helped to madden with false statements, to fight and die in order that they might lounge around, in comparative safety on their cotton plantations.

Robert Tharin's is just one link in the long tale still greatly in a need of the telling.

in a land of plenty:
no copyright (1982–85)

Editors' Note: This essay appeared in the last collection of West's work published during his lifetime, In a Land of Plenty *(1982).*

No Copyright:

Purposely this book is not copyrighted. Poetry and other creative efforts should be levers, weapons to be used in the people's struggle for understanding, human rights, and decency. "Art for Art's Sake," is a misnomer. The poet can never be neutral. In a hungry world the struggle between oppressor and oppressed is unending. There is the inevitable question: "Which side are you on?"

To be content with things as they are, to be "neutral," is to take sides with the oppressor who also wants to keep the status quo. To challenge the power of oppression is the poet's responsibility. Such action helps to preserve and build faith and hope in humanity. Nothing raises the spirit of a people more. This is the major mission of the poet or artist.

Thus no copyright, no effort to restrict use. Groups or individuals are welcome to reproduce or use any or all parts of this book.

selected poems

Don West reading poetry on the stage at the 1988 Appalachian South Folklife Center
Music Festival.

from *crab-grass*
(1931)

Editors' Note: Published in 1931 by the Art Print Shop, Trevecca College, in Nashville, Tennessee, West's first collection of poetry is an undersized fifty-page limited edition hardback with a cover design by the artist Julius Lee Rayford. The book includes a foreword by Harry Harrison Kroll and an introduction by West's fellow student, the writer Jesse Stuart.

Dedication

To
My mother and father,
Mountain woman and man
Who dug crab-grass
And sour-wood sprouts
From between the corn rows
With a goose-necked hoe
While, as a baby, I lay
On my back in a
Deep-plowed furrow
Kicking at the dirt,
This humble volume of verse
Is affectionately dedicated.

Crab-Grass

It wonders me whut fer
Ye'r made,
Crab-grass,

Allus pesterin' aroun',
In th' corn down th' creek
An' taters in th' new-groun',
Crab-grass,
Allus pesterin' aroun' . . .

Did'n ye hear thet squrrul
A-barkin'
Yan-side uv Still-House-Holler,
Don't ye know my ole houn' dawg
Ez ready fer to foller,
An' my rifle-gun ez-clean,
Crab-grass,
Allus pesterin' aroun' . . .

Martha want let me see
No peace,
Crab-grass, while ye
Cum a-peekin' thru th' corn
An' th' sun-ball burns me so
It's a botherment I'm born,
Crab-grass,
Allus pesterin' around' . . .

Bill Dalton's Wife

It shore wuz pitiful
Th' way Bill Dalton's wife
Lay up thar on Bull Creek
An' suffered out her life.

Th' granny-wumurn, from
Over on Bad-Creek's hed,
Cum to tend th' labor,
An' thar foun' Lizzy ded.

Th' babe wuz crossed, Bill sed,
The doctor wudn't cum,
Bill wuz powfly in debt
An' cudn't pay th' sum.

Ole Kim Mulkey[1]

Might nigh ever new uv th' moon
Ole Kim Mulkey
Got his nine lazy sons
Out on Sassafras mountin
A-grubbin' up sassafras sprouts.

"Git a-hustle on, sons,
These sprouts'ul never grow
Agin, if grubbed on
Th' new uv th' moon,"
Ole Kim wud say.

But ole Kim's sons
Loved moonshine-licker
An' when ole Kim wuz gone,
Horace, the youngest, brainiest,
Biggest, an' laziest
Uv all Kim's lazy sons,
Stole down th' creek
To Lige Mealer's still,
With a long-handled
Yaller gourd.

When I Am Old

To my class at Hindman, 1930–31[2]

When I am old, gray days shall come,
But my dreams shall ride into memory
Where young voices laugh and play
In springtime when the crocus creeps up.

When I am old, I shall look back,
Each rose-colored day a memory
Gold-shot with columbine pink or blue,
Rose-shot with corn-flower blue and sunset's glow.

When I am old, bright eyes of love
Shall call me back to morning joys—
Blue eyes, gray eyes, brown eyes,
Eyes of little children shall call me back.

When I am old, I shall laugh and live
Like mountain azalia or arbutus,
For one short season of memory
Shot-through with the joy of living.

Denmark

On the North Sea[3]

Like a mocking phantom
Your shores merge
With the sea.
I see the last of you blotted out
In nothingness.
But with you I have left something.
That walks in the night-time
Out where the corn-blades
Sigh for the whispering song
Of the winds,
And Heather sobs
For an unreturning voice.

Mountain Reverie

I shall foot it,
Down Troublesome[4]
And up Trace,[5]
Where lean
Hungry figures,
Ghosts of mountain dwellers,
Are known to wander . . .

I think when
Chilly winter comes
And dusky night
Brings trembling stillness
To lonesome dwellings,
My spirit shall stalk by
Peering behind closed doors
Of mountain homes,
Where once I was
A welcomed friend . . .

And it may be
They can hear me sing,
Joining with the
Sad music of
Troublesome's waters,
Or playfully, with
The rippling laughter
Of the corn blades
In the new-ground hill side
Above the barn . . .

Anyhow, I shall be there,
Down Troublesome
And up Trace
In autumn
When leaves are browned
And fodder is pulled . . .

Mountaineer's Desire

I have no passion
To be deep
Scented down
In a black coffin,
Silk lined
And cushioned . . .
But this flesh
Shall be burned
To grey embers

And strewn
High up in
The Mountains
Among the
Hard faced
Silent rocks,
Where time
Has gnawed
Cracks and
Crevices,
Where stunted
Mountain trees
Send roots down
Against the
High wind's fury,
And where
Mountain people,
Silent,
And solitary,
Like the rocks
And trees,
Pass by . . .

To—

Heather sobbing in the night-time,
And you were there
At the death of day
When corn-flowers bend
To the whisperless voice
Of sun-down skies,
When earth is held
In the labor
Of a new night's birth.
We felt the cold caress
Of dusky fingers
And heard hungry voices
From broken bodies
Of women and men

Who said our love, too
Must go down in
Embers of shame
And be scattered
Through the night-time . . .

Prayer

They said I didn't pray,
The people in the church . . .
I saw a silver spray
Bathing a slender birch,
Saw a sycamore tree
With white leaves caressing
Pools colored like the sea,
Deep blue and blushing.
I saw cows quiet feeding
On the sweet pasture grass,
Saw birds at the mating
And a lad and a lass.
An old farmer working,
Digging weeds from the corn,
Heard his daughter singing
At the birth of the morn . . .

Feeling these, I bowed, and stayed,
But they say I never prayed.

In Potters Field

In Potters Field
The rag-weeds grow
With red-nosed briars
Along the row
Of hedge and thorn
Which circles in
The rotted dust
Of earthy men.

In Potters Field
No rich man lies,
No marble tombs
Point to the skies,
No prayers were made
Their lives to save
Before they met
The pauper's grave.

They sleep there now
Soft dust to dust
In earth's cold breast
As all men must.
Six feet of dirt
Is life's whole yield
To those who lie
In Potters Field.

from *deep, deep down in living* (n.d.)

Editors' Note: Published in 1931 or 1932, this pocket-sized paperback chapbook consists of twelve pages; it does not list a place of publication, publication date, or publisher. The collection is dedicated to "G. G. Ward, Poet, Philosopher, and Mountaineer," an educator and local historian from West's native Gilmer County, Georgia.

Deep, Deep Down in Living

Deep, deep down in living
Is something I desire,
Deep in ages smoldering,
An ever living fire.

Surging human passion
That I cannot define.
I feel it in the masses,
Mysterious . . . divine.

Deep, deep down in living
These mighty breakers roll.
The spell of living people
Has clutches on my soul.

Mountain Widow

I

Shadders on Burnt Mountain.
Night a-comin' on, dusk dark.

Curtains bein' pulled like actin'
Over the sleepy hills.
Me a-settin' out so lonesome
Listenin' to whippoorwills.

Wonderin' whur my man is—
He went away last morn.
Workin' in Lick Log Narrers
Runnin' a moonshine still.
Wish it wusn't so risky
Over th' Lick Log Hill.

Wish I'd see my man now
A-trompin' over th' ridge.
Wish my man had money
An' didn' haf to be
A-workin' in Lick Log Narrers
Allus away frum me.

II

Fetched him home by moonlight
Frum over th' Lick Log Hill.
Down th' trace by Mealers,
My man so cold an' dead.
Revenues raided th' Lick Log.
Thur bullets went thru his head.

Wish it wusn't so risky
Over th' Lick Log Hill.

Mountain Boy

You are more than a dirty child
In patched overalls.
You mountain boy . . . !
The hills are yours.
The fragrant forests,
The silver rivers
Are your heritage.

Dreamers. Thinkers.

Rise up, young hillmen.
Sing your ballads.
Dream your future.
Up and down your valleys,
Over the ridge-roads.
Climb your jagged mountains.
Gaze into blue space . . .
Turn your thoughts free.
Nourish your imagination.

What will you do for your hills,
You mountain boy?

Love the soil.
Your father's blood
Made it rich.
His sweat has caused fruit to grow.
Sift the coarse soil
Between your fingers.
Exult when it runs between your toes
Through brogan shoes
As you follow the plow.
Yours is the poet's life.
You rhyme the soil,
Dig and plant
And watch the corn grow.
You are the heart of a nation—
Even America.

O farmer boy,
Rise up!
Sing your songs,
Live your life
Even as you know how!

Harlan Portraits

I've seen beauty in Harlan,[6]
In the trailing arbutus,
The dog-fennel and pennyrile
In the fence corners,

And in the forests dressed
In a foliage of
Rattleweed and ditney.
I've seen beauty when
Grey winter strokes his beard
With bony-white fingers,
And trees are skeletons
Of summer's glory.

But beauty never visits
The coal diggers.
They live in the coal camps—
Dirty shanties,
Stinking privies,
Grunting pigs,
And slop buckets.

Hollowed-eyed women
With dull hopeless faces
Cook soggy wheat biscuits
Without grease or milk.

Tall gaunt men
Eat soggy bread
And fat meat.
Gulp down black coffee.
Work all day—
Digging, digging.
Everlastingly digging.
Grime and dirt
And digging.
In their dreams they dig
And smell unpleasant odors.

For beauty
Is a stranger
To the coal camps . . .

Brown Brother

To Langston Hughes[7]

I heard you, my brown skin brother,
Sing the songs your people think,
Saw the fire that we would smother
And the gall that you must drink.

We are proud and boast the whiteness
In the pigments of our skin,
Never think to measure rightness
By a soul that burns within.

Now I know you seek no pittance
From a condescending clan
That has failed to give admittance
Or to treat you like a man.

How can you sing songs of gladness,
Full of hope and growing cheer?
When your people live in sadness
With the white man's curse to fear.

Epitaphs

For Myself

Bones rest here of a mountaineer.
His place another fills.
He gained from life all that he sought.
The friendship of the hills.

from *between the plow handles* (1932)

Editors' Note: Published on September 25, 1932, by the Highlander Folk School in Monteagle, Tennessee, this undersized paperback chapbook consists of thirty-two pages and notes West as being the "author of Crabgrass *and* Deep, Deep Down in Living." *The collection is dedicated to "M.C.W.," West's wife, Mabel Connie (Adams) West. The chapbook acknowledges the editors of eight periodicals for prior publications.*

A' Callin' Home th' Hogs

"Pig-o, pig-o, pig-o-o-ee,
Pig-o, pig-o, pig-o-o-ee."

"Whut's thet echo, Lurey,
Whitherin' down Oak Hill,
Over Devil's Holler
Whur' th' night's so still?
See them whick'rin' shaders
Wimplin' by thet tree,
Goin' toward th' echoes—
Wonder whut they'd be . . . ?"

"Pig-o, pig-o, pig-o-o-ee."

"Nother gin, Lurey,
Cross th' marshy bogs!"
"It's ole Kim Mulkey
Callin' home th' hogs."

"Since last mast season
When chestnut burs was spread,
Ole Kim Mulkey's
Been livin' with th' dead.
Nearly bout a year now
Ole Kim's been away—
Sumpen calls th' hogs home,
Eve of ever' day."

"Listen, Lurey girl,
Th' hush of them frogs
When ole Kim Mulkey
Comes to call his hogs!"

"Lurey, hain't hit lonesome,
Whutherin' through th' fogs—
Sound of ole Kim Mulkey
Tollin' home his hogs."

"*Pig-o, pig-o, pig-o-o-ee,
Pig-o, pig-o, pig-o-o-ee.*"

"It's ole Kim Mulkey
Callin' home th' hogs."

Dark Winds

Dark winds,
Winds creepin' down frum th' mountins
To stinky mills,
Callin' my longings
Back to th' hills.

Smoke winds,
Fouled with dirt frum th' sutty stacks
Of a fact'ry,
A-scrougin' fer room
An' blackin' me.

Deep winds,
I feel them blowin' in th' streets
An' when alone,
Dulled by th' fact'ry's
Dull monotone.

Sad winds,
They've blowed sorrow an' sufferin'
Frum northern mills,
An' drug my people
Down frum th' hills.

Scratching in Memory

Kim Mulkey, old man Kim,
Scratching in ashes
Of memory
For a rusty nail
To spike the slabs
Of eternity
Onto his soul.

Kim Mulkey, old bent Kim,
Nodding in dreams of
A yesterday,
A silent man
On an outward trail,
A lonely way
Toward the sun-down west.

Old Kim Mulkey,
You've scratched long
And tried
To find a song
In memory
Crisp and dried.

But memory is a lamp,
An old brass lamp
With a sputtering wick
That soon burn out.

I've Seen God

I've seen God—
I've seen him smile
In the several hues of a rainbow.
I've felt his warm breath
In the mists
The sun sends up
From the plowed dirt
After a summer rain.
And God was free.

I've seen God—
In the gaunt eyes
Of a factory worker,
Bound by chains
Of circumstances.
I've felt God's pulse beat,
I've seen his soul
And heard him groan
From the hungry throats
Of miners' children
In a Kentucky coal camp.
And God was in prison!

Highlander Youth

I hear the dumb groan
Of convulsive pain
Scouring the hills
With a crimson stain
Of mountain blood.

And—
A heartless power,
O Highlander youth,
Now grips your throat
To kill the truth
I'd have you see.

Up, you Highlander!
And hear what I tell,
In a world of plenty
Is a world of hell,
While you sleep on!

You Highlander youth,
There's yet a new way
To dream your dreams
Of a coming day
And hills at peace.

Up, up, you sluggards,
You mountain men,
Who fear no devil
Nor snare of sin—
Shake off this hell!

Between the Plow Handles

Between the plow handles—
Dawn-break—
Furrow on furrow.
A stubble field,
Dirty sweat
Streaking the belly,
Dripping from overalls
Mixing with dust,
All day, all day.

Dusk—
Tired horses
Stench of foaming sweat
And stable manure.

Supper—
Corn bread
Sow-belly
Pot-licker.[8]

Sleep—
Smell of rye straw
From a bed tick[9]
And dreams:
"Between the plow handles,
Four 'clock—
Sweat oozing under arm pits—
A deep plowed furrow
Between the plow handles."

from *toil and hunger*
(1940)

Editors' Note: Published in 1940 by the Hagglund Press of San Benito, Texas, this is an undersized ninety-nine-page paperback. The book includes reproductions of woodcuts by Stanley deGraff, linoleum cuts by John C. Rogers and Howard Swenson, as well as an illustration by Frank Zartman. The collection is divided in two parts: "Toil and Hunger" and "Dialect Poems." It features a prologue by West, dealing with his family background and view of Mountain South history, and an updated introduction by Jesse Stuart. The book is dedicated to West's daughters, Ann and Hedie Grace, and also acknowledges the editors of eight periodicals for prior publications.

Funeral Notes

We're burying part of him today
In Hickory Grove Church Yard.
We can't put him all here,
For his grave
Spreads over a few rocky acres
That he loved—
Where peach blossoms bloom, and
Cotton stalks speckle the ground
On a Georgia hill.

Forty years he's been digging
And plowing himself under
Along these cotton rows.
Most of my Dad is there
Where the grass grows
And cockle-burrs bristle
Now that he's gone . . .

We're covering him in March days
When seeds sprout.
And I think next Autumn
At picking time
The white-speckled stalks
Will be my old Dad
Bursting out . . .

Anger

    Words of the toiling south—

"It came unbeknowence to us.
Don't know when
May have been when death
Gnawed through to the heart
Of our least one
With hunger's keen teeth.
Or maybe when six mouths
Asked for food
And six stomachs stayed empty.
Must have been slow,
And we don't know when—
But it stays, and we like it?"

The slow, groaning anger
Of the south—
Born of toil and hunger,
Tearing at a million hearts,
Taken in with bulldog gravy[10]
Or pinto beans,
Sucked up with coal dust or lint
Into the belly of the south,
The great, gaunt belly
Of a smoldering south!

No anger's in a dead man—
But it's in the south,
Slow, groaning anger
In the toiling south!

What Shall a Poet Sing

What is a poet saying
Down by a Georgia pine
Where a broken body's swaying
Hung to a cotton line . . . ?

With his folk all burdened down,
Pinched by hunger's pang,
Whether he's white or brown,
What shall a poet sing . . . ?

Symbols

They were symbols,
The preacher said—
The bread and wine
In memory of him,
Of Jesus the Toiler . . .

I see other symbols.
Hungry and cold
They tramp America
Like ghosts passing by—
In the coal camps,
Dirty with dust,
Begging a crust,
A nickel, a dime,
Or an old coat
For winter time.

Toilers' children,
Gaunt and tired,
With rickets and flux—[11]
These are the symbols I see . . .

Visit

We didn't say much.
Jim's table had a few scraps
And an old bone
On it.
The landlord came
A-cussing for rent . . .
We didn't say much.
Jim was all down in the mouth,
And I was down, too.
Jim had a nickel.
I had eight cents.
We didn't say much,
There wasn't much to say.

Toil and Hunger

Toil and hunger
Took him away—
My old Dad.
While he ripped up
The sad red earth
His life dripped down
In the furrow,
And Georgia's clay hills
Sucked it up.

Plum trees blossom
From sweat-salted earth
And sorrow climbs up
Through the leaves
To scent the flowers
On the blooming trees.

Toil and hunger
Attended his birth,
And bury him now
In the sad red earth!

Southern Nights

Southern nights in Georgia—
You know them, comrade—
Cling like down
Under the eagle's wing.
Moon rides low over ridge tops
Flicking pine needles
At the sky rim . . .
Rivers, old and brown,
Slither and slide
Down the valleys of Dixie—
Till corn blades and cotton blossoms
Shiver in the wind
And night-time kisses
The earth with dewy lips.

    Beauty is southern nights,
    Beauty is a tall sycamore
    On the bank of the Chattahoochee.
    Beauty is the somber face
    Of a southern Negro,
    And the rhythmic lines of the mountains,
    A wild music
    Etched on a dusky sky . . .

Poets have sung of her beauty
And I sing.
But I say southern nights
And southern ways
Are deceptive—
Some are liars!
I speak hard words
Because soft words
Hide a cruel south,
A cold-hearted south
With flesh in her teeth
And blood on her mouth.
Slow southern rivers
Murmur gently over bones
Of dead Negroes.

The river covers many a lie
And so does the soft drawling voice
Of the ruling south.

Soft southern nights—
Sharecropper's shack
Blends into red plowed fields
Mine shanties in Harlan
Hide their ugliness
Till sputtering lights
Gleam like spikes of gold
Half hammered into the mountainside.

Dark Night

My brain is an old pile
Of scrap iron to-night.
My music is the jangle
Of rusty plows banged together
On a Georgia farm—
My songs are twisted pieces
Of old cast-off iron
And steel
Corroding . . .

I've wanted to heat them
In a white-hot forge
And hammer them
Into long keen blades
The color of steel
Dipped in blood . . .

But to-night my songs
Are rusty pieces of iron
With edges snarled
And twisted
To bruise and lacerate
Sensitive fingers . . .

Soon in the morning I shall rise
To hammer a new song
Out of these old pieces!

Hungry Old River

The little ripples of the River
Purred gentle and smooth
Like a house cat,
Or the soft feet of a jungle beast
Stalking the forest edge.
Summer's moon glittered
From the waters
Like little diamonds
Speckled out
Across a velvet bosom . . .

"I shall never forget that night
On the River,"
A man said.

Hunkered in the shadows
Toes on the banks,
The people waited
And watched.
The great warm Heart
Of the people
Bled
And sorrow dripped down
To be licked up
By the forked little tongues
Of the sparkling waters . . .

Out there—
Beneath those flickering diamonds
On the velvet bosom,
One of the people was caught
And the hungry old River
Guarded his prey
With jealous jaws,
While the big warm Heart
Of the people
Bled . . .

"I shall never forget that night
On the River,"
A man said . . .

Song of the Saw

Ever hear about the song of the saw,
Ever hear of
John McCarty?

We were working a saw mill
Twenty miles from nowhere
On Troublesome Creek . . .

John was a sawyer
Ran a hot steel saw
Sixteen hours
Through long Georgia pines.
Loved to hear
The song of the saw
Ripping through the guts
Of a yellow pine—
Loved to sing about his
Wife and baby
Back home . . .

John was young—
Muscles bulged out
Like iron hoops
On a whiskey barrel—
Soft blue eyes
That laughed like a child's . . .

Belt was bad.
John wanted it fixed.
Boss said wait until Monday—
Finish the job . . .

Saturday the belt slipped.
John's belly struck the saw.
Ripped him open
Like a yellow pine log,

Straight through the belly.
Boss said
"Mighty good sawyer,
Too bad I lost him—
Get Kim Mulkey Monday."

We picked up the pieces—
One on the saw dust,
One on the slab pile.
We tried to fit
The bleeding things together
Before burying them under
A tall Georgia pine.
But somehow they wouldn't fit—
Our hands were red with blood
And grime.
We were clumsy
And felt cold
Under a broiling sun . . .

Somebody wanted to pray
But it looked crazy
With John's belly
Split wide open
And his guts hanging out.
We looked at each other.
One man cursed
And we all felt better . . .

Nobody wanted to go
Tell John's wife and baby
Twenty miles up Troublesome.
We pulled straws
And it fell my lot . . .

Nancy didn't cry
Or scream.
Just hung her head
Down low
And stroked the hair
Of John's baby.
She looked out through the trees

And it didn't seem like
She looked at anything . . .

The kid pulled at her apron—
Asked for daddy.
Seemed like it couldn't understand
That John's belly was split
Wide open and worms were gnawing.
His wide blue eyes—
The kid didn't understand . . .

But Nancy just looked
And said nothing—
Looked out through the pines,
Tall yellow pines
Like John loved to saw.
I wondered if she listened
For the song of the saw,
For John's big voice
Singing about his wife and baby
Back home,
If the splotches of sky
Clutched by the little fingers
Of the pine trees
Reminded her of John's blue eyes
And his laugh
Soft like the sound
Of a Southern wind
Walking through the tree tops.

Stillborn

I wasn't lonely then, Little One.
I could feel you there,
Felt you kick and claw inside
And your kicks filled me full,
So full I thought my heart
Would burst
And joy
Drip down

Like rain-drops
In April . . .

So I made a song
To sing—
A song of creation.
The song was full of you, too,
As April was full of violets
Breaking through.
And I thought the whole world
Was pregnant,
Bursting out.
It throbbed
Like I throbbed,
Full of you . . .

But you are still, Little One,
And I am empty
And my song is gone—
The song I made to sing
So full of you . . .

Seeker

I've always been a seeker,
Restless and wary.
I've sought beauty
In a morning fog
Sleeping on the bosom
Of a sluggish southern river,
In the mists of a rainbow
Climbing up from plowed dirt
After a summer's shower,
And in the silence
Of mountain stillness
Before a storm . . .

I have also sought love
And found it—
In a tenement house,
A lonely mountain cabin.

I have found love,
Joy
Sorrow
Fear—
Leaning on the bowed shoulders
Of a toiling mother,
A southern field hand
Grabbing the white locks
That speck the red hills
Like a spotted hound's back . . .

Yesterday I found dreams
In a ditch digger's mind,
And poetry on the lips
Of a cook . . .
I looked again
And found music
In the rhythmic throb
Of toiling millions—
Feet beating the earth in unison—
And I thought
It is like the pregnant feel
Of a highland evening
Before a storm
Breaks on the mountain . . .

They Take Their Stand

For some professional Agrarians[12]

Some poets live in Dixie Land
   Who never to themselves have said
We'll wash the star-dust off our hand
   And wipe the cobwebs from our head.

In books so learned they have writ
   Praise to a system dead and gone.
And like old Buddha, here they sit,
   Proclaiming how they mope alone.

In Dixie Land they stake their stand,
    Turning the wheels of history back
For murder, lynch and iron hand
    To drive the Negro from his shack.

They never delve in politics,
    That's all too commonplace, they say.
Their thoughts must go to subtle tricks
    Befitting noble gents like they.

In Dixie Land there's many an ass
    Braying loud in every school,
But never sees the growing grass
    That might be had by any mule.

Come, sift the star dust off their stars—
    See coal-dumps where our children play.
They sing of ancient Greece and Mars,
    We'll show them starving kids today!

Clodhopper

I'm the Clodhopper—
Have you heard about me—
The lump that feeds the world.
A lowland Georgia Cracker,
Song singer from the mountains—
A cotton-picking Brown Skin—
I'm the Clod-hopper
That puts clothes on the world . . .

Who said:
"Clodhoppers of the world,
Unite!
You have nothing to lose
But your clods—
Unite!"

Was that Jesus or Marx?
Or maybe it was me
Said that
And:

"Down with the clodhopper joke?
Up with the dignity of the clod.
To every clodhopper a clod
To wiggle between his toes!"

Isn't it written:
"The laborer is worthy
Of his wage,
And the Hopper
Of his clod?"

If it isn't,
I'll write it now . . .

Oh, I'm the Clodhopper
That makes the tall corn grow,
The artist that smears dignity
Through the speckled cotton patch.
I'm the man that fills
The belly of the world,
And slips a petticoat
Over her nakedness . . .

Night on a Mill Hill

Dark scrambles down between ridges
And hugs the village
To her bosom . . .
Around the edges
Sounds squeeze out
And float for a while . . .

Then listen to a Southern night,
Listen to old ballads
Full of misery
Throbbing on the dusk—
"Twenty-one years
Is a mighty long time."
"Will you miss me?"
"Left my home in Georgia"
And "That lonesome valley."

Songs pour out the sorrows
From the lives
Of Southern toilers,
And songs wake up new hope . . .

The huge mill lies slumbering
By the creek bank,
Furnace half a-glow—
Like the blazing eyes
Of a tiger
Waiting to tear the limbs
Off its prey . . .

Homecoming

And I've come back to you,
Mountain Earth,
Come to laugh
And sing
And sorrow,
To dig my songs
Up from your dirt
And spin a melody
Of corn-blades,
new grounds,
Crab-grass
And a crooked furrow.

I've come to sing
And grope
With a people
Who stagger
Up a long
Dark road . . .

I've come because
Your great silent agony
Echoed everywhere
And the weary footsteps
Of my old Dad

Still sound upon the mountain
Where his sweat dripped down
To wet your clay . . .

My South

Of soft flowing rivers
With slender willows
Clutched hungrily
To your bosom—
And red Georgia hills
Where cotton patches
Speckle the ground
With downy snow balls
Like a spotted hound's back,
And lazy pools
The deep green of corn blades
In June
Glisten under a Southern moon—
You are my South.
I found life deep in your womb
And I love you . . .

I love the sad solemn beauty
In your mountains—
The great Blue Ridge,
Cumberlands
Smokies
Unakas—[13]
That stand like sentinels
To witness the surge
Of human passion
Flowing through your ribs,
Laughter and hate
Of Southern toilers . . .

I love you who toil
In the dirt
And factories
And mines—

You whose skin is ebony
From a tropic sun
And my own bleached brothers . . .
I love the slow drawl
Of your Southern voice,
The way you love the sound
Of silence
And the easy swing
Of your bent shoulders . . .

I've felt your deep sorrow
In songs you sing
And I've wanted to sing
With you,
To turn your songs
Into keen blue blades
Slashing at your chains,
The cruel chains of hunger.

But your eyes were blind
And your hate was old;
Your brain was warped
And your heart was cold.

Oh, my South,
My cold-blooded South
With a Negro's blood
Smeared over your mouth
And a Negro's bones
Which you blindly make
A few charred coals
By a burnt-off stake—

You have drunk poison
And it turns you mad
Like a rotten cancer
Gnawing at your brain.

And I am grinding
The blades of my songs
To a tempered edge
To whittle on
Your cancerous brain . . .

Tomorrow you must wake
And white hands will clasp
Ebony
Bowed over a few charred bones
By a burnt-off stake!

You are my South:
I'll hammer you
Into a beautiful song
For I love you . . .

Georgia Mother

I heard my mother laugh
And sing
Like the wind's song
Rustling fodder blades
In a hillside corn patch.
I felt her smile
And kiss my face,
Wet from a mountain rain.
My mother was young—
Fleet as a winging bird,
Straight as a bamboo cane
And the temper of steel . . .

I was a little boy—
Thought my mother
Eternally beautiful,
Fresh like mountain dew
And graceful as jalap vine.
I was a little boy—
I didn't understand . . .

Today I gazed
On the anemic face
Of a textile slave—
Gaunt eyes,
Sunken cheeks,
Bent body . . .
A numb and senseless creature

Peered up at me
Beseechingly.
Sighs and sobs rent the air.
And I thought:
Is this the woman,
The lilting singer—
My mother,
When I was a little boy . . . !

O my brothers!
You who sweat and toil and bleed,
Sound the union trumpets!
Beat the drums of rebellion!
Bind our hearts with steel bands,
Scatter the dogs
Who tear the vitals
Out of women,
Who turn toiling mothers
Into gruesome creatures,
Joyless,
Half dead . . . !

O steel of Unity!
O warmth of power . . . !

from *clods of southern earth*
(1946)

Editors' Note: This 148-page collection was published in hardback and paperback editions in 1946 by Boni and Gaer in New York. It features an "appreciation" and introduction (reprinted on pages 3–8 of this book) by West, which focuses on what he calls the "other history" of the Mountain South, and a blurb from the novelist Henrietta Buckmaster. The noted artist Harold Price adds the cover illustration and drawings throughout the book. The poems are divided into three parts: "No Anger in a Dead Man," "Folks A-Living," and "No Lonesome Road." The book is dedicated to Alva Taylor, West's mentor at Vanderbilt University.

Look Here, America

I want to tell, America,
About victory—
About sharecroppers, tenants,
Black men and Crackers.
And you must listen
And look
And think deep . . .

For tomorrow
You must lift your head,
America—
Proud of yourself,
Proud that a Georgia Cracker
Can clasp the hand of a black man
And say:
"Brother!"

Look here, America,
Bend your head toward me
And listen.
Make your dreaming eyes to look
For I have tales to tell
And little pieces
Of twisted life
To show. . . .

You must look, America,
And listen
And think deep.
For even I, a Georgia Cracker—
One of your own mongrels—
Am grieved
By looking
At what I've seen . . .

Miner's Widow[14]

Take your pious prayers,
You preachers of God!
I'll bury my man
Under coal blacked sod.

Killed him while a-slavin'
As you see him there;
Jest another miner gone,
Take away yore prayer!

See the workers murdered,
You yellow-streaked men;
Shout of hell's damnation
And a poor man's sin!

Barney, loved leader,
Murdered like a dog;
Shot you in the back, boy,
From behind a log.

Barney, hated leader,
Blood was on yore brow;
Super's gunmen got you
An' starve our younguns now.

Kid's a'cryin', Barney,
Cupboard's cold and bare;
Preachers come a-peddlin'
Thur tales about a prayer.

Leave me here a-grievin',
You have done yore share;
You preachers of the bosses,
Take away yore prayer!

Should I Have Said

I said I would ask nothing of you
    especially love
But you should love me only if you
    found no escape,
    if it filled you full
    to overflow
On a pungent grey December night . . .

What was it, then, we touched that night
    in the stillness
Where a pulsating fog tantalized
    a sad-faced moon,
When soft shadows of stars were in your eyes—
    we touched and heard,
Like a low sob-moan from the throat
    of a dying wind-song
    in the tree tops—
A broken song crying in the dark . . .

Why, in such ineffable moments
    could I not say
That asking nothing is just a way
    of wanting all—
    a tilted face

with deep warm eyes
a laugh, half pain,
a word unsaid,
and the ecstatic feel
of touch of flesh
and two white jasmines
that are your breasts . . .

Or should I have said, O my Love,
    you've come too late,
For I have nothing left to give,
    or, how many times
    can your heart ache
    for an absent face?
How many years can your love penetrate
    the mist
    and dark
    and leaden dusk?
How long can you feel the touch
    of absent lips
    and hungry hands
    the cryptic pulse
    of responding love
    palpitating
    deep inside
    your slender self . . .

Or should I have said my road is long
    I camp beside many more
    who follow it
    hungry as I,
Asking nothing save the memory of
    a broken song
    to keep—
    a face
    a smile
    a meaning look
From deep, warm eyes.

And I Have Loved

I have loved—
The bigness
Of everywhere . . .
Of living.
And the little things—
The soft beauty
Of a flower in bloom.
And a blood-red sun
Caressing the swollen breasts
Of a pregnant spring earth . . .

I have loved the mystery
Of dark, somber rivers
With little ripples gnawing
At the red earth,
And a splashing mountain stream
Splitting its heart
On jagged stones
As it slips to the bosom
Of the deep green river . . .

And I have loved
The callused hands
Of a Kentucky coal miner,
The sad, solemn eyes
Of a hungry child.

The bent shoulders of a
Georgia sharecropper
Digging crabgrass from
His new-ground corn patch;
The splash of the Mississippi
Against a tow of straining barges,
The strong words of river boatmen
And the way hard men can
Love each other;
The clash of steel on steel,
And the sizzle

When men pour liquid steel
Into puddling troughs . . .

And I have loved
The trusting grip
Of a little child's fingers,
And the soft, yielding feel
Of a lovely woman,
Body close to mine,
Eyes deep and warm . . .

Harlan Coal Digger, 1934

Home . . . a box . . .
on four pegs . . .
Oozy, drippy shoes . . .
Acrid odors
From under the car-scorcher . . .

Gummy clothes . . . aching body . . .
A little whiskey . . . warms up
the damp spots . . . soothes . . .
makes hurt places quit aching . . .
Makes you feel good. . . . forget . . .
laugh . . . laugh in the face of a
big black pit . . . laugh at ragged kids . . .
hunger . . . ugliness . . . love . . . the smell
of a woman . . .

Harlan, Kentucky
December 25, 1934 . . .
Church bells ringing . . .
Jesus, born
in a stable with mule
manure . . . Jesus . . . died for us all . . .
laugh . . .
Sweet land of freedom . . . watch out for
company gun thugs . . . if you're a
union man . . . if you are not a union man . . .
you ought to be . . . Charlie Lewallen[15] shot . . .
at night . . .

thru the back . . .
Charlie's wife has nine kids . . .

It takes unity . . .
to build the union strong . . .

Watch out!
It could happen here!

These I Remember

These I remember:
Amber skies
Hooked onto a sundown earth,
Moon shadows
In a mountain valley
And flickering lights
From a cotton mill town
Across the river—
Sticking out like
Golden spikes
Half hammered into
The sides of night . . .

And I remember you—
A working woman—
Who told me
Joy always mated pain,
Toil lived with hunger
And sorrow slept
In the bed with love . . .

The wind in the cedars
Sang of sorrows
It had known;
And you said it
Picked them up
From the door-steps
Of the cotton mill homes
Across the river . . .

And I remember the wind
That sang of hate
As it played with the
Little fingers of the pine trees;
And of smoldering embers
Fanned to blazes.
And you said it sang
For the workers
In the cotton mill town—
Of blood . . . and fire,
And a new dawn
Of hope and joy,
Red, like a morning sun-ball . . .

Voice of the Cracker

I'm the voice of
The Southern Cracker,
Once silent, inarticulate.
But I'm learning to look
And talk straight now,
Listen to me . . .
For you've listened to others—
Unfriendly voices.
Because I was quiet,
Laboring with arm
And back muscles
Beside the silent slave,
My voice was not heard . . .

I'm learning that
The blood of my fathers
Made revolution
And hammered beauty
Out of wilderness,
That America's dirt
Has sucked up my sweat
To keep soft hands soft
And make pot-guts potted,
While hunger and rags

Disease and illiteracy
Shriveled the souls
Of my own children . . .
Oh, I'm the Cracker—
The Red-neck
Clod-hopper
Mountain hooger hill-billy—
The "white trash" nobody.

And you've heard
That I'm the lyncher
Of Negroes,
The man with hood and night shirt!
But I tell you
You've heard falsely!
For the pattern was set
From the big houses
By those who now point
The unfriendly finger at me,
Who taught me to hate
And say, "nigger,"
And the Negro to hate
And say, "white trash,"
And both of us
To despise the Jew . . .

Oh, I'm the Cracker,
And I'm learning—
Of *unity,*
Not *hate,*
To look
And talk straight . . . !

No Lonesome Road

For Byron Reece[16]

Once I too said that all men walk
A solitary road
And that each one must grope alone
And drag his little load.

I thought that I must walk forlorn
Upon that lonesome street
All hedged about the granite walls
Of pride and self-conceit.

But now I've learned that all can trudge
Upon a common way
Thru moonlight night and stumbling dark
Or in the flaming day.

And men cry out in word and name
As they are passing by
To those whose faith and fortitude
Have shoved them near the sky

Like Galileo at the stake,
Jesus nailed to a tree.
Cold bleeding feet at Valley Forge
Are on that road with me.
And I would not forget the men
Who dig and plow the soil
And those who fight that all shall live
With simple lives of toil.

It is no lonesome road we tread
Though so the cynics say.
The poet, farmer, working man
Must walk a common way.

from *the road is rocky*
(1951)

Editors' Note: Published in paperback by New Christian Books in New York, this eighty-page collection does not list a publication date; the introduction by Roy Smith, a Georgia labor activist, is dated June 1951. The book features a cover illustration of West by Bill Lytle and drawings by Ida Scheib. The poems are divided into three parts: "A Time for Anger," "A Time for Rejoicing," and "A Time for Love." The book includes blurbs from the poets Langston Hughes, May Justus, and Byron Herbert Reece as well as from West's fellow activists Alva Taylor and Rev. Claude Williams. The collection is dedicated to the Texas labor organizers Harry and Grace Koger.

There's Anger in the Land

Note: In the summer of 1950 I picked up a Negro hitch-hiker in South Georgia and brought him across the Chattahoochee at Eufala, Alabama. As we crossed the river he began telling me the story of how his brother was lynched and his body cut down from the limb and flung across the door-step of his mother's shack—broken, bleeding and lifeless.

Oh, there's grieving in the plum-grove
And there's weeping in the weeds,
There is sorrow in the shanty
Where a broken body bleeds . . .

For there's been another lynching
And another grain of sand
Swells the mountain of resentment—
Oh, there's anger in the land!

And a woman broods in silence
Close beside an open door
Flung across the flimsy door-step
Lies a corpse upon the floor!

You'll not ask me why I'm silent;
Thus the woman spoke to me.
Her two eyes blazed forked anger
And her throat throbbed agony.

Let the wind go crying yonder
In the tree-tops by the spring,
Let its voice be soft and feeling
Like it was a living thing.

Once my heart could cry in sorrow
Now it lies there on the floor
In the ashes by the hearth-stone—
They can't hurt it anymore!

Did you ever see a lynching,
Ever see a frenzied mob
Mill around a swaying body
When it's done the hellish job?

Yes, the night was full of terror
And the deeds were full of wrong
Where they hung him to a beech-wood
After beating with a thong.

Oh, there's grieving in the plum-grove
And there's sobbing on the sand,
There is sorrow in the shanties—
And there's anger in the land!

Sad, Sad America

Oh, America—
Sad, sad America!
Once you stirred the souls of men
In dark places
And shook the smug oppressors
By declaring equal rights for all men!

Oh, my country,
Land that I love!
You have known glorious days
In your morning years!
The strength of your rugged arms—
Sinew of the pioneer—
Was raised against the tyrant,
To breathe your name
Roused hopes in bruised breasts
Of the humble in every land
And despots cursed you
With angry hearts!

But now, my country,
You eat a bitter fruit,
And I must eat with you!
You are betrayed by those
Who breathe your name
With honey love-words!

And I, at this moment,
Walk in silent sorrow
By this rumbling river of time,
For these are sad hours—
Saddest in my country's history!

Oh, America!
Sad, sad this hour
When you rattle the atomic sword
And your bombs blast
Innocent brown babies
Eight thousand miles from these shores!

Question Mark

Why . . . ?
The question mark!
Dangerous!

Why . . . ?
Why hunger?

Why poverty?
Why slavery?
Why so few rich people?
Why do those who work less get more?
Why do those who work more get less?
Why so many poor people?

Why . . . ?
Why war when men love peace?
Why must a Georgia plow-boy
go shoot a brown boy
five thousand miles from
the furrow he plows?
Why do corporations make profits
from war, from the blood
shed on battlefields?

The question mark
shakes the world!
Sows seeds of rebellion
among slaves,
and freedom germs.
Sprouts doubt weeds in the field
of holy war!

Why . . . ?
Why blind obedience?
Why not scrape away
scales of prejudice
and see—
See who fastens them there?

Oh, Pity Those

> For those who back down under pressure

Pity not the poor,
The hungry mass
Who fight for bread midst human tears,
But pity those
The liberal class
Once brave with words, now cowed by fears!

Oh, pity those,
The liberal men
Whose words were brave when times were fair
But now their lips
Are tight and thin—
We cannot hear them anywhere!

Advice to Would-Be Poets

Note: On a bright Sunday in 1950 I sat in a meeting of "Texas poets" in San Antonio and listened to a lot of verses about a lot of things— a lot of things beside life and people with their hurt and trouble and hope and pain. I heard poems in praise of practically nothing, and poems in praise of MacArthur as the great Christian gentleman and champion of democracy. And I thought: "O Lord, how long? How long, O Lord, until poets learn to go to the people for inspiration, for poetry?" And I wrote these lines there.

Away with pious references
To patriotism and to prayer,
As the naked child is born,
Let the truth lie cold and bare!

If there is a thing to tell
Make it brief and write it plain.
Words were meant to shed a light,
Not to cover it up again!

Where Tears of Sorrow

My word and my life are one.
My life is in my word,
And I refuse to be chained . . .
I will clamber across
The highest mountains
And I will fall down and curse
And fight and get up again . . .
I will not shun dark places,
Nor those who are called bad people.
In dark places I shall find

The buried hopes of other men.
I shall go there
And you shall come there to meet me—
You, the woman I have chosen
From all others—
And we together will grope our way
Through the night
Where echoes of broken songs
Linger, like low sobs
From a hurt man,
Where tears of sorrow
Make rivers run down
Between the valleys . . . !

Four Gifts for Man

I am he who sings
of the beauty of living—
the life process—
two cells united
from whence come many;
the inner surge
compelling male to seek
the female
and she him;
the love of a man for a woman
and she for him . . .
The sex in it, I say,
is clean and holy.
I say no function under the sun
in the life process
is unclean . . .

And I speak of death, too—
the ugly places—
the changing of death into life
and their unity.
I say there is no life
without death

and no creativity
without blood and struggle . . .

I will lay no yardstick
to the life process
nor attempt to measure
the rumbling river of imagination
flowing into a sea of eternity
and the half-sick joy
of old memories
burgeoning up from inside . . .

I will erect no formula
to cramp the dreams of men
nor will I preach obedience
to any law that blinds the eyes
of adventurous man
and dams off the stream
of creation . . .

And I say I know no sorry people[17]
on this good earth
nor mean.
I only know the strong and the weak,
with pride and without,
rebellious and defeated,
human, with love, or without . . .
is!

Four gifts I crave for man:
Love, that makes him human,
Imagination, to realize it,
Pride because he is,
and Courage to be . . .

The Dangerous Ones

The dangerous ones—
Find them, and they are
The dissatisfied
The cross-breeds of love and sorrow

Of hope and anger—
The prodders and goaders,
The provokers, agitators,
Trouble makers
And the lovers . . .

Dangerous to the few,
The parasites
Who suck the blood of the people!

Such a one is the peace-maker
And builder, too.
He's the little man at the bench
And the poet who speaks to the little man.
He's the black man in the furrow,
Who sees the sun coming up
Soon in the morning
From between the plow handles,
The red of the sun seeps down
Through his eyes to the heart.

The man in the furrow
Knows the power of the sun
To break open a seed,
To make it sprout and grow.
He knows the power of hope, too,
And of sorrow—
To break open a human heart,
To break the shell of an old world
And sprout anew!

These are the dangerous ones!
The woman of passion,
The man with a dream
Who sends words as tormentors
To stir the souls of hungry men,
Who weld the twisted old scraps
Into a chain of links
Strong with the strength
To drag the world
Toward her future!

These Things

These things I've hungered for—
Books,
Books to read and ponder,
And friends,
Friends to talk and visit with,
To be quiet with—
And the love of a woman . . .
These things I hunger for,
And need. . . .

Remember Me

For my children

Remember me, my children
As one who loved you
With hope
And a limitless tenderness,
Who saw in you
The blossoms of dreams,
Who watched your first
Stumbling steps
With pride—
But who insisted
That you stand
And walk
On your own feet . . . !

These Songs of Mine

For one who went away

These songs of mine will wind themselves
around you like the jasmine
twines around the cypress bush . . .

In evenings whenever you wait alone
my thoughts will tread lights
across your door to stir a memory . . .

These songs of mine with the rough edges
of a southern sharecropper's hands
have also the tender feel
of the southern heart . . .

When your way is dark and night is long
you'll feel their gentle touch . . .

Desire, like our never-to-be born baby,
hidden in your heart,
is stranded now in deathless eternity . . .

And it will be like violets in spring,
or the first snow of winter,
compelling your attention . . .

When I am gone, my songs will linger—
in the evening smoke twirling up
from mountain cabins,
in the agony, pain and hope
of the mothers of hungry children,
and they shall speak to you—
to the heart you thought dead,
to the thing you tried to kill there.

from *o mountaineers!*
(1974)

Editors' Note: Published in 1974 by the Appalachian Press in Huntington, West Virginia, this 242-page book was printed in both hardback and paperback editions and illustrated with reproductions of oil paintings by Connie West. It contains an introduction by Aubrey Williams, the New Deal activist and publisher of the Southern Farmer, *and reprints West's introduction from* Clods of Southern Earth *(reprinted on pages 3–8 of this book). Largely a collection of West's previously published poems, the book is divided into two parts: "Of Hurt and Anger" and "A Time for Hope and Love." The book also reprints blurbs by Langston Hughes, Rev. Claude Williams, and May Justus. It is dedicated to "Connie, Ann, Hedie, Mildred and Vicky, Appalachians."*

Obituary for Despair

After a long spell when no poems came

These empty years you fogged out eyes
With fall-out waste of cynical lore.
In errant disheartenment
Our feet have trod on somber soil,
Lips half whispering
The un-sung songs, still-born
Of dull aches
Muted by conformity's stale aura . . .

But not for long you held your sway
No hand can desolate strong hearts
No leash hold back their quickened urge
Nor empty now these brimming ewers.
The silence breaks,
We sing again . . . !

The Kennedy Baby

Conversation in a West Virginia Clinic

"You heard the news about
The Kennedy baby bothered by reporters?"
The miner's widow asked.

"I did, and got all choked up
Waiting there in a Kanawha clinic[18]
For Molly Brackenridge
To have her full-time child.
Molly from up on Jumping Branch
And Hetty Hatfield from Cabin Creek
Each had her child full-time
and dead . . .

"They say pintos and molly-grub[19]
Don't set well
On pregnant bowels.
The baby's feeble breath
Whispered out
On the third hour . . .

"Too bad the Kennedy child
Had to be bothered by questions."

Automated Miner

An automated miner
From Cabin Creek,
Said automated miner
From Cabin Creek
Ain't got no job
That's what I seek.

Now I used to dig coal where
The mine was damp.
Said I used to dig coal where
The mine was damp.

Load sixteen tons
By carbide lamp.

But since automation came
The times got tight.
Said since automation came
The times got tight.
They put me on
A special diet.

O molly-grub and gravy on
The welfare roll.
Said molly-grub and gravy on
The welfare roll.
Can't get no job
To save my soul.

Walked all the way to Charleston
My feet got sore.
I walked all the way to Charleston
My feet got sore.
And then I went
To Baltimore.

But twenty years a miner
It's all I know.
Said twenty years a miner
That's all I know.
No job, no home,
No place to go . . .

Confession

For Carl Braden.[20]

I saw him walk through
The prison gate
And heard the iron bars clang
Against his freedom.
Accused, character assassinated,
Condemned and forsaken
By those unfit his shoes to tie,

He went to serve time in prison,
And there, but for my cowardice,
Walked I . . .
Walked I . . . !

Stereotypes

Redneck, Cracker
Goober picker
Eat poke sallet
Drink pot licker.

Wool hat, hooger
You're my brothers
All of us had
Poor white mothers.

Linthead, white trash
Red dirt eaters
Lonesome water
Makes repeaters.

And hillbilly,
Do you think we should
Class ourselves with
The Peckerwood?

Or "Mountain Whites,"
That sound better?
Then write it down
In scarlet letter.

We are the ones,
The big folks claim,
Why lynch the blacks
And bring them shame.

The Blessed

Blessed is he that considereth the poor

Blessed are the poor
the hungry
the meek
the merciful
and peacemakers
the persecuted
slandered and reviled . . .

For they are God's children
and shall be found:
on the picket line
the peace walk
freedom march
sit-in
the prisons . . .
wherever the stumbling feet
need the dangerous
little candle lights
of human dignity
held aloft
by humble hands . . .

For These Sad Ashes

News Note: In Georgia, Ku Klux Klan elements burned three houses
at our farm home on the river just outside Atlanta. One was our li-
brary with a life-long collection of books, papers, manuscripts and
such. Another housed a craft shop with tools, antiques, etc. The fire
was set on a Sabbath day in February, 1958. My first reaction was
stunned disbelief. Just now in the following lines, I have begun to put
down a more articulate, if unfinished reaction.

They burned my houses
And all my books,
Workshop and old tools,
Valued for their memories—
A life-time collection of rare things

Personalized by long acquaintance—
A whiteoak maul whittled by my Dad
Handled smooth by his own weary hands,
The frow old Kim Mulkey used
To rive boards for my first school,[21]
Books re-read and cherished
For the comfort they sustain.

Coming home at dusk-time
Weary from the plow-handles
Sweat salt stinging the eyes
To settle down to caress the shelves
With looks
Too tired to read, but comforted
By the presence of books
The awareness that they were there
As old friends
Waiting to be visited
Talked with, loved.

In the east corner Shakespeare
Quietly challenged
And Milton crowded against
Keats and Shelley
The brooding spirit of Tom Wolfe[22]
Stirred uneasily
In a multi-volumed set by the west wall
And Bobby Burns, barnyard philosopher[23]
Of the little folk
On the middle shelf
Understood the way a man
Followed the plow all day
And returned to his bed
For a well-earned night.

And there were also the later ones,
The Olive Dargan[24] books
She of the rare and lovely spirit
Bursting through the bindings
"A Stone Came Rolling," she wrote
From her "Highest Hill,"
A great big roundly rough stone

With notches and scars on it,
Came rolling across the land
Sparking a fire that kindled
The hearts of men and women,
Came rolling across the South
In the nineteen thirties—
To Gastonia, to Happy Valley
At Elizabethtown in Tennessee
To Harlan County in Kentucky
Where coal-blacked skins
Failed to hide man's dignity,
Where company commissaries and gun thugs
(Documented by the LaFollette Committee)
Failed to wipe out man's self-respect and human hunger
Which craves more than bread
For satisfaction, but needs bread also.

Across the great Appalachians
The stone came rolling
Gathering men up and binding them
Together in bundles of unity,
Calling to dignity
Feeding the blaze that makes men human
Stirring the ex-hill farmer
To "Call Home the Heart"
At the humble hearthstone
Of a mountain cabin
A miner's shack staked to a hillside
On uncertain stilts
Or the gray monotony
Of dull rows of workers' homes
On a cotton mill hill,
To call home the heart
To where beauty lives with human dignity.

Olive Dargan at Asheville in North Carolina
Where Tom Wolfe's troubled spirit broods
Over the tops of blue-fogged mountains,
Still trying to come home.
Olive the rare and beautiful one.
In her will she left me her library,

Books she had cherished and loved
And lived with
Books sprouted from her own heart's weeping
And laughing.

It took three truck loads to move them
And I stacked them with great love
And expectation of future perusing.

But they burned them
And their ashes are part
Of Georgia's red dirt
Where wind-bent weed roots now feed.

And I walk here by these sad ashes
Reflecting on each dull gray speck.
Has that dancing whirlwind
Caught up the complete works of Shakespeare,
Planting his seeds out across my fields
To where tall pines
Turn the plowed furrows?
Is that wisp of smoke
Scattering Milton through the tree tops
Leaving poems on the pines
To drip down and root in this red earth
Next spring?
And are those grass blades
Sun-dancing across the lespedeza pasture
With Lanier to where the river's ripples[25]
Murmur softly
"The Song of the Chattahoochee"?

Henrietta Buckmaster[26] wrote of this river
This "Deep River."
It rolls by my farm
Growing in sullen anger at the fields.
This Chattahoochee rising
In the hills of Habersham
From springs in the valleys
Whose branch waters nourished
Gentle spirits of a mountain people
Opposed to slavery.

Her books were there on my shelves
With ten thousand others
And half-finished poems and stories
Of my own musing, laid aside
For future touching.

Weep now by these sad ashes
Where the big elm tree
Lop-sided from the fire's fierce blazing
Stands lonely by these chimney stones.
Weep deeply,
But not alone for the burning.

Mourn more for what has happened
To Sandburg's "People,"
"The People, Yes," the people,[27]
For what happens to men who set fires,
Who threw the home-made bomb
At the window of Lee Peery's house
Past midnight with three small ones sleeping
Breathing sweet air
Needle-scented from Georgia pines.

Lee and Ann Peery
Of the Jesus spirit
Enriching the dirt of my gardens
Because they loved.
Lee Peery, the man is to me
As a brother,
Mourn not for him
But for the hurt spirits of men
Who sneak in the night-time
To bomb his dwelling.

Weeping, walk here
By this red river
Reflecting on Albany, Atlanta, Oxford
Birmingham, Greenwood, Attica
Route 40 in Maryland
And Bill Moore,[28] murdered.
Go grieve of Hiroshima and Nagasaki,
That our country's conscience

Is not burning,
Fearing her conscience is dulled
Beyond shared feeling
By the bias of bombs
For human extinction . . .

Be made sad by an arrogance
Assuming "manifest destiny" of affluence
At the cost of death
To peasant peons
Of Guatemala, Bolivia, Peru, Santo Domingo
And other lands where our country
Supports decaying dictators
Grieving that only dictators
Now look to America with hope
In their eyes . . .

Though weeping, also rejoice—
For the love in man
For Bill Moore, the gentle
And peaceful one, who lay down his life
On an Alabama road
That man's humanity might live,
For the strength of men
To endure the Star and Gas Chamber
The stake and burning cross.
For this, rejoice, and far more—
For the humility of great men
Who submerge themselves
In the fountain of the people for renewal
Feeling there the pulse-beat
Of the people's yearnings
To be human . . .

For the gentle heart of the Negro people
And for the brave hope
They have brought to our land—
Frederick Douglass and his people,[29]
Under the whip-lashes
Of haughty masters
Kept hope alive

That now stirs the heart of our nation.
For this, rejoice.

And—
For Roger Williams[30] whose dream
Has not yet arrived
Thomas Paine with the world[31]
For his country
And a religion to do good.
For Jefferson and Lincoln
Who bent and doubted
But came back to the people—
Pegs to hang our hopes on
From history . . .

And rejoice even today for
The white men and women of the South
Of humility and truth
Close to the oppressed—
Aubrey Williams[32]
Giant among pygmies who yap at his heels,
Aubrey who never learned to double-talk
And who walks on a rocky road
With the great of history.

For Carl and Ann Braden,[33]
Tuned to the under tow depths,
Who listen and look and see
And dare the prison walls.

For Claude Williams[34] and Joyce
Who preach the Jesus Gospel
And live it,
Who walk with violence and fear
Close by—
And never thought to turn back.

For Floyd Buckner and Jean
Who question, and in dark hours
Of discouragement
Keep close to the bothered spirit
Of the common folk
As they search with love and hope.

Walking here by the white-barked birch
Lost in the river's rolling
Weep and rejoice
As fog hides the tear drops dripping.
Mourn these days
While men must mourn
Confused, in alienation.
Mourn, but not alone,
Lifting high the Pilgrim hope
In a Manifesto of Man
Rejoined to himself . . . !

If I Could Make You

For Linda[35]

You would be
A hungry one
So dissatisfied
You'll never know peace of mind
So disturbed you'll never
Accept old ways
And philosophies
Hoary with rust . . .
You would be a questioner
A digger and searcher
And a traveler
On the way to becoming . . .

You would see
With the artist's eye
Feel with the poet's heart.

Nor would I shield you from tears
Or the bitter you must taste.
For from them the heart of the poet
Will squeeze the true.

You would see raindrops in summer
As a young maiden's tears
From heart-break crying

Falling to ease
The world's great hurt . . .

And the misty winds
As the restless breath
Of lovers
Breathing beauty
Into its human form . . .

Hospital Waiting: May 8, 1963

For Connie[36]

Five hours now you've been unconscious
Under the surgeon's knife
And I wait here, lacking patience
A nerve bundle, raw-edged
Remembering, remembering—
Now that nothing else matters
And other things are dropped
I wait, remembering—
The sound of your foot-fall
On door-step, floor, stairway
Remembering years of hard going
And the good . . .

Spring-time in Kentucky
Rhododendron blossoms on Cumberland
And the teasing blue eyes
Of a laughing girl
Daring me in a climb
Up the big mountainside
To where the Pinnacle looks out
Over the Holston.[37]

We were the foolish ones
Where was the cliff to daunt us?

There, on the mountain peak
Above Cumberland Gap
Overlooking Boone's Trace[38]
And Tennessee Valley

With five states in view
We made a pledge . . .

You were the foolish one—
Joining yourself to sorrow and hurt
And hard times ahead
But you were smelted
From strong ores, tempered
For bearing bruises
On the troubled way
With a man dissatisfied
With his world . . .

Remembering Kentucky
At the forks of Troublesome Creek
And Tennessee . . .

And then the children
And pinched bellies.
Remembering Atlanta
With mattress on the floor
Of a basement room
And five dollars a week!

And the children—
Ann, the gentle, the sweet one
Skipping onto our way
Like a puckish elf
Singing the sweet songs of the young
Ann, who grew so much like you
She could never hurt another being
She, the unselfish—
Ann, the first benediction to our love!

Then Hedy
With the stubborn chin, yours—
And mine.
Hedy of the singing lips
And compulsive drive—
Gathering snakes and lizards—
And to whom all mountains
Were invitations to climb

A bundle of questions
Asking for answers
Hedy, the hungry one
Strong with the strength to take life
By the hand
And walk with it in light places
And in the dark.

Remembering, remembering—
The hurt places we found.
Your feeling heart knew
Cotton-mill poverty—
Children, pinch-faced, resigned
To hunger
Women, hiding their hurt
Under stolid faces
A Negro boy sent to a Georgia chain-gang
Because he asked bread for the needy.
Pain and hurt and love walking
On a Carolina mill-hill
Up the valleys of Harlan
In Kentucky
On Cabin Creek in West Virginia.

Your quiet patience
Bore my own raw impatience
With the courage of love

So much I remember here, waiting
Waiting for the surgeon's verdict
And then the long, lonely nights
Of uncertainty, waiting

The pain there
In a hospital bed
And telephone calls—
Mama from Georgia,
She who taught us to sing
When hurt,
Sis in New York
Buddy in West Virginia
Belle in Colorado

So far away, so long, I don't
Recognize voices
Reaching out across space
With tender touch . . .

And the children—
Hedy in California, she with music
In her restless fingers
And your own image on her face.
Hedy the strong and tender hearted
Whose troubled thoughts course deeply
Beneath a smooth surface.
Ann, in Ohio, Ann the warm-hearted,
Who taught Hedy to sing
The old songs
Ann, who has in herself the quiet strength
To walk the dark valley
With hurt and sorrow
And who is so much like you she moves
With your own sweet unoffensive step,
A blessing to all who know her,
Ann, the first benediction of our love!

And a helpless void inside
All of us.
For none can bear another's suffering,
Each must taste the gall
In his own . . .

I reach out and touch your face
But I cannot take the pain away
Other times I've seen you suffer
Body broken near death
And have walked alone in the night
Cursing
That the pain could not pass to me,
That I could not take it into myself—
You of the generous heart
You the gentle human
You with courage to face and live
The hard life with a restless one
You about whom I am passionately personal

You the woman I love
My tears now cannot reach
Or heal you . . .

Old Homeplace

    For Hedy[39]

We stood silent there
Watching wimpling shadows
Of Big Burnt Mountain
Creep across Turkey Creek
By a crumbled rock chimney,
Homeplace grave marker
Whose hearthstones had tales to tell
Of lowly doings
Of days when a scant cupboard
Was never too bare to share
With a tired stranger,
Of the pack-peddler
And pull of lowland cotton mills,
Of a strong man with hope
And a singing blue-eyed girl
Who lived and loved,
Made a crop with two bull yearlings
And bore nine children
To feed and dress
As the mountain earth sucked up
Their flesh, burying
In salty sweat drippings
Covered by bulltongue and mattock

And the blackberry bier had tales
And the sarvis bush
Crowding the unfurrowed fields:
That the woman and man were still there,
Her eyes in the blue of the violets
Lips in the sarvis berries
Face in the sweet-scented trailing arbutus
And songs of the bending willow,

That the man, loving his fields
And babies, plowed himself into the lip sap
Of their own gray roots
Sucking deeply there on the mountain

You said it was strange
To see a man's fields grown
To bush and weeds,
A strong man.

And the wind came over the mountain
Laughing with a wimple of oak leaves
Talking secrets in soft whispers
As low bending willows
Plucked the sparkling creek waters
For music
To sing the silent songs
Of the sleepers.

There'll Be a Tomorrow

For Clifton and Mary Bryant[40]

In all my wanderings
I've gone most to the poor
Who are adept at hiding pain.
Sometimes the mountain man
does it stolid, ox-like,
revealing scant emotion.
But I know there is a cry inside
a flute song hungering for words
and maybe a curse . . .

On Cabin Creek I eat and sleep
in the makeshift home
of a disabled miner.
Hurt lies heavy on the house
But the deepest hurt is still unworded.

There is a today on Cabin Creek—
ghost-town mining camps
miners who sit idle

drawing DPA checks[41]
while machines drag coal from under the mountains
and bulldozers tear the mountains down
mixing with cess-pool creek filth—
a today swallowed in poverty's greedy gullet.

There was a yesterday on Cabin Creek
Paint Creek, Matewan, Logan[42]—
a yesterday with heroes, heroines and hope—
Mother Blizzard, Mother Jones
and women ripping up rails and crossties
that the Baldwin Phelps armored train
might not pass;
A yesterday with Bill Blizzard[43]
and a hundred others indicted for treason
by courts doing corporation bidding;
A yesterday with Steve Mangus shot dead
and the long march to Logan.
Seven thousand Kanawha Valley miners
with rifles, shotguns and pistols
on the long march to Logan . . .

There was a yesterday of hurt and hope
and solidarity
when a virgin Union's inspiration
stirred mountain men and women
to heroic feats.
Born on Cabin Creek,
"Solidarity Forever"
went on to stir lowly hearts
in all parts of the land.[44]

And there may be a tomorrow
On Cabin Creek
a clean tomorrow,
child of hope and hurt and solidarity.

Mountain Heritage

Listen
You mountain kid
Old woman or man,
I would call you back
To your own heritage . . . !

Must we, too, be lost
As America is lost
In a thicket of violent greed?
Are we too lost to recognize
Our own broken image?

I would point you back
To an uncertain time in history
When the values Appalachia gave to the South
And America
Were rooted deep
In independence and freedom!

At an uncertain time in history
When civil war clouds darkened the land
Appalachia held a blazing torch
On the freedom road . . . !

Appalachian Blues

Down here in Appalachia,
government designated "poverty area,"
blue thoughts stagger
up the valley
whisper on mountain fogs—

First:
    To you who come to study us
    to see what is wrong with us
    that we are poor,
    who look for the cause in us.
    (For in this opportunity wonderland

isn't it all agreed
any man can be president?
and if he hasn't a job
and can't feed his kids
he's just no 'count!)

My word,
and we do have faults
a plenty of them:
    Poor schools
    Bad government
    Poor roads
    Politicians
    Poor people
    Corporations
    Corporation native flunkies
    Etc., etc. . . .
And dirt, trash, beer cans and whiskey bottles
rusted automobile bodies
decorating road sides
piled in back yards
and men on welfare in beer joints!

But don't look closer,
don't look too close.
It might be dangerous
You might see our colonial status—
outside corporation control:
    Consolidation
    Continental Oil
    Island Creek
    U.S. Steel
    Dupont and Ford
    Union Carbide and Mellon
    Rockefeller
    and the bought and paid for
    native lackeys
    etc., etc. . . .

"Yesterday's People,"[45] didn't look that close
so it was safe.

It was given to VISTAS, Appalachian Volunteers
and other varied assortments
of "Poverty Warriors"
as a Bible
that they might understand us hillbillies.

The fault of a poor man is all in himself,
verily.
And the dove is killed
because she flew in front
of the shot gun pellets.
The doe fell because
she ran into the rifle bullet.
And the rabbit,
of course,
the trifling silly rabbit!

Verily, verily I say
look to the victim
for causes
of why the victim
is a victim—
You who come to study us!

Second:
    You do-gooders
    missionaries of numerous persuasions
    soul-savers who paint outside privies
    poverty warriors who play at being poor
    and gather us together
    to tell us what our troubles are,
    long haired hustlers
    expert at proposal writing
    lengthy verbiage
    for Federal grants:
    Descend upon Appalachia
    as the great black raven
    from superior heights
    hovering wings clouding the sun.
    Find an articulate hillbilly,
    for front man,
    prime him

trim him
use him
to do your thing
to us . . . !

Third:
   Folksy ballad hunters
discoverers of mountain music
and mountain musicians
Columbuses discovering Appalachia—
Culture diluters
Culture polluters
Culture exploiters
Circuit riding freaks
Builders of spurious communes
pulling on your weed
running away from your own drug culture
but bringing it to Appalachia,
buyers of mountain land
builders of summer homes:
Your Appalachia is not Appalachia
but a life-style travesty
a foreign thing!
Yours was a revolt in patterns
counter culture
counter revolutionary
counter poor people!

from *in a land of plenty*
(1982–85)

Editors' Note: Published in 1982 and reprinted in 1985 by the West End Press in Minneapolis and then Los Angeles, this 221-page paperback is the only book by West to include several of his prose pieces along with his poetry. Largely collected from earlier editions, the poems are divided into four parts: "Works from 1932–1946," "Poetical Works from 1947–1951 and Prose from 1962–1966," "Poetical Works of the Recent Period," and "Prose of the Recent Period." The 1985 edition includes an additional fifth part, "Poems Added to the Second Edition," as well as a blurb by Dave Roediger from Northwestern University. Both editions include a cover photo of West in overalls and a straw hat and make note of West's desire for "No Copyright." The book is illustrated with sketches by Constance Adams West.

When I Read the Report[46]

When I read the report of the Committee
uncertainty engulfed me.
I knew fear, and acknowledged it,
with no apology intended.
I who loved America
who cherished the dream deferred
was accused by the Committee.

Plowing fields
on the banks of the Chattahoochee
the federal marshal found me.
His unaccustomed toe
tangled in turf,
sprawled him belly down
on the upturned sod . . .

Blushing, he opened his bag
to hand me the subpoena.
I must report to Memphis
on the order of Senator James O. Eastland
of the Senate Internal Security Committee.
My beliefs and doings
were in question.
My name was among the accused.

Alone in a remote farm field
I pondered sadly—
not alone for myself
but for my family
and my country . . .

Born to the poorest of the poor—
red-neck, cracker, hillbilly—
proud of ancestors
who never bought or sold a human body
but lived by sweat of their own skin,
that some among us
can clasp the hand of a Black person
and say, "Sister, Brother!"

In the 1930's
I had started Highlander Folkschool
and helped to free
a Black lad in Atlanta
from a 20-year chain-gang sentence.
He had led hungry people
to ask for food.
Two years in Fulton Tower—
protests, midnight handbills, legal action—
Angelo Herndon was free!

Now I was guilty.
Senators Eastland, McCarthy, McCarran[47]
and other upholders of Nazi ideology
said so.
Atlanta authorities
took a bench warrant with word out to
"Get him dead or alive!"

Little security could my friends offer,
Black or white.
There was no hiding place.
A Black preacher's wife
pushed me by trap door into her basement
a poor white mother shoved me
out the back door
under a bramble thicket
when the cops came looking.

Leaving Atlanta and the state I love
under crocker sacks,
driven by a Black man,
dropped by the Great Stone Mountain
to thumb a ride northward.
I who have an intense dislike
for Chase Manhattan
and Wall Street imperialism
found haven with yankee workers.

Girl of Matoaka[48]

Come, Pamela, girl of Matoaka,
come to me
to where I am
on these Appalachian heights
where our people's roots sank deeply
in mountain-top granite
eagles once rested
and ravens built nests . . .

Eagles are gone now
and the raven,
nests fallen like crumbling clay
of old chimneys
parted from log walls
of homes long desolate . . .

Come, Pamela,
hurt child of the hollow,

let us learn together
of a people
now dispossessed
who lived and loved
dug life from these rocky hills
and coal from under,
wove and spun to keep bodies warm
hid refugees on the Underground
groping a way toward freedom,
took up guns against human bondage
shed tears and sweat and blood,
faced company gunmen
and refused to be human clods . . . !

Come, Pamela,
tend your roots
spread your wings
rise
look
see
and possess your heritage!

Poor Little Rich Kids

At the universities in the 1960's
I read poetry to audiences
dressed in bib-coveralls
with multi-color patches.

Playing at poverty
poking fun at the poor
by shaggy assumption
of dirt and unwashed dress
they "did their thing"—
and the poor kept
getting poorer
and the rich richer . . .

Funeral Notes 2

We gather in Hickory Grove Church Yard
to bury part of her
beside our old Dad
laid here long ago . . .

Dust to dust benediction
mingles with red clay dull thudding
from shovels to coffin.

We're only burying a memory
a memory already out of the grave
up in the tops of tall maple trees
singing to banjo string music
on limber limbed willows.

Her teasing laughter sparkles
down Cartecay cataracts
by Ellijay to Coosewatee's shoals
and sluggish Chattahoochee

Her rugged womanhood
stirs the sap of tan-bark chestnut-oaks
on Turkey Creek
Sourwood sprouts rustle
to the rhythm of her goose-necked hoe
grubbing crabgrass
from the Long Hollow new-ground patch

Strong Mother
who taught us to sing when saddened
with always a song on her own lips.
Mountain Mother
sharing the sorrow of those who wipe silent tears
while wry jokes eased the hurt.

She cannot leave these hills
while a spark of her
is in Ann's gentle touch
in Hedy's restless fingers
tuned to banjo picking
and Talitha's puckish protest.

Lolita Lebrun

> Lolita Lebrun, Puerto Rican patriot, spent 25 years in the Alderson, West Virginia, Federal Prison for Women. She was guilty of the same crime committed by George Washington and the Boston Tea Party participants.

Lolita, gentle being
freedom fighter
epitome of eternal woman-kind
reservoir of human dignity,
we greet you and would welcome you
to our mountains with no prison handcuffs
you are one with us . . .

Twenty-five years
you look across Alderson's prison walls.
Iron gate and barbed wire
where 700 women count the minutes
of the hours of the days . . .

Like the wounded raven
born on the crippled wing
toward the balsam mountain top
you make hope a living thing.
Across daisy-speckled meadow
limber willow limbs
bend to kiss lilting lips
of the Greenbriar.[49]
Freight trains laden with a hundred
coal cars are a monotonous growl.
Trains drag a part of us
by Alderson Prison toward Wall Street
where handcuffs for freedom
are forged and fastened.

Freight cars clatter
a morose monologue
with tales of human flesh
and sweat and blood on coal.
Cry of the cripple-winged raven
resounds, indomitable,

over the prison walls.
Lolita inside listens
speaks with her God
and sends us the warning:
"Bury the bomb!"

Her God says: "A-men!
Let it be!"

Visit to Lolita Lebrun's Home

In the home land of warm hearts
on the streets of Lares,[50]
birthplace of patriot revolution,
along coffee-bush shaded trails
worn deep on the mountain
by human feet,
I walked across fields
where old peasants tell tales
of patriot love,
a laughing child playing there
free in his child-heart reverie
free in girl-time beauty
free in her woman love,
feet helping wear deeper trails
by trees reaching limbs up
to taste sweet rain waters
whispering the wind's song
that Lolita in prison
is forever free!

Great Day A-Coming

We'll call beauty on that day
and she'll come home
Scars are healed
work is everywhere—
for Ester and Mildred of Harlan
for Donald and Gary of Matoaka

and for women and men everywhere.
All who breathe
find useful doings.

Leaves flutter in growing corn fields
of verdant valleys
Food abounds
even for Floyd Fowler
whose daddy drowned
in a six-inch mud hole
No child nurses a hurt
No person knows want
of body or spirit
Black-lung, holding the
hand of greed, followed by ugliness
slunk out of our hollows.

Great day a-coming . . . !

They Who Exploit

They who exploit the poor
have soft hands
voice modulated.
(The poor's hands
are hard
voice a growl
of inarticulate protest.)

They who exploit the poor
make Foundations
with charity gifts
to dull the sharp edge
of rebellion.
(The poor take hand-outs
with bitter taste.)

They who exploit the poor
make wars in far-off places
and profits in the USA.
(The poor fight, die in battle

and come back to welfare
and uncertainty.)

They who exploit the poor
cause mountain-top plagues
to slide down the valleys.
(The poor know
Buffalo Creek[51]
and its bitter waters.)

They who exploit the poor
make wholesale deals
in pot and LSD
that sons and daughters
of affluence
may "do their thing"
peddle their "revolution."
(The poor have their own revolution
needing no dope
for inspiration.)

All of Them

Red-neck, hillbilly
dago, wop
got the red from plowing a crop
of Georgia cotton.

Cracker, ridge-runner
Jimmy Higgins[52]
gully jumper
and a lot more.

Massacred at Ludlow[53]
I tore down the convict stockades
at Coal Creek.[54]
My blood made Harlan bloody.
My sweat wet the cement
of Detroit and Atlanta.
With pain and tears
I made Greece and Rome.

I was the gladiator in gory arenas
and now the boxer
bruising and slugging
to amuse the sick people
conditioned to cry for blood.

My Poem

I am a mountain man
my history has life in it,
a people who cared.
My poem is collective
like Harlan miners in secret meetings
from gun thug terror
or cotton mill workers
at Gastonia and Marion
in 1929.[55]
And my poem is personal
as personal as Burl Collins[56]
wheezing black-lung breath
after thirty-five years in the mines
and Rosie's agony
waiting at the mine mouth
for Burl's broken body,
as personal as the pinched belly
of a hungry child
looking upon hollows
where trash speaks a dead language
of despair
a place where beauty shed tears
and went away,
a stranger to our hills . . .

My poem has hurt in it,
the bent bodies of strong men
legs gone, arms severed
striving to stand straight
and stooped women lending their bodies
to the striving.
My poem has hurt in it . . . !

I am brother to these—
the poor, the hurt, the crippled—
all of them . . .

And I am brother
to the eternal glimmer
sparking dark places,
remembering green mountain spring-times
and the resilient fibre
of twisted chestnut oaks
straining toward a ridge-crest plumb line . . .

My poem stays close
where the poor of the earth share life
and cherish beauty,
brother to hope.

My poem lives
to negate lunatic ravings
of nuclear madness . . .

My poem has life . . . !

Something of America

A friend once said:
"If you want to be a good patriot
don't read your country's history
too closely . . ."

But something of America I know
love and cherish
with warm pride
and something I intensely dislike.

The Great Dream
Like the rising of a fair morning
with Thomas Paine
had never been equaled.
But the recording made it
a dream deferred—
left slavery unmentioned

made a Bill of Rights for white men.
Black and red men, women of all colors
were omitted . . .

In the hearts of the lowly
Thomas Paine never died.
There no slavery lived,
no grabbing of red people's homeland.
John Burnett[57] walked the trail
of tears and suffering with the Cherokee.
Appalachian-rooted John Fairfield[58]
laid his own life down
on the shadowy underground
of thousands of Black folk
toward freedom.

Numerous unknown headlines
annals of unrecorded history
speak of justice and peace.
Workers, the humble poor, plain people,
producing life substance
plan no battles, make no wars
for blood to drip
that profits may continue
in undiminished flow . . .

Many I know who now harbor
peace and justice and suffering:
John Woody[59] and Effie
keep hope a-flicker
in desolate Matoaka.
John Woody, a man I know of 48 years
waiting to die of black lung,
never knew the school room,
went to the mine at nine.

Effie and the children
robbed of his manhood
grieve silent tears
on the sad Matoaka hills.
But John's courage stands tall,
remembering Blair Mountain,

Cabin and Paint Creeks,
Ludlow and Coal Creek[60]—
years when miners held
union meetings in secret places.

Once at strike time I found John's body
unconscious, beaten
on a rutted trace.
An empty coffin, a warning,
was left in his yard
labeled "John Woody" in large letters.
When told what the letters said
he smiled.
"That's the last thing I need," he said.

Cabin Creek, alive in heroic tales,
unrecorded.
There Clifton and Mary Bryant
fuel the flame in their humble hut.

Blair Mountain, 1921
Ten thousand miners in struggle
bombs dropping from the air.

West Virginia knew Debs[61]—
in Moundsville Prison,
and in 1912 elected fifty-five
of his party to public office!
West Virginia mountaineers
seceding from slavery in 1863
enslaved to corporate power later—
Consolidated, Continental,
Peabody, U.S. Steel,
Rockefeller . . .

And Ludlow—
bitter in memory Ludlow!
Hungry miners
evicted to tent colony
fearing Rockefeller police bullets
dug an under-tent pit
for women and children's safety.

Rockefeller guards drenched and set fire.
Thirteen children and a pregnant woman
burned to death.
Five men and another woman shot.

O, celebrate the risen Christ
Easter Sunday, 1914
Celebrate the murder of 19 workers!

Ludlow . . . !
Map makers leave it off now.
A stone-carved miner
with wife and slain child at foot
mark the spot to:
". . . the men, women and children
who died in freedom's cause
April 20, 1914."

Ludlow, bitter in memory Ludlow!

And Coal Creek, Tennessee,
blotted, too.
Pleasure-seeking tourists at
"Lake City" don't know
the bitter—and glorious—
story of Coal Creek.
Change the name
blot the memory . . . !

Hope and hurt, blood and terror
lie heavy in Coal Creek memory.
Mountain men there lit the spark
destined to destroy
the convict labor lease system.
In 1891 they were called "Communists!"

In 1934 in a Kentucky jail death cell
with three men sentenced to die
I learned the song:
"Shut up in the mines at Coal Creek"
from one on his way to the Chair.
Stanzas were found when 28 bodies

were excavated
on a scrap of paper blood smeared
between lumps of coal.

Something of America I love
and cherish with warm pride
and something I intensely dislike

Ludlow . . . !
Coal Creek!
Clifton and Mary Bryant!
John Woody and Effie!
Bill Blizzard!
Florence Reece![62]
Cabin Creek!
Bloody Harlan—corporate profits!
John D. Rockefeller[63] the fourth:
"Too rich to steal."

Ludlow . . . !

afterword

George Brosi

A tall, slender, conventionally dressed man in his fifties walked into the group of disheveled college students gathered in 1962 at Pine Hill, New York. He did nothing to attract attention to himself. When he spoke, it was with an unassuming southern accent, and those who talked with him soon discovered that he had grown up on a small farm in the North Georgia mountains and that he had been active in struggles for poor and working-class people since the 1930s. Thirty years after he began working for a better world, not only did he remain as undaunted and committed to those struggles as he had ever been, but he was looking for ways to connect with others who shared his concerns. He had clearly endured persecution and prosecution. He had suffered failure and frustration. He had faced adversity and apathy. Yet he had persevered. He was an inspiration, a symbol of the power of a purposeful life. His name was Don West.

I was one of the students at that gathering who was awed and impressed, perhaps particularly so since I had grown up in the East Tennessee mountains less than 150 miles from his birthplace. Although West was approximately the age of my father, in many ways his life paralleled mine. I had walked my first picket line in the summer of 1961 in my Tennessee hometown to protest a segregated laundromat, and I met Don West the following year while I was attending my first nationwide gathering of student activists, a National Council meeting of Students for a Democratic Society (SDS). SDS made a point of calling itself the "New Left," and the spirit of the times could too often be summed up with the expression, "Don't trust anyone over thirty." Activists of my generation sometimes tended to be disdainful of what they called derisively the "Old Left"—meaning the progressive movements of Don West's generation. Thus his attendance at our meeting, despite our youthful disregard for his generation's struggles, impressed me. His unabashed regard for the Mountain South, where I had grown up, stirred me. Don West's presence that day convinced me that any commitment to social justice and meaningful change has to be lifelong and intergenerational. I had no way of knowing that this, my first encounter with Don, would be the beginning of a thirty-year friendship between us, a bond that would not be severed until his death in 1992. Yet over the following decades, our paths would cross many times with every conversation revealing to me more and more ways that Don West had contributed, not only to progressive forces in the South, but to American society as a whole.

While attending another SDS National Council meeting in Pine Hill the following year, I was delighted to see Don West again. We talked more. I learned that he was teaching in Maryland and saving money to move back to the Mountain South. At a time when many people with roots in Appalachia and the South were ashamed of their region and strove to escape its endemic problems, Don was committed to a strong vision of a progressive South ushered in by native southern activists. He had learned on his grandfather's knee that deep down a progressive legacy had survived in the South for generations, and his subsequent research had confirmed that legions of brave southerners had fought injustice throughout its history. Don West saw the beauty of old-fashioned mountain values and of the religious tenets he was raised to uphold. He felt that those of us who came from the South and from Appalachia were in a unique position to encourage lasting change. He rejected the trendy calls to join the "vanguard" of the various protest movements in Mississippi or California or other hot spots. Don's strong commitment to our region influenced me more than anything else I learned from him.

During the 1960s I worked full-time for SDS, the Council of the Southern Mountains, and other organizations that were part of the social justice and protest movements of that volatile decade. I even spent a couple of years in California creating a job clearinghouse for "the Movement" called Vocations for Social Change. By the summer of 1973 I had returned to Tennessee and married. My new wife, Connie, and I were living on a fifteen-acre farm in Sequatchie Cove in Marion County, Tennessee, near the Alabama and Georgia lines and not far from where Don West cofounded the Highlander Folk School in 1932. By this time Don and his wife, also named Connie, had created the Appalachian South Folklife Center near Pipestem, West Virginia. Both Don West and I had returned to the Appalachian South, and both of us were living on the land. Raised by mountain farmers, Don was one of only a handful of nationally known activists who had ever earned a living from the soil. His farm work and gardening in this period was dramatically innovative, employing farsighted organic and sustainable agricultural practices. I appreciated Don's willingness to do farm work. I recognized that a balance between manual labor and intellectual tasks could provide an enduring and meaningful connection to working people and to the land. Don West's thoughtful and energetic way of life shattered any tidy divisions between "reds" and "greens" in our society. Thoroughly pro-union, anticapitalist, and class-conscious, Don's politics were on the Left or "red." Yet his abhorrence of strip mining and corporate control of our food supply also made him an environmentalist or "green."

Raised in a preindustrial mountain culture, baptized by fire during the tumultuous struggles for labor and civil rights in the 1930s, 1940s, and 1950s, West was thoroughly sympathetic to the dispossessed and the working class, but he was simultaneously deeply committed to the earth from which he and his forbears had wrested a living for centuries.

This balance occurred on other levels. As a farmer and gardener, Don West often lived exactly the kind of day-to-day life that many "back-to-the-land" adherents adopted as a full-time vocation. He admired Clarence Jordon and the multiethnic followers of the Christian-based Koinonia Farm in Georgia. He respected progressive individual homesteaders like Helen and Scott Nearing in New England, Anna and Harlan Hubbard in Kentucky, and Elizabeth and Ernest Seaman in Tennessee. But Don was never content to simply set himself or his family up as prophetic examples. While devoted to "alternative institutions" on a practical level, he felt compelled to transcend borders and reach out directly to people in need, especially those who were displaced or oppressed by the broader economy.

In the summer of 1972 I visited the Folklife Center for the first time to attend the Council of the Southern Mountains Annual Conference. Arnold Miller, then conducting an inspirational and eventually successful grassroots campaign for the presidency of the United Mine Workers, put in an appearance, as did leaders of the victorious effort to obtain compensation for black lung disease and lots of youthful "movement people." The gathering was quite diverse; people from many backgrounds were working on a multitude of important issues. Don consistently realized that social change comes about realistically as a result of many forces, not just one. He never wasted energy in attacking specific groups working for change; instead he refused to disassociate himself from any individual or group working on an issue he cared about. As a result, he was often attacked by more narrow partisans both to his right and his left on the political spectrum. He worked with fundamentalist Christians in Dalton, Georgia, with Jewish activists in New York City, and with anybody who shared his perspective on a particular struggle. Because he was willing to work with groups that included Communists, some who didn't understand his openness to *all* groups assumed he was therefore a Communist and refused to work with him. Ironically, he sometimes incurred the wrath of Communists as well because he was willing to work with anticommunists. Yet Don never wavered. He was always comfortable working with whoever shared his goals on particular issues.

The occasion for my next trip to the Folklife Center was for the annual music festival held there in 1973. My wife, baby son, and I drove up with a couple of our neighbors from Sequatchie Cove. Many of Don's neighbors attended as well. It was a great weekend. The crowd consisted of local people—both black and white—and folk music enthusiasts, as well as people attracted by Don's politics. Don's younger daughter, Hedy, whom I had worked with previously, was one of the performers. Don walked easily in the crowd. He wore bib overalls because they were practical—after all, he was on his own farm and might have to tend to one of his cows at any point. Yet I also believe he wore overalls as an emblem of solidarity with the people he had grown up with and working people in general. Don was equally at ease with all of the people in attendance. Our neighbors were relaxed and enjoyed the music and the crowd. They had not been exposed to protest movements, and I cannot imagine any other "movement" event where they would have been so comfortable. Don West was an activist, but his political values stemmed directly from his Christian values and from his patriotism, his desire for his country to live up to its own basic founding principles. While some organizers for change alienate people by seeming to push "foreign" ideologies, Don West always made his patriotism clear. He saw himself as the legitimate heir to a long tradition of fighting for the common people in his country and region, and he worked hard to build awareness of the positive aspects of our heritage. Don had a way of expressing his political views that emphasized what he was for, not what he was against, and that connected easily with his audience. Our neighbors were as impressed with Don West as any college-educated veteran activists I ever introduced him to.

During this time I was working for the General Convention Youth Program of the Episcopal church giving away youth grants in the Appalachian region. I made arrangements while I was at the festival for our board to meet at the Folklife Center later in the year. When we arrived for the board meeting, the festival crowd was not there, yet lots of young people ate at the dining hall with us. Don was continually reaching out to all kinds of people throughout his life, providing desperately needed direct social services. One of the first Folklife Center programs was a summer camp for local kids, many of whom came from mountain families that struggled to provide enough nutritional support. In West Virginia, Don also served as a local representative of the Heifer Project, an international effort founded by one of his distant cousins that assisted rural people through a livestock exchange program. While many deeply committed activists tended to be disdainful of such social service work, Don West saw this side of his life as a concrete way of caring for people in need. He wanted the lives of people to be improved not only through eventual social changes but also by little things that could be done here and now. One of Don's first campaigns for social change incorporated these elements of protest and social service. During the bitter miners' strike at Wilder, Tennessee, in the early 1930s, not only did Don join students and faculty members at Vanderbilt Divinity School in providing clothes and food for the striking miners, he also joined the picket lines.

When my family moved to Berea, Kentucky, in 1979, initially to run the Council of the Southern Mountains Bookstore, Don, and sometimes Connie, would stop by and visit us. We would feed them simple meals—perhaps soup with garden ingredients and homemade bread—and they would be genuinely pleased and grateful. They were comfortable with our messy house and our growing family—Don had been raised among seven siblings, and we had seven children. He would send us autographed books as presents on various occasions, and, once, when he took his wife to the Soviet Union for breast cancer treatment, he sent a whole packet of books from there. A sense of international consciousness pervaded Don's life and work. While deeply rooted in the Mountain South, he saw the need to rise above narrow provincialism. He toured the country and the world, seeking ways in which our local communities could educate themselves—in the successful manner of the Danish folk schools, for example—or improve health care, as he believed had happened in the Soviet Union. He opened the window to an international perspective that could teach us lessons from its diversity without knocking us off our feet with foreign ideology.

In the 1980s my family again attended an annual music festival at the Folklife Center. By this time, these events were drawing hundreds of people from around the country and presenting some of the most important names in folk and mountain music. Yet festivals were only one of several ways that Don West sought to bring together politics, art, and fun. All of these enterprises were part of Don's values as a literary artist, a poet, and an activist. He understood the power of music, visual art, and literature to inspire and even transform a person's consciousness. His wife Connie fostered the same values with her paintings, and Don never missed an opportunity to promote her work. The two of them actively envisioned ways that artists and organizers could reinforce each other.

The last time Don and Connie visited our home, Don had just bought a miner's shack in Cabin Creek, West Virginia, about a half-hour's drive from his daughter, Ann, in Charleston. Connie was distraught that they were leaving the scenic surroundings of the Folklife Center for a place that she knew was inconvenient for elderly people. But Don had an exceedingly strong sense of history, and Cabin Creek had been a landmark community in struggles for labor rights. Throughout his life, Don had researched and written about historical personalities who had the courage to stand for their convictions. He wanted to live in a place that was imbued with the spirit of an inspiring struggle for a better tomorrow. I have often thought that Don's ability to feel the history of a place may also have influenced the decision years earlier when his wife was pregnant with Ann. At that time they retreated from the intense and dangerous organizing Don was doing in eastern Kentucky to Pleasant Hill,

Don West, age eighty-one, at a folk music festival at the Appalachian South Folklife Center, Pipestem, West Virginia.

Tennessee, for Connie to have the baby. This community was located near Wilder, Tennessee, where Don had first worked with coal miners striving for a better life. Likewise, in his old age, I think he felt that if he couldn't be as active as he wished, he could at least be in a place that was a symbol of what he stood for. I have never met anyone whose sense of history was as real and concrete and personal as Don's.

When Don's wife Connie died, I drove to West Virginia to attend the services at the Folklife Center. Don's first funeral as a preacher, joined by other Vanderbilt Divinity students, had been for Barney Graham, the leader of the miner's union in Wilder, Tennessee, who had been shot to death on the steps of the company store. The funeral for Connie was the last and the most difficult he ever preached. Don and Connie had married while they were undergraduate students at Lincoln Memorial University, and he had told me more than once the story of their honeymoon—Connie rode a mule they had borrowed in Pineville, while Don walked alongside, traveling over ten miles to celebrate their marriage for a few days at the remote Redbird Mission. Don believed deeply in marriage and the family, and he never recovered from the death of his life-mate whom he had married in 1928. Some people who become disenchanted with the status quo feel superior to society and all its restraints and thus feel free to do as they please, disdainful of common courtesy or even morality. Don West was emphatically not one of those people. The basic Christian values that made West care about changing society also made him care about people as individuals and care enough to lead a personally exemplary life. Don's role as a preacher was not incidental; it was integral to his life. He graced several church pulpits throughout his life and worked briefly as a full-time pastor. Don preached his politics and his educational values, and he tended his flocks of fellow activists.

Late in Don's life, my friend Jim Still, the novelist and poet, stopped by to see me. He had been Don's classmate at Lincoln Memorial University, and they had worked with the same Boy Scout troop as students. Jim mentioned that he was planning a trip to the Yucatan Peninsula. I had recently been in touch with Don and knew that he was at his St. Petersburg, Florida, home, so I encouraged Jim to stop by and see Don on the way. The next time Jim visited me, he said he had enjoyed a good time with Don. I'll always remember that Jim called Don "the last American cowboy." I thought that was a fitting tribute to Don's old-fashioned values, to his masculinity, and to his tenacity. Don was very much like a cowboy—handsome, strong, doing vital work, but also a real loner, in a class by himself.

Don West was a preacher, an educator, a poet, and an organizer, but these were never separate roles for him. His poetry preached and inspired his audience to action. He educated like a true minister, seeking creative ways to build

Don and Connie West in front of one of the concession stands at the Appalachian South Folklife Center's annual Music Festival in 1988.

awareness of the need for justice and sustainable communities. He organized people into movements that had artistic, spiritual, and educational substance.

Those of us who teach, write, preach, and organize for social justice have a great deal to learn from Don West. From him we can learn that these roles do not need to be separate but can be mutually reinforcing. We can learn that social change and social service go together and that living in harmony with the land must go hand-in-hand with getting involved in struggles outside our immediate communities. We can learn that patriotism, in the deepest sense, must come from a thorough understanding of our heritage and our history and how each generation has played a role in challenging the injustices in our communities and abroad. We can learn to balance our lives between worthwhile physical labor and intellectual pursuits. We can work to meet not only the basic but also the artistic needs of our fellow citizens. We can promote caring in the family and the community and beyond. Together, our love for the land and for each other can inspire us to change the world.

In 2001 the Appalachian Studies Conference created, for the first time, three T-shirts honoring regional "heroes." Don West was one of those chosen. I wish Don had been alive to witness this recognition of his contribution to our region. Thirty-nine years after I first encountered Don at an SDS meeting, it was unnerving to walk around at a very different conference and see scholars wearing Don West T-shirts, obviously as awed by Don as the SDS kids had been decades before.

In the forty years since I first met Don West, I have had ample opportunity to reflect upon his life and times. I am amazed that he never became nationally famous because he was a truly innovative Christian leader, an outstanding educator, a sterling poet, and an inspiring activist. He was dismissed for being a Communist *not* because he wanted the Soviet Union to conquer America or even because his ideology was communistic. He was one of the most patriotic Americans I ever knew, and he was often more "green" than "red" and always more "Christian" than "Marxist." He was red-baited precisely because what he stood for was so American, so Christian, and so compelling that the forces for backwardness could not use reason to defeat him.

I am proud that Don West considered me a friend and a comrade and feel lucky to have been inspired by him. His legacy rests securely in my heart, a place forever branded by "the last American cowboy."

notes to the prose and poems

Selected Prose

1. The Cumberland Mountains, a portion of the Appalachian Mountains west of the Tennessee River Valley.

2. James Edward Oglethorpe (1696–1785) founded Georgia in 1733 and later served as the first colonial governor.

3. "Pided" is mountain dialect for having a sickly pallor. In this context, "moccasin" refers to a water moccasin snake.

4. Granville Sharpe (1735–1813) was a leading British opponent of slavery.

5. The town of Darien was the site of the first English settlement in Georgia.

6. A large depression or sinkhole in the ground that usually occurs in areas containing primarily limestone rock.

7. In mountain dialect, "furren," or foreign, can mean from anywhere beyond the familiar territory, not necessarily from a different country.

8. "Pretty Saro" is a traditional Appalachian love ballad. "Single Life" is a popular folk ballad extolling the single life from the perspective of a woman.

9. Tom Watson (1856–1922) was a Georgia politician who served as a U.S. senator and was the Populist candidate for the U.S. presidency in 1904 and 1908. His politics took a decidedly anti-Semitic and anti-Catholic turn at the end of his career.

10. Richard Dyer-Bennett (1913–91), hailed as "the twentieth-century minstrel," was one of America's most popular folk singers in the 1950s and 1960s.

11. Lowell, Massachusetts, was the scene of dramatic textile mill strikes by young women workers in 1834 and 1836. Falls River, Massachusetts, was the scene of a dramatic textile mill strike in 1903. "Brown lung" is a disease endemic to mill workers, caused by small lint particles in the air of the mill irritating the lungs of workers. In 1934, the United Textile Workers of America organized a general strike in all of the textile mills in Georgia. "Flying pickets" were groups of union advocates who attempted to spread the strike. Labor unions strongly prefer "closed shops," where all employees must be union members, over "open shops," where only employees who so choose have union dues deducted from their paychecks. Between 1963 and 1980 the Textile Workers Union of America attempted to organize the textile giant J. P. Stevens. The effort was widely known at the time this article was published (1979) because of a well-publicized boycott of J. P. Stevens products.

12. Textile mill strikes took place in Gastonia and Marion, North Carolina, and Elizabethton, Tennessee, in 1929. Cabbage Patch was the name given to one of the best-known "poor white" neighborhoods of Atlanta. The neighborhood was so-named

because low-income people often ate cabbage, an inexpensive food, which, when cooked, emits a distinctive odor.

13. *Tobacco Road* (1932) by Erskine Caldwell (1903–87) is one of the best-known American novels depicting southern sharecroppers.

14. James Still (1906–2001) was one of the most respected Appalachian authors in the twentieth century, best known for his novel *River of Earth* (1940). Jesse Stuart (1906–84) was one of the most popular and prolific twentieth-century eastern Kentucky authors, best known for his novel *Taps for Private Tussie* (1943), which became a bestseller.

15. West is referring to the Berry School, in Rome, Georgia.

16. This gap in the Cumberlands, specifically in Walden's Ridge that runs from Alabama into Virginia, provided relatively easy access from the South and East to the Bluegrass Region of what is now Kentucky for many early settlers, most famously for Daniel Boone in the late eighteenth century.

17. Hindman is the county seat of Knott County, Kentucky. The town is also the site of the Hindman Settlement School, which was founded in 1902 to serve youth in the mountain region.

18. Bad John Wright (1844–1931) was one of the most colorful characters near the border between eastern Kentucky and southwestern Virginia. Wright was a circus performer, a Pinkerton detective agent, a Confederate soldier, and the Sheriff of Wise County, Virginia.

19. John Fox Jr. (1862–1919) and Lucy Furman (1869–1958) were two of the more notable writers to publish stories about Appalachia in the early 1900s. Furman also taught at the Hindman Settlement School. She was the author of several books, most notably *The Quare Women* (1923).

20. Hindman, Kentucky, is located at the forks of Troublesome Creek.

21. Leather shoes commonly associated with poor working people.

22. Kim Mulkey was Don West's maternal grandfather, a Radical Republican since Civil War times, who exerted a powerful political influence on West.

23. Jim West was Don West's father.

24. The *Daily Worker* was the official newspaper of the Communist Party USA. It was published from 1924 to 1957. At its peak, the circulation was thirty-five thousand.

25. Clarence Senior (1903–74) served as the executive secretary of the Socialist party in Georgia during the 1930s. Norman Thomas (1884–1968) was a six-time Socialist party candidate for president and a cofounder of the American Civil Liberties Union.

26. Clarence Hathaway (1894–1963) served as the editor of the New York–based Communist newspaper the *Daily Worker* in the 1930s.

27. John Spivak (1897–1981) was one of the twentieth century's leading "muckrakers" or investigative journalists. His book, *Georgia Nigger* (1932), is widely credited with bringing reforms to the long-standing southern practice of using prisoners in chain gangs.

28. The *New Masses* was a leading periodical of the Left from 1926 to 1948. *The Liberator* was a leftist periodical founded in 1917 by Max Eastman (1883–1969) and others when the radical publication, *The Masses*, was shut down. *Labor Defender* was a month-

ly magazine published out of Chicago and the official publication of International Labor Defense, a Communist-led effort to defend workers, especially those involved in challenging industry and government. It was published from 1926 to 1937.

29. The Scottsboro Boys, including Olin Montgomery, were nine young African American men who were wrongfully tried and convicted for the rape of two white women aboard an Alabama freight train in 1931. Their case became a compelling cause for progressive citizens during the many years it was in the courts.

30. *Mulatto* was a controversial play by Langston Hughes (1902–67), the celebrated African American author, which made its debut on Broadway in 1935.

31. *To Make My Bread* (1932) by Grace Lumpkin (1892–1980) was one of the most famous novels based on the dramatic Gastonia Strike of 1929.

32. A coal mine opening on the side of a hill.

33. A miner who ingests too much coal dust is likely to cough up black phlegm, a probable sign of "black lung" disease.

34. Shoats are young pigs, which at this time ran free in the mountains and ate "mast," or acorns, chestnuts, and other natural forest foodstuffs.

35. Roy Harris (1895–1985) served as speaker of the Georgia House in the 1930s and 1940s and was the campaign manager for four different successful candidates for governor. A close ally of Herman Talmadge (1913–2002) and an ardent segregationist, he staunchly supported the White Democratic Primary.

36. Georgia populists at the turn of the twentieth century often referred to themselves as "Wool Hat Boys."

37. Ellis Arnall (1907–92) was governor of Georgia from 1942 to 1947. One of the most progressive Georgia politicians of his era, he was a supporter of Franklin Roosevelt (1882–1945) and pushed for election and prison reform.

38. Joseph McCarthy (1908–57) was a U.S. senator from Wisconsin. When he became chairman of the Committee on Government Operations in 1953, he launched a "witch hunt" for suspected Communists.

39. The Congress of Industrial Organizations (CIO) was first organized as a more progressive and militant alternative to the American Federation of Labor (AFL). The CIO attempted to organize all workers of particular industries, not only those of a particular trade, believing this would give them more power to confront their employers. The AFL and the CIO merged in 1955.

40. Dwight David Eisenhower (1890–1969), later the thirty-fourth president of the United States, was the leader of the American forces in the European theater of World War II. General G. K. Zhukhov (1896–1974) served the army of the Soviet Union in a similar position.

41. Henry A. Wallace (1888–1965), the former secretary of agriculture and vice president under Franklin Roosevelt, ran for president in 1948 as the Progressive party's candidate.

42. West served as a delegate from Georgia for the Progressive party in 1948, despite bitter opposition from local Communist Party elements who supported another candidate.

43. In 1954, in the case of *Brown v. Board of Education,* the U.S. Supreme Court ruled that racially segregated schools are unconstitutional.

44. See Proverbs 15:16–17: "Better a dinner of herbs where there is love, than a dinner of fatted calf where there is hatred."

45. In 1780, southern mountaineers and other American Revolutionaries defeated the British in the decisive Battle of King's Mountain on the border between North and South Carolina near present-day Charlotte, North Carolina.

46. The Tennessee Valley Authority (TVA) was founded in 1934 initially with an emphasis on power production, flood control, and community development. Estes Kefauver (1903–63) was a U.S. senator from Tennessee from 1948 until his death.

47. Montgomery, Alabama, was the site of the boycott of segregated buses sparked by Rosa Parks (b.1913) and Martin Luther King Jr. (1929–1968) in 1955.

48. William Holland Thomas (1805–73) was a European-American trader in the 1830s who served the Cherokee in North Carolina. The legal basis for the "removal" of the Cherokee to the West was that they were not allowed to live on land that wasn't privately owned, and, as Indians, they were forbidden to own land. Thomas registered land deeds for Cherokees in his own name so that they could continue to stay in their homes in the area, near the present town of Cherokee, North Carolina.

49. Founded in 1902, the Farmers Union is a national organization that works to improve the lives of farmers through political and economic action. It is still active in some states.

50. From 1892 until 1908, the People's party, or Populists as they were called, attracted a large following for their platform, calling for more control for ordinary farmers and workers. In 1904 and 1908, Tom Watson (1856–1922) of Georgia ran as their presidential candidate against the Democratic and Republican nominees.

51. Organized in 1955 in opposition to the Supreme Court's ruling favoring school integration, the White Citizens Council became a powerful organization of southerners who supported racial segregation throughout the 1950s.

52. See James 2:26: "For as the body without the spirit is dead, so faith without works is dead also."

53. "Black Belt" refers to areas of the South with a majority black population.

54. Clarence Jordon (1912–69) was a Baptist minister who, along with his wife, Florence, founded Koinonia Farm near Americus, Georgia, as an interracial, peace-loving community in 1942. Habitat for Humanity was founded here.

55. The "wage differential" refers to the fact that corporations with facilities in both the North and South typically paid lower wages in the South.

56. See John 4:17–18: "perfect love casteth out fear."

57. Amos, a shepherd from Judah, prophesied the downfall of the corrupt reign of Jeroboam II. Social Gospel preachers such as West often referred to passages in the Book of Amos, including 5:14: "Let justice roll down like waters and righteousness like an everflowing stream."

58. Luke 18:20 and 6:24.

59. Matthew 23:23–29.

60. Luke 4:18 and 4:23–30.

61. Senator James O. Eastland (1904–86) of Mississippi was a member of the Senate Internal Security Subcommittee, which investigated "subversives" in the South during the 1950s.

62. Spartacus was a Roman slave who organized tens of thousands of slaves into a revolt that lasted from 73 to 71 BCE before it was crushed by the Roman army.

63. Union General Oliver Otis Howard (1830–1909) played a major role in the U.S. government's establishment of Howard University in Washington, D.C., of which he served as president from 1869 until 1872. In 1895 he founded Lincoln Memorial University in Cumberland Gap, Tennessee.

64. Piles of mine waste, typically composed of the slate rock that often accompanies coal deposits.

65. The Appalachian Volunteers was an organization founded in 1963 by the Council of the Southern Mountains. At its height, it brought thousands from outside the region to assist regional poverty programs. The Southern Conference Educational Fund (SCEF) was founded in 1946 as the educational arm of the Southern Conference on Human Welfare, an advocacy and activist organization. The Volunteers in Service to America (VISTA) was a federal agency created in 1965 as part of the federal government's "War on Poverty." Community Action Programs (CAPS) were the branch of the War on Poverty that encouraged poor people to form organizations to solve their own problems.

66. Dogpatch is the fictional mountain community in the comic strip "Li'l Abner." Created by Al Capp (1909–79), the strip was syndicated in American newspapers from 1934 until 1977. Much of its humor derived from hillbilly stereotypes.

67. Theodore Dreiser (1871–1945), an important novelist in the early twentieth century, organized public hearings in 1932 to investigate the labor unrest in Harlan County, Kentucky.

68. The Office of Economic Opportunity (OEO) was the official name of the government agency created to wage the War on Poverty in 1965.

69. During the Harlan County, Kentucky, mining conflicts in 1931–32, Florence Reece (1900–86), the wife of a coal miner and organizer for the National Miner's Union, wrote the words to the famous union anthem, "Which Side Are You On?" "Solidarity Forever" was written by Ralph Chaplin (1887–1961), a labor activist and leader in the Industrial Workers of the World (IWW).

70. In 1969, Joseph Yablonski (1910–69) ran for the presidency of the United Mine Workers Union against the incumbent, Tony Boyle (1902–85). Weeks after Boyle won the election, gun thugs from the union's East Tennessee District 19 burst into the Yablonski home and murdered him, his wife, and his daughter.

71. Jack Weller (1923–2000), a Presbyterian minister in Hazard, Kentucky, published *Yesterday's People* in 1965. It contrasted mountaineers with mainstream Americans in a way that implied that middle-class values were superior to mountain values.

72. The first European-American settlers in what was to become the state of Tennessee lived in the Watauga River Valley beginning in 1769.

73. The *Manumission Intelligencer* was a newspaper published in 1819 in Jonesboro, Tennessee, by Elihu Embree (1782–1820), a Quaker industrialist who ran an ironworks

and was active in the Tennessee Manumission Society. In 1820 Embree founded *The Emancipator,* the first periodical in the United States dedicated solely to abolitionist issues.

74. Published continuously from 1831 to 1865 by William Lloyd Garrison (1805–79), *The Liberator* was the most prominent abolitionist newspaper in America. Benjamin Lundy (1789–1839) was a prominent abolitionist and editor of the newspaper *Genius of Universal Emancipation.*

75. Dr. Samuel Doak (1749–1818) was a Presbyterian minister and educator. John G. Fee (1816–1901) and Cassius Clay (1810–1903), both native Kentuckians, founded Berea College in 1855. John Rankin (1793–1886) was a native of Jefferson County, Tennessee. Henry Ward Beecher (1813–87) was an abolitionist Presbyterian minister and the brother of Harriet Beecher Stowe (1811–96), author of *Uncle Tom's Cabin* (1852). Charles Osborne (1808–89) was a member of the Tennessee Manumission Society.

76. General Sam Houston (1793–1863), the first president of the Republic of Texas, was born in Timber Ridge, Virginia, and lived at times with the Cherokee in Tennessee.

77. In 1861, Winston County, Alabama, attempted to secede from the state when Alabama voted to secede from the Union. Dade County, Georgia, the state's northwestern county, was the scene of organized conflict over secession.

78. William Lowndes Yancey (1814–63) worked as a lawyer and served as the editor of the *Greenville Mountaineer* during the early 1800s. Following the election of Abraham Lincoln, Yancey wrote Alabama's ordinance of secession, and in 1861 he was sent by Provisional President Jefferson Davis (1808–89) as the Confederacy's first commissioner to England and France to gain support.

79. Levi Coffin (1789–1877) was a native of the North Carolina mountains who became a leader in the Underground Railroad in Ohio and Indiana.

80. Hinton Rowan Helper (1829–1909) of North Carolina authored *The Impending Crisis—The Impending Crisis of the South and How to Meet It* (1857).

81. More commonly termed "broad-form deeds," long-form deeds were the instruments that outside mining companies used to purchase the right to extract minerals while allowing the landowner to continue to occupy the land.

82. In the 1890s, Coal Creek (since renamed Lake City) and Tracy City were the sites of struggles by free miners against prison labor in the coal mines. The Battle of Blair Mountain occurred in August of 1921 when law enforcement officials in Logan County, West Virginia, a stronghold of opposition to coal mine unions, confronted approximately ten thousand armed union miners marching from Kanawha County to Mingo County. The fighting lasted ten days and came to an end only when the U.S. army intervened by dropping bombs on American civilians for the first time in history.

83. John L. Lewis (1880–1969) was the charismatic and autocratic leader of the United Mine Workers of America from 1920 to 1959.

84. Francis Marion (1732–95) was a hero of the American Revolution from South Carolina. The elusive and daring tactics he employed during several battles against the

British and their American sympathizers, called Tories, earned him the nickname "The Swamp Fox."

85. John Calhoun (1782–1850), who served as vice president of the United States under John Quincy Adams (1767–1848), was a staunch South Carolina supporter of state sovereignty and a firm believer in the rights of individual states to nullify acts of Congress.

86. Edmund Ruffin (1794–1865) was born into a prominent Tidewater Virginia family and became an outspoken proponent of slavery and secession during the 1850s.

87. George Fitzhugh (1806–81), a Virginia planter and lawyer, was the author of several pamphlets and two books, *Sociology for the South* (1854) and *Cannibals All!* (1857), that strongly advocated the use of slavery.

88. Christopher Sheets (1839–1904), the Winston County, Alabama, state representative, opposed the secession of Alabama from the Union and attempted to persuade county representatives to vote against the action, declaring that if Alabama had the right to secede from the Union, then Winston County had the right to secede from the state.

89. Daniel Reaves Goodloe (1814–1902) was a North Carolina native who actively opposed slavery. He wrote several pamphlets against slavery and served as editor of the *National Era,* a leading antislavery newspaper.

90. Francis Lieber (1798–1872) was a German-born professor of history and political economy at South Carolina College. An ardent abolitionist, Lieber resigned in 1855 from the school after the Board of Trustees refused to select him as university president due to his political views. Benjamin Sherwood Hedrick (1827–86) was a chemistry teacher at the University of North Carolina and a staunch abolitionist. He lost his job because he supported John C. Fremont (1813–90), the Republican party candidate for the presidency who ran against James Buchanan (1791–1868), the Democrat, in the 1856 election.

91. "Millerism" refers to a religious movement in the United States during the 1830s and early 1840s. Followers of William Miller (1782–1849) believed that the bodily arrival of Christ was imminent. "Spirit-rappings" became popular in 1848, when the sisters Catherine Fox (1836–92) and Margaret Fox (1833–93) claimed to hear signals from the spirit world emanating from a room in their farmhouse. A religious movement known as "Spiritualism," which insisted that communication with the dead was possible, grew up around these "rappings," even though the sisters later admitted that the signals were a hoax.

92. Robert Augustus Toombs (1810–85), a staunch supporter of slavery and states' sovereignty, served as a U.S. senator from 1853 until Georgia seceded in 1861. Another U.S. senator from Georgia, Alexander Stephens (1812–83), initially argued against Georgia's secession from the Union but eventually shifted his stance. He was elected vice president of the Confederacy in 1861.

93. John C. Breckinridge (1821–75) was the Democratic candidate for president against Abraham Lincoln (1809–65) in the 1860 election. He was a native of Lexington, Kentucky, and an advocate of slavery.

94. William Henry Seward (1801–72), a native of New York, served as Abraham Lincoln's secretary of state during the Civil War.

Selected Poems

1. Kim Mulkey was Don West's maternal grandfather, a Radical Republican since Civil War times who exerted a powerful political influence on West.

2. West taught eighth grade at the Hindman Settlement School in 1930–31.

3. West toured the folk schools in Denmark in 1931.

4. Troublesome Creek forks at the Hindman Settlement School.

5. The Trace Fork is one of the branches of Troublesome Creek that comes together at the Settlement School.

6. Located in eastern Kentucky, Harlan County was the site of numerous coal mining labor conflicts. Harlan is also the name of the county seat.

7. Langston Hughes (1902–67), a leader in the Harlem Renaissance literary movement in the 1930s, maintained a friendship with West over several decades.

8. Pot-licker is the water left after vegetables are cooked.

9. A bed tick is an inexpensive bed filled with straw or feathers.

10. Bulldog gravy is a cream gravy or white sauce made with whole milk and a grease and flour mix.

11. Rickets is a disease caused by a vitamin D deficiency that can lead to skeletal deformities such as bowed legs. Miners were particularly prone to the disease when they worked long hours and seldom saw sunlight, the most common source of vitamin D before the invention of supplements. Flux, or dysentery, is a potentially deadly condition that produces bloody diarrhea and vomiting and is often seen in areas with poor sanitation and crowded living conditions.

12. A literary movement that emerged out of Vanderbilt University in the 1920s, the Agrarians published a collection of essays, *I'll Take My Stand,* in 1930, taking a decidedly southern and conservative stance toward life and their discipline.

13. The Blue Ridge Mountains are the Appalachian Mountains to the east of the Great Valley—comprised of the Tennessee and the Shenandoah Valley. The Smoky Mountains reach their greatest heights along the Tennessee–North Carolina border. The Unaka Mountains lie between the Tuckaseegee Valley and the valley of the Little Tennessee River in North Carolina.

14. The widow referred to in the poem is the wife of Barney Graham (1886–1933), the union leader murdered during the Wilder, Tennessee, mining strike in 1933.

15. Charlie Lewallen was a miner and labor activist in Harlan. When West published this poem in *Clods of Southern Earth* in 1946, he was sued by another Charlie Lewallen in Georgia for defamation of character. The case was eventually dropped.

16. Byron Herbert Reece (1917–58), a critically acclaimed north Georgia poet, grew up on a small farm in Union County, Georgia, less than fifty miles from Don West's birthplace. Reece committed suicide in 1958.

17. In mountain dialect "sorry" means lazy.

18. Kanawha County, West Virginia, is the home of Charleston, the state capital, and was the site of several labor disputes during the first half of the twentieth century.

19. "Molly-grub" is a colloquial term for food eaten by the poor.

20. Carl Braden (1915–75) was a field organizer for the Southern Conference Educational Fund. He served eight months in prison in the mid-1950s after he and his wife Anne Braden (b.1924) helped an African American family purchase a house in a segregated area in Louisville, Kentucky. Braden served an additional nine months in prison in 1959 when he refused to cooperate with the House Un-American Activities Committee.

21. To rive is to split wood.

22. Thomas Wolfe (1900–1938), a native of Asheville, North Carolina, was the author of the critically acclaimed novels *Look Homeward, Angel* (1929) and *You Can't Go Home Again* (1938).

23. Robert Burns (1759–96), immortalized for the traditional Scottish ballad "Auld Lang Syne," is widely considered the national bard of Scotland for his poems dealing with the lives of common farmers and the political and religious issues of his period.

24. Olive Tilford Dargan (1869–1968), a native of Grayson County, Kentucky, and a longtime resident in the Smoky Mountains of North Carolina, wrote three proletarian novels under the pen name Fielding Burke, as well as poetry, drama, and short fiction. Her works include *A Stone Came Rolling, From My Highest Hill,* and *Call Home the Heart.*

25. Sidney Lanier (1842–81) was a poet and musician from Macon, Georgia.

26. Henrietta Buckmaster (b. 1909), best known for her historical novels on the Underground Railroad, used West as a prototype for the protagonist in her 1944 novel, *Deep River.*

27. Carl Sandburg (1878–1967) was a Pulitzer Prize–winning poet and labor organizer. His best-known poem, "The People, Yes," was published in 1936.

28. Bill Moore (1927–63), a civil rights activist, was murdered during a freedom walk in Gadsden, Alabama, in 1963.

29. Frederick Douglass (1817–95) was an African American abolitionist and journalist who escaped from slavery.

30. Roger Williams (1603–83) was an English cleric who founded Providence and obtained a Royal Charter for the Colony of Rhode Island.

31. Thomas Paine (1737–1809), a British-born American revolutionary, wrote the landmark texts *Common Sense* and *The Rights of Man.*

32. Aubrey Williams (1890–1965) headed the National Youth Administration for President Franklin Roosevelt. After World War II, Williams, along with Gould Beech (1913–2000), purchased the newspaper *Southern Farmer,* based in Montgomery, Alabama.

33. Carl Braden (see n.20 above) was often joined by his wife Ann in their work for social justice in the South.

34. A divinity student at Vanderbilt University with West, Claude Williams (1893–1977) was a radical preacher and activist, based mainly in the South and in Detroit.

35. Linda Williams McCarthy is West's granddaughter.

36. Connie West was West's wife.

37. The Pinnacle is the mountain that forms the northeast edge of Cumberland Gap. The Holston River forms the valley to the south of Cumberland Gap, where Don and Connie West attended college at Lincoln Memorial University.

38. Boone's Trace is the Wilderness Road that runs through Cumberland Gap, and the Tennessee Valley is formed by that river and its tributaries, including the Holston.

39. Hedy West is West's youngest daughter.

40. The Bryants were labor activists in West Virginia.

41. Department of Public Assistance (or welfare) checks.

42. Locations of important labor conflicts.

43. A longtime labor leader during the West Virginia coal wars in the early twentieth century, Bill Blizzard (1892–1955) was tried for treason for his role in the Battle of Blair Mountain, a mining conflict in the 1920s.

44. "Solidarity Forever," one of the labor movement's best-known songs, was written by Ralph Chaplin (1887–1961), a labor activist who was involved in West Virginia conflicts.

45. *Yesterday's People* (1965) by Jack Weller is a book about Appalachian poverty.

46. In the 1950s, West received several subpoenas to appear before congressional investigation committees, including the House Committee on Un-American Activities.

47. Pat McCarran (1876–1954) was a Democratic U.S. senator from Nevada, who served as the chairman of the Senate Internal Security Subcommittee. One of the Senate's most powerful anticommunists during the McCarthy years, McCarran sponsored the Internal Security Act in 1950 that required members of the Communist Party USA and affiliated organizations to register with the attorney general.

48. Matoaka is a town in southern West Virginia.

49. The Greenbriar River flows near Alderson Prison in West Virginia.

50. Lares was Lebrun's home in Puerto Rico.

51. On February 26, 1972, Buffalo Creek in West Virginia became the site of one of the nation's worst flooding incidents. It was caused when three "gob pile dams" made of mine waste left by Buffalo Mining Company, a subsidary of Pittston Mining, burst and left 125 people dead and 1,100 injured in a matter of minutes.

52. In the novel *Jimmy Higgins* (1919) by Upton Sinclair (1878–1968), the title character is a union man who spends his days folding pro-union leaflets to be passed out at the gates. Thus, the basic and more tiresome organizational work of unions became known as "Jimmy Higgins" work.

53. Twenty members of mining families, including miners, wives, and children, died at the hands of hired gunmen in the Ludlow Massacre in 1914 during a coal mining strike in Colorado.

54. In 1891, coal miners in Coal Creek, Tennessee, burnt down the stockades used to corral prisoners who had been brought in to work the mines as part of a brutal convict lease system in the South.

55. In 1929, Gastonia and Marion were the sites of two of the largest textile strikes in American history.

56. Burl Collins was a friend and colleague of West in West Virginia.

57. A native Tennesseean who grew up among the Cherokee, John Burnett (1810–1893) was a private in the U.S. army and served as an interpreter during the relocation march of the Cherokee in 1838–39 that later became known as the Trail of Tears. Later

critical of the treatment of Native Americans, Burnett wrote a personal account of his experiences during the relocation.

58. The son of slave owners, John Fairfield was one of Ohio's legendary conductors on the Underground Railroad.

59. John Woody was a coal miner, labor leader, and a friend of West who died of black lung disease.

60. Blair Mountain, Cabin and Paint Creeks, Ludlow, and Coal Creek are all locations of important labor battles.

61. Eugene Debs (1855–1926) won nearly one million votes as the Socialist party presidential candidate in 1920 while imprisoned under the Espionage Act for speaking against the First World War.

62. Florence Reece authored the labor ballad "Which Side Are You On?" during the Harlan labor conflicts in the 1930s.

63. New York City–born Jay Rockefeller (b. 1937), great-grandson of the Standard Oil industrialist John D. Rockefeller (1839–1937), is currently a U.S. senator from West Virginia.

a don west bibliography

Between the Plow Handles: Poems. Monteagle, Tenn.: Highlander Folk School, 1932.

Clods of Southern Earth. New York: Boni and Gaer, 1946.

Crab-Grass. Nashville: Art Print Shop, Trevecca College, 1931.

Deep, Deep Down in Living. N.p., [1932].

Freedom on the Mountains: Excerpts from a Book Manuscript on Southern Mountain History. Huntington, W.Va.: Appalachian Movement Press, 1973.

In a Land of Plenty. Minneapolis: West End Press, 1982. Reprinted with additional poems, Los Angeles: West End Press, 1985.

"Knott County, Kentucky: A Study." Bachelor's thesis. Vanderbilt School of Religion, 1932.

O Mountaineers! Huntington, W.Va.: Appalachian Press, 1974.

People's Cultural Heritage in Appalachia. Huntington, W.Va.: Appalachian Movement Press, 1971.

The Road Is Rocky. New York: New Christian Books, 1951.

Robert Tharin: Biography of a Mountain Abolitionist. Huntington, W.Va.: Appalachian Movement Press, [1973].

Romantic Appalachia; or, Poverty Pays If You Ain't Poor. Huntington, W.Va.: Appalachian Movement Press, [1972].

Songs for Southern Workers: 1937 Songbook of the Kentucky Workers Alliance. Huntington, W.Va.: Appalachian Movement Press, 1973.

Southern Mountain Folk Tradition and the Folksong "Stars" Syndrome. Huntington, W.Va.: Appalachian Movement Press, [1972].

A Time for Anger: Poems Selected from "The Road Is Rocky" and "Clods of Southern Earth." Huntington, W.Va.: Appalachian Movement Press, 1980.

Toil and Hunger: Poems. San Benito, Tex.: Hagglund Press, 1940.

In addition to his own publications, Don West's poems and prose have appeared in the following books:

Crowell, Suzanne. *Appalachian People's History Book.* Louisville: Mountain Education Associates, 1971.

Ergood, Bruce, and Bruce E. Kuhre, eds. *Appalachia: Social Context Past and Present.* Dubuque, Iowa: Kendall/Hunt, 1976.

Hicks, Granville, ed. *Proletarian Literature in the United States: An Anthology.* New York: International Publishers, 1935.

Higgs, Robert J., Ambrose N. Manning, and Jim Wayne Miller, eds. *Appalachia Inside Out: A Sequel to Voices from the Hills.* Knoxville: University of Tennessee Press, 1995.

McKinney, Irene, ed. *Backcountry: Contemporary Writing in West Virginia.* Morgantown: West Virginia University Press, 2002.

McNeil, Nellie, and Joyce Squibb, eds. *A Southern Appalachian Reader.* Boone, N.C.: Appalachian Consortium Press, 1988.

People's Appalachian Research Collective. *Appalachia's People, Problems, Alternatives.* Morgantown, W.Va.: People's Appalachian Research Collective, 1971.

Plumley, William, and Marjorie Warner, eds. *Things Appalachian.* Charleston, W.Va.: Morris College Publishing, 1976.

Smith, Barbara, and Kirk Judd, eds. *Wild Sweet Notes: Fifty Years of West Virginia Poetry, 1950–1999.* Huntington, W.Va.: Publisher's Place, 2000.

Walls, David S., and John B. Stephenson, eds. *Appalachia in the Sixties: Decade of Reawakening.* Lexington: University Press of Kentucky, 1972.

index

DON WEST (1906–92) was a best-selling poet and literary phenomenon, Appalachian historian, political militant, mountain farmer, ordained minister, and nationally recognized educator.

JEFF BIGGERS is a writer based in Illinois and Italy.

GEORGE BROSI teaches English at Eastern Kentucky University and is an independent scholar, bookseller, and authority on writings about Appalachia. The editor of *Appalachian Heritage,* a regional literary magazine published by Berea College, he was a longtime associate of Don West.

The University of Illinois Press
is a founding member of the
Association of American University Presses.

_____

Composed in 10.5/13 Minion
with City Bold display
by Celia Shapland
for the University of Illinois Press
Designed by Dennis Roberts
Manufactured by Thomson-Shore, Inc.

University of Illinois Press
1325 South Oak Street
Champaign, IL 61820-6903
www.press.uillinois.edu